LINKAGE INC.'s BEST PRACTICES IN LEADERSHIP DEVELOPMENT HANDBOOK

Case Studies • Instruments • Training

EDITORS

David Giber
Louis L. Carter
Marshall Goldsmith

Foreword by Warren Bennis

Copyright © 2000 by Linkage Press. Published by Jossey-Bass/Pfeiffer and Linkage Inc.
ISBN: 0-7879-5237-0

Library of Congress Cataloging-in-Publication Data
Linkage Inc.'s best practices in leadership development handbook:
  case studies, instruments, training / editors, David Giber, Louis
  Carter, Marshall Goldsmith; foreword by Warren Bennis.
     p. cm.
  Includes bibliographical references and index.
  ISBN 0-7879-5237-0
  1. Leadership Case studies.   2. Strategic planning Case studies.
I. Giber, David J. II. Carter, Louis L. III. Goldsmith, Marshall.
IV. Title: Best practices in leadership development handbook.
HD57.7.L564   2000   99-42894
658.4'092—dc21

Printed in the United States of America

Published by

JOSSEY-BASS/PFEIFFER
A Wiley Company
350 Sansome St.
San Francisco, CA 94104-1342
415.433.1740; Fax 415.433.0499
800.274.4434; Fax 800.569.0443

| www.pfeiffer.com |

LINKAGE *INCORPORATED*

One Forbes Road
Lexington, MA 02421
(781) 862-3157; (781) 862-2355

| www.linkageinc.com |

Acquiring Editor: Matthew Holt
Director of Development: Kathleen Dolan Davies
Senior Production Editor: Dawn Kilgore
Manufacturing Supervisor: Becky Carreño

FIRST EDITION
HB Printing   10 9 8 7 6 5 4 3 2

 This book is printed on acid-free, recycled stock that meets or exceeds the minimum GPO and
EPA requirements for recycled paper.

CONTENTS

LIST OF EXHIBITS

ACKNOWLEDGMENTS

Linkage Team

Susan Brady, Louis Carter, Lynda Davey, David Giber, Taavo Godtfredsen, Lori Hart, Jonathan Lehrich, Melissa McLaughlin, Derek Smith

Contributors

June Abramson, Candy Albertsson, Brian Anderson, Jay Conger, Bridgit Courey, Michelle Fellenz, John Ferrie, Marguerite J. Foxon, David Giber, Elizabeth Haight, Pat Hurton, Don Kraft, Margaret Latif, Cheryl Lazzaro, Ursula Lohmann, Lou Manzi, Donna McNamara, Mimi O'Donnell, Antonia Pennisi, Jean Patton, Pat Sabine, Alan and Deborah Slobodnik

ABOUT THIS BOOK

The principal goal of this book is to provide you with a world-class cookbook of the best ingredients that go into successful leadership development programs. Through a case study approach, this book provides practical, easy-to-apply tools, instruments, training, and competency models that can be used as benchmarks for the successful implementation of a leadership development program.

Within each case study, you will learn how to:

- Analyze the need for leadership development
- Build a business case for leadership development
- Determine the competencies for leadership
- Identify the audience for leadership development
- Design the leadership development program
- Implement the design
- Evaluate the effectiveness of the initiative

HOW TO USE THIS BOOK

Direct Application

Because this book contains actual forms, guides, training, competency models, and methodologies for implementing a leadership development initiative, you can immediately apply many of its parts directly to your job. Many of the evaluation forms, reference guides, and training exercises can be easily implemented and customized to fit your specific organizational needs.

Master's Degree or Executive Workshops and Seminars

This book is ideal for a master's degree or executive workshop or seminar on designing, implementing, and evaluating a leadership development system. The case studies can be used as actual examples of leadership development systems. For more information on Linkage on-site or public workshops on leadership development systems, or to purchase a leadership development participant guide, contact Linkage Customer Service at (781) 862-3157.

On-line or Virtual Team Learning

This book can be shared with members of teams or students across long distances who are not able to attend.

Getting the Most From This Book

1. Read over the frontmatter to get a feel for the book's landscape.
2. Skim over the table of contents for each chapter, mining for information on the types of leadership development initiatives, key features in each program, competency models, strategic objectives of programs, critical success factors, and evaluation methods.
3. Examine all of the exhibits.
4. Go back and choose specific case studies and read them over carefully
5. Work with a team of people to develop a list of the components in a few case studies that do and don't fit your organization. Design a customized plan or blueprint of what your organization's leadership development system looks like based upon this list. Analyze why these components are most applicable to your organization and its strategic objectives.

FOREWORD

Warren Bennis

O ver the past few years, there has been an explosion of interest in leadership development. Companies have recognized the shortage of talented managers, the importance of building their bench strength, and the need to widen perspectives in order to compete globally. In 1998, Linkage, Inc. and I collaborated in completing a study of more than 350 companies involved with leadership development. We found that:

- Nearly all respondents recognize the need to create internal bench strength, yet less than 44 percent have a formal process for nominating or developing high-potential employees.
- Companies that do successfully build their high-potential employees use structured leadership development systems.
- The programs that make a difference include some or all of three critical components: formal training, 360-degree feedback, and most important, exposure to senior executives, including mentoring programs.

The programs shared many of the key features or components shown in the tables on pages xviii and xix. The different combinations of these components formed the critical ingredients for unique success in each organization.

**MOST IMPACTFUL KEY FEATURES OF LEADERSHIP
DEVELOPMENT PROGRAMS OF EIGHT MAJOR
MANUFACTURING AND PHARMACEUTICAL FIRMS**
(*by key feature in order of impact*).

1. Action Learning
2. Cross Functional Rotations
3. 360-degree Feedback
4. Exposure to Senior Executives
5. External Coaching
6. Global Rotations
7. Exposure to Strategic Agenda
8. Formal Mentoring
9. Informal Mentoring
10. Internal Case Studies
11. Executive MBA
12. Accelerated Promotion
13. Conferences

Major Findings

This year we talked to many of these companies to compile this book, and we asked them to share the approaches, tools, and specific methods that made their programs successful. We wanted to obtain stories from a variety of industries and to include firms that ranged in size, age, and where they were in the business cycle. Perhaps more important, we chose companies that have succeeded in developing a "teachable point of view"[1] on leadership. These are the companies where leaders are "made," though integrated, multi-mode programs that include the following features.

Leadership Competency Model

Almost all of these programs have an explicit leadership model, usually using behavioral competencies. These range from SmithKline Beecham's twenty-one competencies to the nine or fewer factors favored by Barclays Global Investors, SIAC, BP Amoco, AlliedSignal, and others. Bose has three sets of leadership competency models for first line, middle, and senior management levels. These models frequently form the basis for 360-degree assessments and often provide a focus to the flow of the program itself.

LISTING OF BEST PRACTICE CASE STUDIES
(BY COMPANY, INDUSTRY, NUMBER OF EMPLOYEES,
AND GROSS REVENUE).

Company	Industry	Number of Employees	Gross Revenue
Abbott Labs	Healthcare/Pharmaceuticals	20,000+	$10B+
AMSC	Government	<250	N/A
Allied Signal	Aerospace/Chemicals	20,000+	$10B+
BGI	Institutional Investments	501–2,500	$10B+
Bose	Consumer Electronics	2,501–7,500	$1B–$10B
BP Amoco	Chemicals/Petroleum	20,000+	$10B+
Colgate-Palmolive	Consumer Goods	20,001+	$1B–$10B
Gundersen Lutheran	Healthcare	2,501–7,500	$251–500M
Imasco	Consumer Products and Services	20,000+	$1B–10B
MathWorks	Software	501–2,500	N/A
Mitre Corporation	Federally funded R&D	2,501–7,500	$251–500M
Motorola	Electronics	20,000+	$10B+
PECO Energy	Utilities	2,501–7,500	$1B–10B
SIAC	Information Technology	501–2,500	$251–500M
SmithKline Beecham	Healthcare/Pharmaceuticals	20,000+	$10B+

Management Support

The multilevel support of the program was critical. In fact, 100 percent of the case studies in this book stated that the support and involvement of senior management was critical to the success of the overall leadership development initiative. The CEOs at Bose, Barclays Global Investors, and AlliedSignal endorsed their programs, and others such as PECO Energy created explicit Management Development Committees. Successful programs were able to get their senior managers to act as "program faculty" and to actively participate in 360-degree assessment and feedback.

Systematic Training

Virtually all of the leadership development efforts we examined took a systems approach, going beyond training to build skills through rotations, coaching and mentoring, and on-the-job training. The sponsors and developers took specific steps to ensure that educational components of the leadership system were reinforced and that the learning was transferred to on-the-job use.

Action Learning

Action learning has emerged as the "hottest" approach in the leadership field. Case studies from Motorola, Imasco, Colgate-Palmolive, and others highlight this dynamic approach. These companies, as well as others in the Bennis-Linkage leadership development study, have found that the fastest and most lasting learning is produced when people are engaged in finding real solutions to real problems.

A Learning Community. The best of these programs, such as Colgate-Palmolive's, build learning communities by training and enlisting graduates and company senior management as instructors and faculty.

A Leadership "Typology"

As we began to review the case studies for this book, we thought about whether various leadership programs fit into a range or category. While a typology may enforce too narrow a set of characteristics for describing these programs, it seems to us that they can be differentiated by the focus chosen by the program sponsors and designers that directly led to the impact achieved. The major choice in designing a leadership program was whether to emphasize the individual, the team, or the organization and its strategy. Development professionals, who flexibly used the elements of the leadership system in ways that considered their relation to the organization's challenges, culture, and maturity as a business, achieved the best impact. They viewed leadership development as a strategic intervention and built a foundation from which to use their program to drive change.

The companies in this book present a grand tour of today's corporate issues, which they chose to address through leadership development programs and systems. It is instructive to examine the recurring and particular areas on which they focused. These included:

Globalization

The challenge of managing globally is a focus of many of the programs. Not only are the participants recruited internationally, but the action learning projects and case studies drive right to the heart of the difficulties of global leadership. Barclays Global Investors, Colgate-Palmolive, BP Amoco, and others provide outstanding examples.

Competition

Abbott Labs uses their leadership program to create knowledge of the company's current strengths. Imasco emphasizes the customer's viewpoint and experience. Both aim to enhance strategic thinking and perspectives while building a competitive, customer-oriented perspective.

Leadership Behaviors

The programs in this book make trade-offs between their emphasis on the individual, the team, and the organization. Even if they begin at the same place, the equation is balanced differently. Many of the authors provide specific rationales for why they adopted certain learning approaches and chose to emphasize particular experiences over others.

While most of the programs put some focus on building an understanding of strategy, for some the driving force is achieving measurable progress on a strategic issue through action learning teams. Here the leadership development issue is achieving organizational impact. The basic assumption is that leaders learn by tackling real problems. These organizationally focused programs, like Motorola's GOLD program, achieved organizational breakthroughs and built strong teamwork. They build credibility for the leadership effort by tying it to tangible business problem solving and innovation.

While almost all of these benchmark programs include an assessment process, several put a major emphasis on personal insight and change as a component of developing leaders. Programs like PECO's offer transformational learning experiences that alter individual styles, behaviors, and effectiveness. Certain programs, like the Army Management Staff College's, target specific leadership skills and behaviors that may close a critical gap or open up a new capability. Other programs invest more time and energy into building teamwork and team leadership, and they emphasize this aspect of leadership work over self-discovery. Gundersen Lutheran Hospital's learning teams are a wonderful example of creating teamwork that facilitates and supports individual learning and growth.

The key elements of the leadership systems are often the same. The difference may be in whether individuals, teams, or organizational change efforts are seen as the best vehicle for carrying the dual burden of driving learning and facilitating organizational change.

A Leadership Development Approach

We have defined a six-phase approach to leadership development, which may be seen in most of the case studies in this book. The phases are listed below:

1. Business diagnosis
2. Assessment
3. Program design
4. Implementation
5. On-the-job support
6. Evaluation

Phase One

The first phase is usually a diagnostic step in which the business drivers and rationale for creating a leadership system are identified. Critical to this stage is creating consensus and a sense of urgency regarding the need for leadership development. A future vision that is supported by management is key. All of the leadership systems have some model as a focal point for their work. The best of these models capture the imagination and aspirations of the organization and its leaders. Designing the leadership system also leads to strategic questions. The following questions are taken from the Abbott Labs example:

- What are the company's current strengths to be leveraged for future success?
- What are the "gaps" that must be bridged to avoid difficulty?
- What new skills or competencies are needed to achieve the intent of new strategy?

As Don Kraft, director of Abbott human resources planning and development, also points out, the program design must also consider "career transition" skills or needs. Where are individuals making difficult leadership transitions (e.g., from function to general management) and what is happening during those transitions? A well-thought-out diagnostic phase is usually connected to an evaluation of the desired business impacts in Phase Six.

Phase Two

Assessment is also a commonly shared element. Clearly, our industries have taken to heart the idea that leaders need to know themselves "from the inside out."[2] Assessments are delivered to both individuals and to teams, resulting in development plans and actions. Assessment has become a norm for business—the question is how we use the assessment to drive change in our businesses and ourselves. Individual coaching often accompanies this assessment. This coaching has been extremely successful for such firms as SIAC, PECO Energy, and others.

Phase Three

Phase Three is program design. These outstanding programs have several unique elements, which are delineated here:

- Colgate-Palmolive uses a learning journal to help its participants capture the immediate application of their learnings, especially in dealing with client accounts.

- Assessment centers and simulations have made a comeback at such companies as PECO Energy, BP Amoco, and Abbott Labs. These assessment centers use highly interactive simulations. These simulations help participants experience the leadership dilemmas of the next level.
- The Army builds a perspective on leadership while simultaneously teaching about key aspects of how the Army manages, operates, and deploys its resources. The Army also has participants choose class leaders, further formalizing the role of leaders in the session.
- Several programs work hard to build in customer perspectives. Barclays Global Investors reports two unique prework assignments, including completing two "client audits" to determine their client's overall satisfaction and how they can help their client meet his or her goals. Imasco actually visits its operating companies to "field test" both customer and employee issues. Imasco participants truly see strategy in action.
- A few of the programs have a unique emphasis on building a sense of community, both internally in the company and externally in the world outside. Abbott Labs began with providing basic physical labor at a community agency. They evolved these community service projects to allow greater interaction with agency staff and clients building to a social event (baseball game, picnic, and so on) by the third encounter. This stretching of the community projects turns it into a genuine opportunity to experience diversity and cultural differences.

Phase Four

The fourth phase is program implementation. In several outstanding leadership systems this includes creating action learning teams which tackle significant business problems and projects. This is the second biggest trend in leadership development after assessment and coaching. The popularity of action learning raises the issue of whether leadership development programs can become too tactical if they are attached to specific projects. These top programs leverage action learning, using it to build insight and provide a growth challenge in themselves. Programs must answer such questions as:

- What is a "doable" project that still expands thinking?
- How do we set senior management's expectations for the business value that the learning will produce?
- How do action teams stay together as "learning groups" over time?

Many programs have outstanding structures for learning teams. Math-Works, The Mitre Corporation, Gundersen Lutheran, Imasco, and Motorola are true standouts.

Phase Five

These benchmark programs reach beyond the classroom and provide on-the-job reinforcement and support. Work in this phase defines the follow-up support that determines whether the learnings of the program will generalize and transfer to the job. In several of the programs, the support system outside of training is one of the most salient elements of the leadership system. AlliedSignal and SmithKline Beecham have successfully built multisource feedback into their performance and career progression systems. The Army and SIAC map their management curriculums based on the leadership models and assessments.

Coaching is another major trend in leadership development. Key questions about these coaching and mentoring systems may include:

- What are the critical skills needed to coach most effectively?
- What are the best coaching tools and methods for developing competencies in others?
- What do the best executive coaches do?
- How can we build coaching into our performance management system?
- What does it take to initiate an effective mentoring program?
- How can we measure success in both individual coaching and an overall system?

Phase Six

Evaluation is the capstone—the point at which the organization can gain insight on how to revise and strengthen a program, eliminate barriers to its reinforcement and use in the field, and connect the intervention back to the original goals to measure success. Perhaps the outstanding example of this is Motorola's GOLD Program, which achieves measurable bottom-line impact. Yet all of these programs are concerned with a longer-term, multiyear approach to creating leaders. Many report lowered turnover among participants and greater numbers of people ready for development. Colgate-Palmolive reports that sales directors and account managers perceived a direct relationship between the program and sales results.

Conclusion

Should companies invest in leadership development? The authors, passionate champions all, would argue yes. While more data on business impacts are needed, the programs in this book have had significant influence on the culture of the organizations. The shift in culture may have eased an important organizational transition, helped anticipate pressures of globalization, or toughened an organization to compete. The value of the shifts, in terms of improved decision making, more attractive recruiting, or better solutions, needs to be understood and tracked.

Clearly, there are prominently shared views and approaches across these various industries of what is needed to address the challenge of developing leaders. The formula for leadership development remains an important goal, which companies need to keep as an asset. We look forward to tracking these and other companies as they continue to write their leadership stories.

June 1999

References

Cashman, Kevin (1998). *Leadership from the Inside Out*. Provo, Utah: Executive Excellence Publishing.

Tichy, Noel, M. (1997). *The Leadership Engine*. New York: HarperCollins Publishers, Inc.

Notes

1. Tichy, Noel, M. (1997). *The Leadership Engine.* New York: HarperCollins Publishers, Inc.
2. Cashman, Kevin (1998). *Leadership from the Inside Out.* Provo, Utah: Executive Excellence Publishing.

CHAPTER ONE

ABBOTT LABORATORIES

This chapter outlines a strategic results and personal change initiative that is designed to prepare the organization for a changing environment within the healthcare industry by developing the competencies of and retaining high potential leaders.

Introduction

Abbott Laboratories, founded in 1888, is one of the most diversified health-care manufacturers in the world. Three of Abbott's four core businesses—diagnostics, hospital products, nutritionals, and pharmaceuticals —are the number one or two competitors in their fields. Abbott is, and has been for fifty years, a global company. Approximately 40 percent of its sales and one-third of its 57,000 employees are outside the United States. Its profit as a percent of sales places Abbott among the top companies in the world (for example, in 1998 Abbott was ranked 129 of the Fortune 500 in sales and 12 in profits).

Cultural Elements Influencing Leadership Development Initiative

Abbott's success is the result of its strategy, execution, and culture. Among these sources of competitiveness are cultural elements that heavily influence leadership development thinking and efforts:

- A passion for the business (improving customers' lives)
- A passion and drive for achievement (and a belief that actions—results—speak louder than words)
- Self-confidence and a desire for self-reliance (historically, a great emphasis on internally generated growth and fierce autonomy of the operating divisions)
- A bias for action (and a bias against forms and processes)
- A belief in "Abbott" (the team or system will deliver results, not individual "heroes")

Strategic and Competitive Business Challenges

The early- to mid-1990s was a period of extraordinary change for healthcare companies around the world. What America experienced as the Health Care Reform Initiative of 1993 was reflective of a global trend to cap rising healthcare costs. Government intervention and cost containment worldwide reduced pricing flexibility and slowed market growth in economically developed countries. Simultaneously, the balance of power between healthcare companies and their customers was shifting dramatically. For the first time, healthcare customers were bigger and more powerful than healthcare manufacturers. Additionally, partly in response to this situation and partly in response to weak product pipelines, there was a wave of industry merger, acquisition, and general consolidation. Driving even greater change was increasing or changing regulatory standards in the United States and around the world.

It was clear to the entire industry that these market dynamics were not "one time" events, but that they represented a new world in which to compete. They provided both incredible challenge and opportunity. Abbott's response to this situation, fashioned in the mid-1990s, was to:

- Remain a diversified company, leveraging its multiple strengths
- Continue its drive to excellence through outstanding execution and productivity improvement
- Drive rapid growth by:
  increasing the effectiveness and efficiency of internal research and development
  maximizing global opportunities, particularly the emerging markets
  effective licensing and acquisition of technology
  acquisition of selected new businesses

While Abbott's sales growth rate did slow during this period, pursuing this strategy provided it a foundation on which to build in the late-1990s and into the next millennium.

Strategy and Leadership Development—Creating a Business Case

This rapidly changing environment had very clear and powerful implications for Abbott's leadership development practices. The key questions it raised were:

- Given its practice and desire for internal promotion, how does Abbott prepare people developed in one world for a radically different one?

- As Abbott continues to grow in size and complexity, how will it standardize and teach the important things people have previously learned by immersion or osmosis?
- Moreover, how would Abbott ensure its leadership was "inclusive" (for example, diversity of thought, perspective, gender, race, and globally) enough for the rapidly changing world?

These questions signaled the need to modify the company's main leadership development instrument, the Leadership Development Program (LDP). In addition to responding to the business's strategic needs, enhancements to the LDP also had to address two "technical" leadership development concerns that program administrators had identified:

- How can Abbott increase the relevance and application of the LDP?
- Has the proper participant audience been identified and pursued?

Against this backdrop, the company's human resources planning and development group began its redesign of the LDP in 1996.

The Leadership Development Program (LDP)

The Leadership Development Program, initiated in 1991, was a solid beginning for the redesign of Abbott's executive education and development efforts. It was a three-week annual process of providing thirty-five high-potential leaders with current thinking from outstanding business school faculty and much of Abbott's most senior management. Participation was by business unit nomination and was considered an achievement in itself. The pool of participants included was high-performing leaders with potential for advancement. Generally, these would be people for whom vice president, the top 140 positions in the company, was the next step. In addition to new ideas and insight, networking among participants was considered a key benefit of the program. This networking was especially valuable given the limited cross-company interaction most participants experienced on the job.

The Plan for Leadership Development

As the program administrators went about redesigning Abbott's executive development effort, they were guided by both business objectives (for example, how can we ensure Abbott's success?) and leadership development objectives (for example, how do we become "world class" in developing leaders?).

Business Objectives

Strengthen Abbott's leadership team by:

- Developing the competencies required for future success (for example, globalization, alliance and acquisition, future orientation, and so on)
- Driving desired strategic cultural objectives (such as greater interdivisional synergy)
- Developing more people faster and earlier in their careers
- Maintaining or enhancing high-potential retention. (Retention was high, but there was concern that slowing sales growth would lead to the perception of slowing career growth.)

Leadership Development "Technical" Objectives

Enhance the programs by:

- Increasing the application and impact in the workplace
- Developing a smooth, seamless curriculum
- Being the source of a stream of new ideas into the organization

The Audience for Leadership Development

An important first step in rethinking executive development at Abbott was "audience." Given the size of the company and even a narrow definition of "leadership team," a target audience of thirty-five people annually was simply too small to provide the learning or impact the company needed in a reasonable time frame. In line with the objective of developing more people sooner, the company initiated a second program called the Management Challenge: Managing Across Boundaries (MC). The MC was designed to provide an opportunity for a broader audience, targeted to their needs. With two programs, it was important to develop a clear distinction between audiences and purposes—to avoid confusion and to maximize the investment and opportunity. Table 1.1 shows the distinct target audiences.

Once the target audiences were developed, it was clear that the programs should be integrated—in other words, the MC should support and feed into the LDP. This concept not only shaped the development of the MC, it drove the redesign of the LDP by asking the questions, "How do we eliminate redundancy with the MC?" and "How does this align with or extend the MC?"

TABLE 1.1.   LEADERSHIP DEVELOPMENT AUDIENCES.

Program	Management Challenge (MC)	Leadership Development Program (LDP)
Participant description	Senior "functional" manager who can benefit from broader general management perspective	Senior leader preparing for executive position—should have general perspective; moving toward creating the future
Typical titles	Senior manager and director	Director and vice president
Performance/ potential	High performer/high potential	High performer/high potential
Total pool of potential participants	Several thousand	Several hundred
Annual participants	70 (two sessions)	35 (one session)

Designing the System

With target audiences established, the design could begin. The same basic approach was used to structure both the LDP and the MC. The team used two "streams" of content to determine the programs' components. The first stream was Abbott's strategic needs: (1) What are the company's current strengths to be leveraged for future success?; (2) What are the "gaps" that must be bridged to avoid difficulty?; (3) What new skills or competencies are needed to achieve the intent of the new strategy?

The second source of program design content was generic "career transition" skills or needs: What are the generic shifts an individual must make to move from functional to general management? From middle management to executive? These sets of questions were answered using publicly available research from Personnel Decisions Inc. (PDI) and the Center for Creative Leadership (CCL), as well as a number of leadership authors.

Answering these questions provided a great deal of potential program content—far more than could be included in either program. Identifying the areas of integration between the two streams was key to the final selection of the program content. For instance, shifting from "developing and implementing mid-term strategy" to "creating the future" is a part of the transition from senior manager to executive. One of Abbott's needs was to increase its external and long-term focus. The complementary nature of these two demands made them a natural to cover in the LDP under the heading "Developing Vision and Strategy."

Identification of Competencies

Working through the two streams of potential content led to the identification of three key competencies to be developed in each program, as shown here in Figure 1.1.

FIGURE 1.1.   KEY COMPETENCIES.

	Management Challenge (MC)	**Leadership Development Program (LDP)**
Competencies	• Understanding and implementing strategy	• Developing vision and strategy
	• Building the team	• Building the organization
	• My leadership	• Leadership or the leader's role

A more detailed description of Abbott's Leadership Development Competency Model can be found in Exhibit 1.1 (page 19).

Once the competencies were settled, the next step was to develop a logical flow and structure for each of the program weeks. The goal was to address each of the desired competencies in each week and to have each week build on the previous one. This resulted in the following weekly themes:

Management Challenge
- Understanding Abbott's strategy and its implications for my organization
- Understanding the general manager's perspective—leading Abbott's business in a new environment

Leadership Development Program
- Expanding horizons—new input and views
- Making sense of the new data—developing strategy
- Responding to the new world and strategy—leading change

Best Practices and Research

These outlines provided a very solid framework and touchstone for the challenge of determining specific content and program format. The desire for program excellence caused program designers to study and consider best practices in executive development as part of the design work. An early and important learning from benchmarking was that "leading edge" is relative; a practice is only as valuable as the quality of its application in its environment. An academic or other company's best practice cannot be successfully laid on an unprepared and/or an unwilling culture. Understanding this, the task in shaping the MC and LDP experiences was to marry innovations in executive development with Abbott's culture. The trick would be to continually stretch the culture and participants beyond their comfort zone, but not to the point of their rejecting the experience as impractical or irrelevant.

The research (including information obtained from university affiliations, consortium participation, web browsing, and benchmarking other companies) and knowledge of the Abbott culture led to the inclusion or exclusion of the elements (see Table 1.2) in the programs' design.

TABLE 1.2.   INCLUSION AND EXCLUSION PROGRAM COMPONENTS.

Inclusion	Exclusion
Simulation	Cross-company action learning teams
Faculty partnerships	Global sessions (one session in the United States, the next in Europe, then Asia, and so on)
Multi-rater assessment and feedback	
Community service	Virtual sessions
Executive involvement and dialogue	
Individual development planning and application	

While the intent of this chapter is to describe "best-in-class" development practices, there may be some value in understanding when such practices may not be appropriate. Among the best practices considered but not implemented because of organizational preparedness are:

• Cross-company action learning teams—because the organization did not commit to deliver the sort of "live ammo" issues required of such teams, partially driven by the diverse nature of the businesses
• Global sessions—because of cost and organizational concern that global sessions might generate a perception of deadlock
• Virtual (electronic) sessions—because the company views the programs as a network-building opportunity and there is no substitute for face-to-face interaction in the early stages of relationship development

Implementation of Best Practices

Of the best practices that Abbott did choose to implement, several— simulation, multi-rater assessment, executive dialogue/involvement, and individual planning—are fairly popular and well-documented in industry, consulting, and academia.

In the MC, Abbott chose to partner with Executive Perspectives to deliver a twelve- to fifteen-hour computer simulation as the cornerstone of week two, understanding the general manager's perspective. The simulation allows participants, in teams of six or seven, to run a fledgling business using the concepts developed through the entire program. The simulation is detailed enough to provide for strong competition and realism. Executive Perspective facilitates the simulation and does an excellent job of integrating it with the course faculty, content, and desired objectives.

Multi-rater assessment is a component of both the MC and the LDP. In a drive to combine simplicity, ease of use, and meaning, Abbott selected the Center for Creative Leadership's *Prospector* for its assessment instrument, a tool that measures an individual's ability and readiness to learn and take advantage of growth experiences that can lead to leadership development. Because of its focus, on learning capability, the *Prospector* matches Abbott's programs' message to participants: "Learning will fuel your continued growth."

Key to the objective of providing participants the skills to lead Abbott's future success is interaction with the company's most senior executives (CEO, COO, and the top ten positions in the company). Like many leadership development efforts, the desired outcomes of this interaction are for participants to:

- Understand the company's direction and need for change—and commitment to supporting it
- See role models or exemplars of the skills to achieve the company's objectives
- Develop a broader perspective about the company

The executive interaction also gives senior managers a platform for sharing their aspirations and expectations while simultaneously scouting talent. The interaction takes the form of "dialogues" with the CEO, COO, and other senior operating people. This element is generally viewed as one of the most positive of the MC and LDP experiences.

"An individual is responsible for his or her career, but the company is responsible for providing opportunity and tools" summarizes Abbott's development philosophy. Toward that end, the programs are designed to provide opportunity for individual development planning and "on-the-job" application of the program content. The MC and LDP require participants to complete the career planning exercise in the appendix of Morgan McCall's *High Flyers* (Harvard Business School Publishing, 1997). It is a nice blending of company direction as well as individual skills and direction.

The programs use a variety of mechanisms to drive learning application outside the classroom. Participants are asked to teach at least one content area of the program to an audience of their choosing (for example, their staff or a team they are on). Additionally, participants create "personal contracts" at the conclusion of the programs, aimed at enhancing follow-up application by committing to a written action plan. Finally, Abbott is implementing a reunion for past participants, part of which will be a discussion of progress against those action plans. Though there is still much opportunity for improvement, these efforts are paying off in increased application on the job as measured by participant feedback, shown in Table 1.3.

There are two elements of Abbott's program design that are either unique or so integral to the process that they merit more detailed discussion. They are faculty partnerships and the use of community service as part of leadership development.

TABLE 1.3.   PARTICIPANT FEEDBACK.

	Before Redesign	After Redesign
Program will make significant impact on my growth	65 percent	100 percent
Program will have practical carryover in daily responsibility	73 percent	90 percent
Supervisor utilized program content	15 percent	54 percent

Faculty Partnerships

Driven by the goal of providing leading-edge thinking and expertise, both the MC and LDP are heavily dependent on external faculty for program delivery (approximately 70 percent of program time). Additional aims of the programs are to marry leading-edge thinking with company strategy and present an integrated stream of content. Given these objectives, program outcomes are heavily dependent on the quality and "fit" of that external faculty.

To maximize its freedom to identify faculty talent to match specific content and strategic needs, the company chose not to partner with any one university or institution. However, recognizing the importance of the faculty, it chose to pursue partnership with individual faculty members. The principles of partnership appear simple, but have paid significant dividends in the quality of learning that takes place, including:

- *Long-term relationship*—Though long-term contracts are not signed, except for an occasional topical presenter, faculty members are approached as if they will be an ongoing part of the programs.
- *Shared understanding*—Much time is spent orienting new faculty members to the background and purpose of the programs; each individual knows where he or she "fits" in the program flow and logic. They develop an understanding of the material and style of the faculty that surround them in the program and link their discussions to that content. For even the most "seasoned" faculty member there is a pre-conference discussion to review objectives, past feedback, and class personalities to ensure the greatest impact in the program.
- *Feedback and communication*—Each faculty member is provided detailed written feedback every time they work in the program. Those that do not respond to that feedback are not invited to return. Likewise, the faculty share their thoughts on the program and input on its continuous improvement.

The benefits of this partnership for Abbott are multiple. First, the quality of instruction in the classroom steadily improves as the faculty gains experience with Abbott's culture and needs. Program flow improves as the faculty understands and works the points of integration. The faculty understand Abbott's goals and needs and begin to refer their own network of peers to the program, much like employee referrals for new employees. Finally, many of the faculty members have, through their introduction in the MC and LDP, engaged in consulting and research projects at Abbott, extending the value of their expertise within the company.

Community Service—A Different Sort of Leadership

The idea of faculty partnerships may not be "leading edge," but the concept is incredibly effective. Likewise, the use of community service in leadership development may not be new, but Abbott's application of it is unique and has been shown to have the potential for powerful impact on the thinking and actions of its high-potential leaders.

Prior to the redesign of the MC and LDP in 1996, community service had been a part of the LDP. It was used for three purposes, as an effective "icebreaker" for the participants (the first day of their three weeks together); as a leaderless team exercise (structuring "fix-it" projects); and to experience Abbott's value of serving the community. Projects were usually physical labor at a social services agency facility. Because the projects were done on Saturdays, they rarely involved interaction with clients of the agency.

The redesign team decided to enhance the value of the community service piece by tying it much more directly to the concept of leadership. The thinking is straightforward: As the market and world change more and more rapidly, the leader will find him or herself in more situations and with more people who are different than what he or she is used to.

Projects are selected on their ability to provide participants a "different" experience and a significant amount of interaction with the clients of the charitable agency. Each program "class" works with the same organization each week it is in session. Generally, the first week focuses on some physical fix-up and limited interaction, allowing both groups to become familiar with one another. Subsequent weeks focus almost exclusively on social interaction designed to address needs the charitable organization identifies. Program facilitators structure the first week's activities, while a subgroup of the class structures the second and third week's activity.

Among the differences program participants must navigate in order to lead the community service project successfully are socioeconomic, race, age, and level of education. The projects challenge participants to think differently about how to lead, how to meet followers' needs, and how to have an impact. While most of the fix-up projects and social interactions are standard (such as painting, minor carpentry, landscaping; sporting events, picnics, bowling) the radically different context provides for powerful learning opportunities. For instance, to experience one's natural approach to delegation as totally unsuccessful in this different setting and to struggle to find other ways to accomplish the task is a great learning experience. For a participant to learn that the difference between career success and homelessness or addiction is not nearly as large as he or she had assumed has tremendous impact.

Community Service Example

One LDP class worked with residents in a temporary residence for men just released from prison. Initially, many of the LDP participants were frightened of the residents and held stereotypical views about the nature of ex-convicts. Through the program's interactions, participants came to understand that the residents were equally afraid of them and that given a chance, many of the residents could contribute very positively to society. The experience of getting to know someone in a new light caused many participants to examine their view of others (especially their subordinates). They discovered their narrow or stereotypical view of their followers was limiting the contributions they were allowed to make. At a personal level, many of the participants "stuck with" the agency long after the program was over, donating time, energy, and money to carry out the work of the residence.

The amount of personal stretch in any of these projects creates apprehension in many participants. There is generally nervous tension and some grumbling before the first experience for each class. Most participants work through their concerns and find great value in the effort. Others reject the idea as too radical or impractical. Many non-U.S. participants are initially thrown by cultural-norm differences. In some countries, the government is responsible for all social work. Despite these difficulties, and occasional administrative opportunities for improvement, this shift has been successful on multiple fronts:

- Participant understanding of and satisfaction with the opportunity to test their leadership in a different environment

- Participants' renewed commitment to Abbott for its commitment to "doing good"
- A genuine opportunity to experience diversity
- A genuine opportunity to make a positive difference for people in difficult situations

The Ideas in Action

The design thinking described throughout this chapter results in a logical program flow within the weeks of each program and between the MC and the LDP. See Exhibits 1.2 and 1.3 (pages 29, 32) for the agendas of these programs.

Evaluation

Abbott values measurement. In a world of limited resources and seemingly unlimited demand, it is natural to ask, "What is this investment's contribution, and can you quantify it?" This task of quantifying the "soft" contribution of leadership development is a challenge. Abbott has committed to developing an appropriate measurement system that is both qualitative and quantitative. This work in progress currently consists of three types of measures. They are, in descending order of control of the facilitators and in ascending order of importance to the business: (1) short-term/process (was the process perceived as valuable?); (2) leadership development objectives (including high-potential turnover, depth, and quality of the talent pool); and (3) business objectives (including accelerated growth, and so on). A brief description of Abbott's progress follows:

Short-term/Process Results

- *Participant satisfaction*—Each participant completes an extensive six-page evaluation of each week of the program. It consists of a numeric evaluation of multiple dimensions of each of the week's modules, a rating of the degree to which the week met its stated objectives, and qualitative feedback about the faculty, content applicability, and opportunities for improvement. The program administrators' goals and performance rating are tied to these evaluations.

- *Participant impact*—Some time after the conclusion of the LDP, participants are surveyed to determine their satisfaction with and implementation of the program learning. The aim in this metric is to determine the degree of applicability in the programs. To see the instrument and data, see Exhibit 1.4, LDP Participant Survey.

Leadership Development Objectives

This data, by its nature, is both quantitative and qualitative. The turnover among program participants (past and present) is running between 3–4 percent annually, and the depth of Abbott's leadership pool, which is the number of "ready now" candidates for corporate asset positions, is expanding. What still needs work is the qualitative side of this piece—are leaders quicker to see and adapt to a changing world? Are they more global in their thinking? Are their followers more motivated? Anecdotal stories from past participants are being gathered, but have not yet been translated into solid measurement.

Business Objectives

This last frontier of measuring leadership development is, for Abbott, the most difficult. Though it is the area richest in data and measurement (such as sales, financial and operational data), the direct links from leadership development to that data are the weakest. Still in the early stages of this development, Abbott is gathering anecdotal data from past participants about the impact of program participation on their business performance. Among the "good news" stories are the transfer of a U.S.-based value-added service to South America, and internal "networks" among program participants that have led to cross-business opportunities that had not been identified previously. Abbott will continue to work at refining these anecdotal stories into more concrete measures of success.

Conclusion

The purpose of redesigning Abbott's leadership development program was to improve its ability to prepare its leaders for a rapidly changing environment. In the eyes of participants, their managers, and the organization at large, much progress has been made toward achieving that objective, yet much more progress still needs to occur. By continually monitoring the process, perception, and impact of the MC and LDP internally, these programs can be continually shaped to meet Abbott's needs. In addition, by continually monitoring the external best practices in leadership development, others' expertise can be leveraged for repeated improvement.

Exhibit 1.1: Abbott's Leadership Competency Model

As previously mentioned, Abbott Laboratory's Leadership Competency
model is discussed here in more detail.

Set Vision and Strategy

Create and deliver a vision of the future to maximize company performance.
Establish and commit to strategies and a course of action to accomplish that
long-range vision. Communicate a clear view of the desired future state.

- Understand trends, their implications and opportunities, in the global
  environment (customer, technical, healthcare, regulatory, and so on).
  Gather information from multiple sources including customers, peers,
  staff, and external experts. Assess information with a global perspective,
  identifying opportunities and threats, and developing long-term strategies to respond. Balance opportunities, resources, and investments to
  maximize Abbott's growth.
- Maintain a strong customer focus. Link the business vision with customer
  needs and marketplace conditions. Develop strategies that convert customer requirements into products and services.
- Identify and capitalize on opportunities to create value from cross-
  divisional capabilities.
- Effectively communicate the business vision and strategies to all in the
  organization.
- Look to the future, using global marketplace, technology, and business
  knowledge to identify and seize emerging opportunities.
- Effectively translate the business vision and broad strategies into concrete or actionable strategic plans and goals, prioritizing goals, projects,
  and plans appropriately.

Linkage Inc.'s Best Practices in Leadership Development Handbook, edited by David Giber, Louis
Carter, and Marshall Goldsmith. Copyright © 2000 by Linkage Press and Jossey-Bass/
Pfeiffer, San Francisco, CA.

Behavioral Anchors

High

- Actively scans environment and develops long-term approaches that redefine problems or market opportunities in anticipation of changing business conditions or environmental trends
- Looks to the future when developing strategy; anticipates potential obstacles, competitive responses, and alternate scenarios; develops contingency plans
- Gains internal and external commitment for strategy by involving broad constituencies (customers, employees, peers, higher-level management) and multiple perspectives
- Drives strategy through the organization by completely integrating organizational and individual goal planning, assessment, and rewards into strategy

Medium

- Recognizes changing environmental conditions that will impact businesses and customers; applies established approaches to address impact; aligns organization (action plans, resource allocations, and so on) to deliver results
- Positions for long-term success when developing plans and strategies to address current issues
- Considers impact on other units, businesses, and divisions when developing strategies
- Regularly communicates strategy and creates broad understanding of direction within appropriate constituencies (for example, has clearly communicated low-range planning direction and goals)

Low

- Conveys unclear or conflicting information on strategy rationales and implementation
- Is slow to incorporate changing business conditions into strategies and plans
- Defines issues or opportunities narrowly, neglecting to consider broader impact (other units, divisions, company); does not adequately "reality check" assumptions and projections

- Uses inappropriate mix of knowledge and expertise in strategy development (does not include employees, peers, higher-level management), or is too dependent on single input

Build Our Organization and Inspire Our People

Attract and grow people to maximize the collective skills of the organization. Inspire and motivate them to achieve the organization's strategic intent, vision, and goals. Create and sustain the organization and structure needed to support the company's people and business strategies.

- Determine and acquire or develop the talents, skills, and abilities needed to achieve the organization's goals; assure a strong talent pool by continuously developing people's skills, knowledge, and ability.
- Staff the organization from various disciplines, backgrounds, and cultures to promote and capitalize on diversity and ensure complementary talents and skills.
- Create a committed organization that acts with integrity; ensure that people understand and are motivated by the strategic intent and value their roles in achieving the company's vision.
- Create a productive organization; encourage people to innovate, collaborate, make decisions, and exercise authority and responsibility.
- Establish clear expectations, provide timely, accurate feedback—both positive and negative—and take appropriate follow-up action, (for example, rewarding, publicizing successes, coaching, and guiding). Recognize, reward, and promote people based on their performance, achievement of results, and development of competencies.
- Serve as a role model by acting in a consistent, fair manner; exude enthusiasm; remain accessible; demonstrate confidence in others' abilities.

Behavioral Anchors
High
- Identifies and matches organization strengths with business opportunities or quickly develops additional capabilities to take advantage of opportunities

- Anticipates talents, skills, and knowledge that will be needed in the organization; seeks out opportunities to grow people's capabilities to meet those needs
- Tangibly demonstrates how products and services help customers; draws connection between individual employee and customer
- Personally invests time and effort in developing and supporting staff
- Proactively works to motivate all employees (exudes enthusiasm; takes every opportunity to speak positively about the organization; articulates sense of purpose and directions; celebrates success)

Medium
- Continually upgrades caliber of organization through selection, training, on-the-job training, development, or rotational assignments
- Creates understanding of organization's purpose and direction by employees through regularly sharing business goals, expectations, timelines, and status
- Builds appropriate cross-functional or multidisciplinary teams to address issues
- Appropriately delegates decision-making authority to others and manages expectations
- Considers impact of organization structure on business success

Low
- Neglects key stakeholders (upward, downward, or lateral) in gaining buy-in for goals, strategies, and direction
- Ignores employee issues and concerns; displays favoritism
- Does not plan for long-term needs of people
- Conveys negative news without discussion of solutions or refuses to acknowledge negative information

Know the Business

Understand Abbott's customers, markets, business operations, and emerging issues. Base decisions on facts, experience, and logical assumptions, taking into consideration opportunity for gain, resources, constraints, risk and reward, and organizational values.

- Continuously secure and evaluate relevant information, identifying key issues, trends, relationships, and cause and effect as they impact the business; appropriately consult with experts; create an environment where information, expertise, and experience are broadly shared and used to create insights that shape the business.
- Learn from and build on business experience to produce success; create organizations capable of learning from both success and failure and applying that learning to future decisions.
- Demonstrate a strong personal capacity for learning new aspects of the business and encourage others to do the same.

Behavioral Anchors

High

- Draws broadly on resources, knowledge, and expertise (for example, through customers, vendors, other divisions, competitors, technical experts) to thoroughly and systematically analyze markets or business opportunities
- Before entering a negotiation, in addition to gathering all relevant facts and data, works to understand the needs, wants, objectives, and constraints of all parties to assure a win-win situation
- Recognizes potential application or implication of unconventional benchmarks, for example, those outside of the healthcare industry
- Maintains awareness of changing business conditions and actively develops contingency plans
- Has a personal learning plan

Medium

- Gathers necessary facts and data before making a business decision; consults with customers, technology, or industry experts, and others in Abbott to assure a clear picture of the situation
- At the end of a project, with project team, takes time to determine what was learned that can be applied to future projects
- Routinely tracks business plans and objectives of internal and external partners
- Creates opportunities for staff to share ideas and information with similar functions across divisions

- Seeks out internal resources, expertise, and knowledge across divisions when trying to resolve business problems

Low
- Works in isolation; does not share goals, results, or activities with or seek out information from others; as a result, duplicates efforts or works at cross-purposes to the work of others
- Fails to learn from experience; continues to replicate a process that has been proven not to work well; ignores suggestions for improvement
- Consistently makes decisions based on first reaction; does not ask questions to clarify or confirm information or to assure understanding of the situation
- Becomes emotionally vested in a course of action; refuses to acknowledge information or experience that indicates alternate courses of action may produce better business results

Drive for Results

Establish high goals for organization success and personal accomplishment. Lead to meet or exceed those goals. Create a nimble organization that executes well and makes speed in achieving high-quality results a competitive advantage for Abbott.

- Collaboratively set realistic, challenging, measurable goals and timetables; keep self and others focused on key performance indicators; be willing to adjust goals to meet changing business needs.
- Set short-term objectives that drive toward longer-term goals or strategies; monitor and adjust activities to meet objectives; stay with a position or plan of action until the desired objective is achieved.
- Support staff with necessary resources to achieve goals.
- Hold self and others accountable for delivering high-quality results.
- Regularly evaluate self and team on goal attainment, process used to achieve goals, and competitive benchmarks.
- Be tenacious.

Behavioral Anchors

High

- Looks for opportunities for synergy and partnership in setting goals; proactively integrates goals with other appropriate functions both inside and across divisions to maximize overall results for division and company
- Consistently sets stretch goals and looks for ways to improve results
- Challenges the status quo in defining desired results
- Works across traditional boundaries to deliver results

Medium

- Persists in pursuit of goals despite obstacles
- Seeks out and implements new ways to increase productivity, improve old processes, and improve results
- Pursues the intent rather than the "letter" of the objective
- Establishes success criteria and metrics at beginning of project; uses metrics to manage and communicate project accomplishments

Low

- Dictates goals without gaining buy-in of those responsible for delivering results
- Focuses on success of own unit, ignoring potential for wider organization benefit
- Creates plans with insufficient detail to monitor progress
- Sets time frames that are overly optimistic or overly generous
- Establishes "safe" goals that promise results comparable to those delivered currently

Make the Difficult Decisions

Make timely decisions in the face of obstacles, difficulties, and challenges. Act decisively, demonstrating confidence and the strength of one's convictions. Commit the organization's resources to achieve the company's strategies taking calculated, well-thought-out risks when necessary.

- Demonstrate the willingness to make and accept unpopular decisions or take opposing positions.
- Challenge status quo or traditional way of doing things.
- Correctly recognize crisis situations and take corrective action at the earliest indication of trouble.
- Recognize errors and make midcourse corrections as necessary; demonstrate willingness to admit mistakes, learn from them, and be held accountable for their impact.
- Make the difficult "people decisions" when necessary.

Behavioral Anchors

High
- Proactively works to improve overall business results even when decisions may be at expense of or not benefit own area of responsibility
- Makes decisions to realign or invest resources to address serious business issues or new opportunities even when such decisions may delay or cancel other projects, require changes in direction or established goals, or negatively impact people
- Promptly makes decision to end or redefine a popular project or program when results, experience, or new information indicate that original objectives cannot be met
- In a crisis situation, will make decisions and set course of action even if available information and expertise does not clearly indicate a solution

Medium
- When problems arise, attempts to improve or correct results; if problem persists, notifies higher-level management and proposes alternate courses of action; makes decisions to act in a timely manner
- Gathers appropriate experts and resources to resolve problems when they arise; based on input from multiple sources, makes final decision on resolution; acts decisively and with a sense of urgency
- Uses task forces or committees to provide expertise, generate options, gain multiple points of view; takes all input into account and makes timely decisions, informing everyone of outcome

- Promptly addresses poor performance from an employee; acts to remove an employee when corrective or developmental actions have not proved successful

Low
- Refuses to acknowledge poor results; continues to invest resources in an unsuccessful course of action in the hope that circumstances will change; does not deliver bad news to higher-level management when needed to support a change in action
- Makes decision to proceed with a proposed project of questionable value because of an unwillingness to disappoint project owner
- Avoids decisions by using committees to address inappropriate business issues
- Delays dealing with employee dissatisfaction in the hope that situation will resolve itself

Encourage Open Communication and Knowledge Sharing

Create a culture of open, honest communication where all are encouraged and feel free to express their views.

- Foster a work environment with continuous open communication and knowledge sharing, leveraging that sharing for positive results.
- Frequently solicit ideas and share information with staff and others.
- Encourage the expression of opposing and different points of view.
- Practice effective listening skills; listen and think about diverse or differing ideas before responding.
- Proactively seek feedback and demonstrate a willingness to learn and change.
- Give honest feedback, positive and critical, both to staff and higher-level management.

Behavioral Anchors
High
- Encourages and rewards disagreement and diversity of opinion in analyzing and discussing issues and opportunities

- Redesigns organizational structure and management systems (goals, incentive, team make-up) to support needed business communication
- Seeks, quantifies, and responds to employee input in large and small issues
- Creates two-way cross-boundary communication networks; routinely uses these networks for decision making and managing the business
- Leverages best practices (other divisions' or companies') for innovation in own area

Medium
- Establishes multiple processes for two-way information flow (town meetings, skip-level meetings, expanded staff, and so on)
- Routinely shares relevant business information with entire organization (strategy, progress versus objectives, competitive activity, and so on)
- Routinely conducts postmortems to determine and apply "lessons learned"
- Leverages technology to facilitate wide exchange of best practices and rapid access to knowledge and expertise
- Seeks and responds positively to personal feedback

Low
- Sets self up as sole information processor or decision maker
- Reacts to negative information by attacking it and/or the messenger
- Tightly controls or hoards information; inappropriately applies a "need to know" approach
- Directs organization to focus exclusively within its current boundaries

Exhibit 1.2: Leadership Development Program Agenda

OVERVIEW OF WEEK 1—1999

Our Changing World: Sharpening Awareness

	3/6/99 Saturday	3/7/99 Day 1 Sunday	3/8/99 Day 2 Monday	3/9/99 Day 3 Tuesday	3/10/99 Day 4 Wednesday	3/11/99 Day 5 Thursday	3/12/99 Day 6 Friday
a.m.		F R E E	Debrief: Leadership (Lance Secretan) Community service project	Debrief: Global economics, trade and investment (Debora Spar)	Global economics, trade and investment (Debora Spar)	Debrief: Future directions in technology (Neil Gershenfeld)	Dialogue with Abbott axecutive (Miles White, CEO)
p.m.	Optional arrival/early check-in	Introduction of program/Week 1 Leadership (Lance Secretan)	F R E E	F R E E		A millenium health imperative (Neal Patterson) Integrating strategy and the environment (Steve Weger)	Week 1 wrap-up Adjourn
evening		Group dinner			Group activity/dinner	Group activity/dinner	

Linkage Inc.'s Best Practices in Leadership Development Handbook, edited by David Giber; Louis Carter, and Marshall Goldsmith. Copyright © 2000 by Linkage Press and Jossey-Bass/Pfeiffer, San Francisco, CA.

(continued)

Exhibit 1.2: (continued)

OVERVIEW OF WEEK 2—1999
The Strategy: Competing From the Edge

	6/13/99 Day 1 Sunday	6/14/99 Day 2 Monday	6/15/99 Day 3 Tuesday	6/16/99 Day 4 Wednesday	6/17/99 Day 5 Thursday	6/18/99 Day 6 Friday
a.m.		Developing strategy (Vijay Govindarajan)	Developing strategy (Vijay Govindarajan)	Debrief: Cooperating to compete: Alliance and acquisition strategies (Ben Gomes-Casseres)	Debrief: Abbott case study	Debrief: Abbott's people strategy (Don Kraft) Synthesis and wrap-up
p.m.	Introduction of program/ week 1	Debrief	Community Service Project		*Leadership (Lance Secretan)	
evening	Reception/ Dinner	FREE	*Group activity/ dinner	FREE	Group activity/ dinner	

30

OVERVIEW OF WEEK 3—1999
The Challenge: Mastering the Game

	9/26/99 Day 1 Sunday	9/27/99 Day 2 Monday	9/28/99 Day 3 Tuesday	9/29/99 Day 4 Wednesday	9/30/99 Day 5 Thursday	10/1/99 Day 6 Friday
a.m.		Debrief: Leading change (John Kotter)	Debrief: Community service project	Debrief panel discussion: The leader's role in leading change (Chicago area executives) — Leading change	Debrief: Abbott case study	Debrief prospector: 360 on learning and leadership leading change workshop: Wrap-up and final commitments
p.m.		Leading change workshop: Choose and assess — Personal initiative	Leading change workshop: Laying the foundation for success — Dialogue with Abbott executive		Leading change workshop: Successful implementation (continued)	
evening	Week 2 Recap — Strategic intent/core competencies workshop	FREE	Reception and recognition dinner	FREE	Group activity/dinner	

31

Exhibit 1.3: The Management Challenge: Managing Across Boundaries Agenda

OVERVIEW OF WEEK 1—1999
Strategy: The Context For Value Creation

	02/07/99 Day 1 Sunday	02/08/99 Day 2 Monday	02/09/99 Day 3 Tuesday	02/10/99 Day 4 Wednesday	02/11/99 Day 5 Thursday	02/12/99 Day 6 Friday
a.m.		Thinking strategically: Competitive advantage in international markets (Debora Spar)	Abbott's strategic initiatives (Gary Coughlan, CFO; Ellen Walvoord, VP of HR) Cooperating to compete acquisitions and alliance strategies	Community service project	Abbott people strategy (Don Kraft) Dialogue with Abbott CEO (Miles White)	Action planning synthesis and wrap-up
p.m.	Week 1 Kickoff/set-up leadership (Lance Secretan)			Managing innovation (Ralph Katz)	Abbott people strategy (continued) (Don Kraft)	
evening	Dinner	Group activity/ dinner	F R E E	F R E E	Group activity/ dinner	

OVERVIEW OF WEEK 1—1999
Functional Integration: Executing Strategy

	05/16/99 Day 1 Sunday	05/17/99 Day 2 Monday	05/18/99 Day 3 Tuesday	05/19/99 Day 4 Wednesday	05/20/99 Day 5 Thursday	05/21/99 Day 6 Friday
a.m.		Debrief: Financial analysis (John Boquist)	Debrief: Operations strategy (TBD)	Debrief: product development (Stefan Thomke)	Debrief: Marketing strategy (Gregory Carpenter)	Business simulation results/ Debrief: (Seth Levenson) Leadership workshops debrief synthesis and wrap-up
p.m.	Introduction of week 2 prospector: 360 feedback session introduce business	Capital budgeting and financial decision making (John Boquist)	Dialogue with Abbott executive (Bob Parkinson, COO)	Business simulation: Team decision making (Seth Levenson)	Business simulation: Team decision making (Seth Levenson)	
evening	Business simulation: Team planning session (Seth Levenson)	Team decision making (Seth Levenson) FREE		FREE	Group activity/ dinner	

Linkage Inc.'s Best Practices in Leadership Development Handbook, edited by David Giber, Louis Carter, and Marshall Goldsmith. Copyright © 2000 by Linkage Press and Jossey-Bass/Pfeiffer, San Francisco, CA.

Exhibit 1.4: LDP Participant Survey

The Abbott Leadership Development Program . . .	1998 Participants			1997 Participants			Past Participants		
	Agree	Neither	Disagree	Agree	Neither	Disagree	Agree	Neither	Disagree
1. Provided new insight into external Issues impacting Abbott and the healthcare industry	100%			95%	5%		97%	2%	1%
2. Gave me valuable perspective about corporate strategy and approach to Abbott's competitive market position	94%	6%		86%	14%		82%	13%	5%
3. Provided me with a different, helpful perspective of the changing environment/ marketplace that Abbott faces	100%			95%	5%		93%	7%	
4. Made me look at myself and my own capacity for change	100%			100%			74%	18%	8%
5. Helped me grow in my level of strategic thinking	94%	6%		100%			86%	12%	2%
6. Provided insight into my leadership style, leading to personal change	89%	11%		95%		5%	64%	27%	9%
7. Enhanced cross-divisional understanding and communication	100%			95%	5%		95%	4%	1%
8. Created a sense of group cohesiveness among participants	94%	6%		95%	5%		93%	4%	2%
9. Improved my understanding about other Abbott divisions	94%	6%		86%	10%	5%	91%	8%	1%
10. Will make a significant impact on my personal growth	100%			100%			65%	28%	7%

Item	1	2	3	4	5	6	7	8	9
11. Will have little practical carryover value to my daily responsibilities and decision making	17%		83%	5%		95%	73%	18%	9%
12. Is highly respected, and selection was considered an honor	89%	11%				100%		9%	91%
13. Tried to cover too much in too little time	5%	28%	67%	14%	24%	62%	52%	29%	20%
14. Was poorly organized and administered	100%			100%			96%	4%	
15. Provided instruction from capable, knowledgeable teachers	95%		5%			100%	2%	2%	96%
16. Has better prepared me for a leadership role in Abbott	95%	5%				100%	1%	12%	87%
17. Left me frustrated when I returned to my regular responsibilities		17%	83%	14%	24%	62%	72%	15%	13%
18. Came at an opportune time in my career	78%	22%		71%	24%	5%	3%	18%	79%
19. Should be available to a larger number of Abbott executives	39%	55%	6%	33%	48%	19%	21%	28%	51%
20. Provided information and skills that my immediate supervisor utilized	54%	23%	23%	10%	43%	48%	51%	34%	15%
21. Ignored some significant corporate issues	N/A	N/A	N/A	N/A	N/A	N/A	N/A	N/A	N/A
22. Increased my commitment to Abbott as a place to work	N/A	N/A	N/A	N/A	N/A	N/A	N/A	N/A	N/A
23. Was worth the time and the corporate expense	N/A	N/A	N/A	N/A	N/A	N/A	N/A	N/A	N/A
24. Built up unrealistic expectations on the part of participants	N/A	N/A	N/A	N/A	N/A	N/A	N/A	N/A	N/A
25. Helped me think through my future plans and values	N/A	N/A	N/A	N/A	N/A	N/A	N/A	N/A	N/A
26. Seemed inconsistent with Abbott corporate expectations	33%	11%	56%	14%	38%	48%	60%	26%	14%

Linkage Inc.'s Best Practices in Leadership Development Handbook, edited by David Giber, Louis Carter, and Marshall Goldsmith. Copyright © 2000 by Linkage Press and Jossey-Bass/Pfeiffer, San Francisco, CA.

About the Contributor

Don Kraft (don.kraft@abbott.com) is the director of human resources planning and development at Abbott Laboratories. Kraft is responsible for leadership development, succession planning, and the redesign of the company's performance management system. In his twelve years with Abbott, he has worked in five different businesses, all within the human resources function. The majority of his Abbott career has been in a human resources generalist position; however, he has had specialist assignments in staffing as well as the current assignment in organization development.

Prior to Abbott, Kraft held several human resources positions at Harris Corporation in Melbourne, Florida. He has a master's degree in management from Northwestern University and a bachelor's degree in business administration from Villanova University.

CHAPTER TWO

ALLIEDSIGNAL

This chapter outlines a 360-degree, assessment-based
leadership development initiative for leaders at all levels of the
organization, designed to work in conjunction with the organization's
human resource strategic plan and performance management process.

Introduction

AlliedSignal is an advanced technology and manufacturing company, serving customers worldwide with aerospace and automotive products, chemicals, fibers, plastics, and advanced materials. The company is organized into eleven strategic business units. With approximately $16 billion in sales, AlliedSignal ranks among the top 100 of the Fortune 500, and is one of the thirty companies comprising the Dow Jones Industrial Average.

The Vision Behind the Initiative

It was clear that AlliedSignal's future called for significant growth and productivity gains. In 1991, the reins for management of AlliedSignal were handed to Lawrence Bossidy, a thirty-year veteran from General Electric. As CEO, Bossidy brought a renewed vigor and energy to the organization. He introduced total quality leadership as a way of life. He caused the many paradigms to begin to shift, encouraging change to happen.

As part of its major organizational-change program, AlliedSignal established its vision: "To be one of the world's premier companies, distinctive and successful in everything we do." Values were defined as central to the vision: "Customers, Integrity, People, Teamwork, Speed, Innovation, and Performance."

To achieve this vision of success, AlliedSignal had to set aggressive goals and had to meet those commitments. One of these goals was in the area of personnel development. AlliedSignal had to identify and develop people who would lead the company and contribute to its growth. This major task required a thoughtful evaluation of the strengths and development needs of current and potential leaders.

Core Review Processes

Strengthening organizational talent is a fundamental building block of total quality at AlliedSignal. In fact, it is one of three core processes. The triumvirate includes: strategic planning, annual operating planning, and management resource review. The strategic planning process drives the company's direction and the annual operating plan identifies the revenues and spending limits. The management resource review (MRR) process is a key AlliedSignal management tool designed to systematically assess and develop the capability of people within its organization.

Management Resource Review Process

The MRR process objectives are:

- Examine business environment, direction, strategies, and associated organization implications, including structure, processes, and people.
- Assess key individuals regarding results, behaviors, and potential.
- Evaluate current depth of succession talent.
- Present action plans for upgrading organization talent.
- Identify high-potential and promotable talent and plans for development and movement.
- Review special topics and status of key change initiatives.
- Summarize organization-wide issues and discuss plans for organization and individual improvement action plans.

The MRR process is integrated with the performance management and career development processes, focusing on the review and development of individual results, behavior, and potential.

Integrated Performance Management and Development Process (IPMD)

This joint process of assessing and evaluating the individual and the organization as a whole is a semiannual, circular program called the Integrated Performance Management and Development (IPMD) process. Each step in the process drives the next and the process is never completed (see Exhibit 2.1). Central to the IPMD process is the concept of continuous development of the employee's career. The career development process starts with the individual and includes seven distinct steps: assessment, research, goal setting, planning, discussion between employee and manager, action, and measurement.

AlliedSignal continues to work to improve the effectiveness and consistency of its MRR process while allowing flexibility for each organization based on different business needs. Consistency in evaluating individuals across the company will enable AlliedSignal to better assess its overall organization and human resource needs.

AlliedSignal developed three foundational building blocks for the IMPD process. Each document is a single-page summary. The Career Profile is a summary of key information about the individual including current position, education, training and development, awards, patents, or recognition, and prior work history. This mini-resume is prepared by the employee and updated as necessary (see Exhibit 2.2).

The second building block is the Continuous Improvement Summary and Performance Objectives Forms, or CIS form (see Exhibit 2.3). This is the primary part of the performance management discussion between the employee and supervisor of the employee's performance. This document is also a focal point of the MRR discussion. It is a summary of the employee's results, behaviors, and developmental needs and plans. The purpose of using the CIS form for both the performance management discussion and the MRR is to eliminate duplication and to ensure greater openness. When employees have a performance discussion with their supervisors, they will know what will be discussed during the MRR. Subsequent discussion of performance, career, and development plans are encouraged and can occur several times during the year, initiated either by the manager or the employee.

The third part of the IPMD process is performance objectives (see Exhibit 2.4). This process involves the review of the four to five most important financial and other business objectives for the employee's review period. These objectives must be specific to the organization's goals and processes as well as measurable in impact and scope. Results might be measured in revenue dollars, productivity improvements, exceptional project completion, process enhancements, or other quantifiable measurements specific to the organization's goals and processes.

Success Attributes and Behaviors

Over time, the values defined in 1991 with the first waves of the total quality swell migrated to patterns of behavior that were expected of all employees. AlliedSignal defined its success attributes and behaviors as the standard for success at all levels in the organization. All human resource processes are aligned to recruit, select, develop, and reward people with these attributes and behaviors. From early 1992 until today, each salaried employee is evaluated annually on these behaviors. The success attributes and behaviors (Table 2.1) are available for all employees.

Rating Scale

To evaluate the employee's behavior, a "developmentally" focused scale is used rather than the numerical performance scale frequently seen in performance appraisal programs. The success attribute ratings are:

- *Exceeds Standard*—Significantly exceeds expectations in this attribute. Others rely on the employee for guidance and help. Truly outstanding performance.
- *At Standard*—Consistently meets AlliedSignal's high standard of performance in this area. Mistakes are few and seldom repeated.
- *Needs Development*—These are areas the individual has had an opportunity to demonstrate but does not meet AlliedSignal standards. This rating may also signify that while the person meets AlliedSignal's standards in his or her current position, he or she needs development in this area to effectively perform in the next position. This rating simply highlights areas for future development.

The Strengths/Developmental Needs Summary on the CIS form (Exhibit 2.3, page 60) is based on the information listed in the results overview and the success attributes and behaviors sections. This area is used to highlight and add greater clarity to the information in the previous sections. The developmental actions and timing area addresses developmental needs outlined during the performance discussion process. AlliedSignal has found that it is critical for development plans to focus on the development needs

TABLE 2.1. SUCCESS ATTRIBUTES AND BEHAVIORS.

Success Attribute	Description of Behavior
Business acumen	• Demonstrates knowledge, interest, and/or aptitude for business • Knows competition • Familiar with strategies and tactics • Manages by fact
Customer focus	• Focuses work processes on customer satisfaction • Meets internal and external expectations • Promotes and maintains strong customer relationships/partnerships
Vision and purpose	• Sees possibilities; optimistic • Creates and communicates compelling vision or direction • Inspires and motivates • Aligns the organization
Values and ethics	• Lives by company values • Adheres to code of conduct • Rewards right behaviors • Ensures that laws are obeyed and that equal employment, safety, and environmental protection are practiced
Bias for action	• Demonstrates a sense of urgency to achieve important goals • Focuses on speed • Sets priorities; seizes opportunities • High energy • Reduces cycle time and bureaucracy • Eliminates waste and unnecessary work
Commitment	• Widely trusted • Takes ownership • Candid and forthcoming • Delivers on commitments
Teamwork	• Initiates and supports meaningful projects • Demonstrates trust in team members • Serves on teams • Celebrates successes
Innovation	• Promotes creativity and informed risk-taking • Strives for technical and market leadership • Establishes processes for continuous improvement
Developing people	• Assembles strong teams • Stretches, empowers, and trains people • Communicates effectively with people • Provides rewards, feedback, and recognition • Demonstrates and stimulates passion and commitment
Performance	• Sets and achieves ambitious goals • Listens and responds • Drives for continuous improvement • Measures the right things • Gets results • Ensures that health, safety, and environmental objectives are met and integrated into business activities
Technical	• Has function- or job-specific competencies

as well as technical competencies associated with missed performance targets. Other topics discussed during the performance interview are also documented on the CIS form. Together this summary provides an excellent review of the employee's performance, strengths, developmental needs, future career goals, and development plans.

360-degree Multi-Source Feedback (MSF) Program

Several organizational trends documented as starting in the early 1990s include more efficient and cost-effective organization structure, reduced bureaucracy, empowered employees, and teamwork. These business trends caused changes in the traditional manager–employee work relationship in many cases. Employees might be matrixed to another department on a project-by-project basis. Some employees elect to telecommute while others might work a flexible schedule in the next cubicle. In most situations, however, not only does the manager see the employee's performance but so do the direct reports, peers, customers, and if applicable, the manager to whom the employee is *matrixed*. To get the most accurate review of the employee's performance, each of these viewers should have an opportunity to contribute to the employee's annual performance appraisal. The logistics of such an approach can be unwieldy without the adoption of a relatively simple system, which is widely known as a 360-degree multi-source feedback (MSF) program.

Building a Business Case for the MSF Program

The number, format, design, definitions, and structures of 360-degree systems within AlliedSignal were growing rapidly. Because the evaluation of an employee's behavior in the success attributes and behaviors was so crucial to the employee's individual performance and to the organization as part of the MRR process, the company recognized the need to reduce variability in the 360-degree systems.

Beginning in 1993, AlliedSignal began implementing a biannual all-employee satisfaction survey process. After the 1995 survey, some businesses continued with quarterly satisfaction surveys with a statistically valid sample of employees. The survey data clearly indicated an employee desire to improve the supervisor–employee relationship and expand the avenues for communication. Employee performance management was targeted as an area for improvement. AlliedSignal initiated a program to ensure that employees receive more valuable performance feedback.

Endorsement from Above. Endorsement from the CEO played an important role in gaining employee "buy-in" for the MSF system. Larry Bossidy wholeheartedly endorsed the 360-degree approach by stating: "At AlliedSignal, effective MSF stands as evidence of our commitment to improving and developing the abilities of all employees. Moreover, it reflects a true team environment, one in which leaders stand not in judgment of subordinates' performance, but rather act as partners so we effectively build on our strengths and eliminate weaknesses to become better leaders and more capable team members."

The Design of the MSF Program

The first step in the design of the MSF program was the identification of a cross-business, cross-functional team to: (1) design the program; (2) develop a survey document and process; (3) identify and select vendors; and (4) make recommendations about the program's continuation.

The team was chartered and began its work. The vision of the MSF program was twofold:

- To assist employees and managers in enhancing the IPMD process by collecting feedback about performance from multiple sources
- To foster an organizational environment that encourages and supports trust, respect, and partnership in a team-based workforce

The MSF program design team communicated several core values to employees to ensure the program's success:

1. Employees will have a significant role in choosing their team of feedback givers.

2. 360-degree data will be used as the foundation for performance improvement and development, not as a disciplinary tool to be used "against" employees.
3. Employees will receive accurate and reliable data that respects the anonymity of the evaluators.
4. Behavior descriptors will be closely aligned with the success attributes and behaviors regardless of position with the organization.
5. A rating scale will be utilized that clearly defines excellence and differentiates between a deficiency and an area that, if improved, would yield improved potential for growth and possible promotion.

Although the CIS form provided an evaluation scale, the AlliedSignal team wanted categories that were more descriptive and user-friendly. The MSF program design team felt that frequency of response was more important than a single, averaged score for each item.

Development of Rating Scales

One of the first tasks in building a new 360-degree tool was to develop new rating scales as shown in Table 2.2.

The rating scale in the MSF program addressed and eliminated a discrepancy in the CIS form used in the IPMD process, the "needs development" rating. During the CIS discussions, it became clear that an individual could benefit from additional development in a particular success attribute without being deficient in that attribute. The MSF program formed two distinct categories: one devoted to improvement of an existing competency, and another stating that immediate improvement is necessary for success in the current job assignment.

Once the categories were developed, the MSF document had to be prepared. The success attributes and behaviors from the CIS form seemed to be the logical source for an AlliedSignal MSF program. The design team had to consider behaviors demonstrated by its more than 70,000 employees. These employees are involved in operations around the world from manufacturing to services to marketing. Plus, AlliedSignal has three core

TABLE 2.2 NEW RATING SCALE.

Continuous Improvement Summary		360-degree MSF Program	
EX (Exceeds Expectations)	Significantly exceeds expectations in this attribute. In this area, others rely on the employee for guidance and help. Truly outstanding performance.	RM (Role Model)	Maintains consistently outstanding performance of this behavior. This person's behavior serves as an example for others.
AS (At Standard)	Consistently meets AlliedSignal's high standard of performance in this area. Mistakes are few and seldom repeated.	CE (Capable and Effective)	Consistently meets AlliedSignal's high standards of performance. Contributions generally meet expectations for this position in the organization.
ND (Needs Development)	These are areas the individual has had an opportunity to demonstrate but does not meet AlliedSignal standards. This rating may also signify that while the person meets AlliedSignal's standards in his or her current position, he or she needs development in this area to perform effectively in the next position. This rating simply highlights areas for future development.	BD (Could Benefit from Development)	Person meets standards in this position but needs development to perform better or to move to the next position.
N/A	N/A	SI (Needs Significant Improvement)	The person has had an opportunity to demonstrate competence in this area, but does not meet AlliedSignal's high standards of performance. Improved performance is required.

businesses (aerospace, engineered materials, and automotive products) with a plethora of research and development, quality, sales, and administrative functions.

The core values of AlliedSignal and associated behavioral expectations dictated the consolidation of behavioral descriptions, which any employee anywhere in the world should demonstrate.

Behavioral Descriptors

The resulting descriptors follow:
1. Business acumen
   - Applies the knowledge of work processes to influence the achievement of business goals
   - Takes action based on knowledge of what the business must do to win in the marketplace
   - Links personal goals to company growth and productivity goals
2. Customer focus
   - Spends time with customers to define their expectations and where improvements can be made
   - Seeks opportunities to do things that have a positive impact on customers before being asked or forced by circumstances
   - Focuses the team on meeting customers' requirements
3. Values and ethics
   - Takes action based on the best interest of the company rather than how it may affect him or her personally
   - Behaves in a way that is consistent with AlliedSignal's values and code of conduct
   - Seeks and effectively uses the different contributions people bring to the job
4. Vision and purpose
   - Clearly articulates a vision for his or her work and inspires others to support it
   - Develops action plans to align his or her work with the goals of the organization

5. Bias for action
  - Sets priorities for his or her action and initiates timely action
  - Conveys a sense of urgency about addressing problems and opportunities
  - Identifies ways to simplify work processes and reduce cycle times
6. Commitment
  - Demonstrates personal accountability for accomplishing work unit goals as well as his or her own goals
  - Persists to meet commitments despite obstacles
7. Teamwork
  - Actively participates in the work of teams; seeks and listens to others' contributions
  - Provides assistance and support to other team members when needed
  - Partners with people from other work units to improve overall performance
8. Innovation
  - Creates and implements improved methods or solutions for meeting business needs
  - Constructively challenges existing work processes and products to enhance value
  - Contributes to change efforts and breakthroughs which advance AlliedSignal's market leadership and growth
9. Developing people
  - Invests time and resources to help others gain skills and knowledge required to succeed in their work
  - Seeks and provides helpful feedback and coaching
  - Recognizes and celebrates others' accomplishments
10. Performance
  - Consistently sets and accomplishes ambitious goals that contribute to business success
  - Uses relevant facts to measure and track progress toward achievement of individual and team goals
  - Continuously improves the team's capability to perform as well as his or her own capability

11. Technical
- Keeps current with technical advances within his or her professional discipline; embraces and applies new techniques and practices
- Willingly shares his or her technical expertise; sought out as a resource by others
- Demonstrates a broad and deep mastery of the technical competencies required in his or her work

The Role of "Feedback Givers"

Once the wording of the behavioral descriptors was completed, AlliedSignal began discussing the number and type of written comment questions. Offering "feedback givers" an opportunity to write comments provides an additional dimension to an MSF process. This is an opportunity for "feedback givers" to speak directly to the employee without the constraints of prescriptive words. This is an opportunity for specific examples and personalized comments. In the long run, this is the opportunity that provides the richest details, the most significant feedback, the specificity frequently lost in the data-rich feedback report, and the most vibrant learnings for the employee. However, written comments take time for the "feedback giver" to construct, time for a vendor to process, and the time for the employee to reflect on and internalize.

Eventually, AlliedSignal constructed a total of six written questions. Two asked for specific examples of success attributes and behaviors, which were a strength or an opportunity for development. Another asked for specific observable accomplishments contributed by the subject employee in the past twelve months. The final three questions were: "What should this person continue doing?" "What should this person start doing?" and "What should this person stop doing?"

Over time, the MSF program design team realized that subgroups in a company as large and diverse as AlliedSignal might have multiple purposes in conducting an MSF program. For example, some units want the employees to own the data and use the program primarily as a tool for individual development. Other units want the supervisor to receive the data first as input for performance development discussions.

The time to complete the MSF instrument can be considerable and the cost can vary. The basic tool was flexible to allow for individual considerations. The tool could be used with each behavioral descriptor being considered as an individual item for a total of thirty-three items. Or each of the eleven success attributes and behaviors would be an item. The number of written responses could vary also. Thus the time and money for the process could vary in accordance with the business unit's desires. AlliedSignal, however, did have a consistent set of behavior descriptors, which bridged a major barrier.

MSF Process

The MSF process is made up of a number of key steps. First, a business unit decides they want to implement the process. Then an MSF process coordinator is identified at the business unit level. The MSF process coordinator clarifies the precise purpose of the process at the unit. This critical step impacts the selection of the MSF tool as well as time and cost. Next, the coordinator prepares a list of participants in an electronic format suitable to vendor specifications. The vendor then prepares packages of survey instruments for each participant. The MSF process coordinator conducts training for employee participants. Then participants and their managers agree on the feedback team. Participants distribute survey packages to the feedback team.

Invariably, participants and feedback team members stop at some point to confirm that the process is anonymous (except for the participant and his or her boss) and confidential. AlliedSignal's vendors assign predetermined numbers or bar codes for each participant. MSF process coordinators clearly articulate the specific process steps during pre-assessment training.

Following the distribution of packages, "feedback givers" complete forms and send documents to the vendor for processing. Working with the vendor, MSF process coordinators can determine the status of adherence to the process for any participant or the business unit as a whole. By actively reviewing status reports, the coordinator can identify participants and feedback team members who are not adhering to the suggested timeline for the process.

Following the receipt of a minimum number of survey forms for each participant in the allowed time period, the vendor compiles data and develops participant reports. Participants go through training to learn how to interpret the data before receiving the feedback report. Process coordinators reinforce the need for both employee and supervisor to review the feedback report and for participants to thank "feedback givers."

Evaluation of MSF Program

While most participants accepted their feedback with initial curiosity and concern, the majority could have predicted the outcome and many were delighted with the depth of feedback in the written questions. Some participants, however, exhibited anger or skepticism with the data and asked for the MSF process coordinator or the human resource generalist to assist with the interpretation of the data. Some questioned how the results could be the way that they were and others were downright hostile. The reactions were closely meshed with the reactions one would expect from a feedback process.

Overall, the goal of the MSF process is to have more consistency and less variability in the assessment of the success attributes and behaviors in the Continuous Improvement Summary for individual and organizational growth and development. The feedback to the individual is personal, specific, and laced with written comments. The individual has real information available about how they are perceived by the boss, peers, customers, and direct reports. They can now compare their self-perceptions against real, factual data.

MSF Links to Management Resource Review (MRR)

For the organization as a whole, any steps taken to improve the assessment of behaviors demonstrated by any one individual improves the entire management resource review process. "In the continuous improvement process, we strive for development; we strive to balance strengths with areas for improvement. We have a philosophy that virtually no employee *exceeds expectations* in all success attributes." Likewise, virtually no employee can continue employment by *needing development* in all areas. And an employee *at standard* in all attributes needs to consider areas for development to expand his or her talent base in the future. With this philosophy in mind, any group, department, organization, or business unit would have a mixture of EX/AS/ND ratings. By compiling a summary of the ratings, the manager could ascertain areas in which the group needs development.

For example, looking at a sample Composite Summary Success Attributes and Behaviors (see Exhibit 2.5) shows that the sample group has adequate business acumen but clearly needs to improve behaviors associated with developing people. This sample group (see Exhibit 2.6) has several individuals (Morris, Ellis, Charles, and Land) who are role models in Teamwork but others (Connor, Baker, Adam, and Frost) who need development. The manager could then suggest that Morris, Ellis, and Charles work with Johns while Adam, Frost, and Land work with Baker to help improve customer focus. Multiple organization analyses could be used to help the group improve.

In addition, in the MRR process, AlliedSignal uses the CIS as one part of a subjective process of reviewing the performance and behavior of the group. The Leadership Assessment Summary is a matrix to provide an overall group assessment of a group or department.

Leadership Assessment Summary

The Leadership Assessment Summary is a powerful device in management's arsenal of development tools. Embedded in the Leadership Assessment is an assessment of potential. The ratings and definitions are:

- *High Potential*—This individual is capable of having two or more assignments with significantly greater scope and responsibility. This is an individual whose career should be carefully tracked and managed.
- *Promotable*—This individual is capable of having one more assignment with significantly greater scope and responsibility.
- *Experienced Professional*—This individual has demonstrated depth and capabilities, which reflect his or her expertise. This professional coaches

those less experienced and less knowledgeable, and is a skilled professional who may be moved to other positions, though the move is likely to be at the same level of responsibility.

- *Too New*—This individual has been with the company less than six months at the time of the review.
- *Placement Issue*—This individual needs to be moved from his or her present assignment within the next twelve months. Possible actions include reassignment or outplacement.

Key Assessment Questions

Key questions add perspective as the manager assesses an individual's developmental needs and potential.

Will this person:

- Develop fast enough to keep up with the rest of the team?
- Take ownership of his or her problems?

Does this person:

- Have the appropriate sense of urgency?
- Have enough experience to take the next job?
- Have the stature of a senior executive?
- Have the skills or credibility to be a senior executive?

Can this person:

- Make tough people decisions that may be necessary to build the organization?
- Build a team?
- Make the transition from a staff to a line role or from a thinking to an implementation role?
- Recover from a bad or slow start?
- Develop a successor?
- Handle the increased administrative load of this position?

- Learn to conduct business more smoothly and effectively?
- Change management styles from "tough leader" to "coach"?
- Move to a new functional area or line of business?
- Manage unstructured people or functions?
- Develop executive perspective?
- Let go? Can he or she let direct reports assume accountability?
- Learn to effectively deal with top management? Can he or she learn to manage up? Can this person influence or manage the boss?
- Have the ability to be effective with less budget, less support, or a leaner staff?
- Constructively leverage outside resources?
- Manage as well as perform functional tasks growing beyond being a personal producer and become more than a technician?
- Really move the business?
- Learn to set higher standards?
- Operate as a stand-alone executive
- Adjust to the AlliedSignal culture?

Is this person:

- Really in the right function, career track, or position?
- Willing to assume a hands-on role?
- Willing to take a more aggressive leadership position?
- In the right business unit?

The Leadership Assessment is a tool used to consolidate the review of individuals in a group, department, organization, or business unit. In the preparation of this matrix, the manager would focus on the distribution of employees in each quadrant. The manager would consider:

- Are the right people in the right jobs performing at maximum levels?
- Is this the mix of personnel necessary to drive the business?
- How does this mix of results and behavior compare with the mix of previous review periods?
- Who needs to be reassigned to another position to improve results and/or behaviors?

- Does anyone need to be outplaced?
- Who could be promoted to further realize career and organizational potential?

Lessons Learned About Multi-Source Feedback Process

The MSF program is one way to improve the foundation of both the performance review process and the Management Resource Review process. AlliedSignal learned that time and dialogues between leaders about the human resources in the organization are also keys to the improvement of the process.

During the first year with the consolidated MSF process, the design team learned that the business unit must establish specific objectives for the program. These objectives must include why the process is being implemented, who owns the data, how much time will be devoted to giving feedback, the budget for the process, and the groups of employees participating in the process.

Some employees and members of their feedback team did not read the printed instructions on the survey instrument. Therefore, the MSF process coordinator needs to give very clear instructions during pre-assessment training. Both participants and feedback team members need to know how to complete the survey form, write crisp, helpful feedback, and return the feedback to the vendor in a timely manner. Following collection of the data and before distribution of the report, the participants need guidance and information about interpretation of the data in the feedback report.

MSF process coordinators reported that building a good rapport with the vendor is important. This relationship can help with lost forms, altering timelines, developing unique demographic reports, rerunning reports, and so forth.

One can ask: Does this process really work? Is a basically subjective process (performance appraisal) really enhanced with the addition of a 360-degree MSF component? Can these processes be accomplished without associated competency studies? Do the leaders of the organization really believe that the review adds value to the business?

For example, AlliedSignal is recognized as a source of talent in the business world. Some would argue that AlliedSignal is prime hunting ground in the search for top talent. It's a nice compliment, but a challenge as well. How has AlliedSignal managed? As promised, it delivered 15-percent earnings per share growth to its investors in 1998—the seventh consecutive time. One business unit, AlliedSignal Technical Services Corporation (ATSC), adopted the MSF program in 1997. This business unit won the 1998 U.S. Senate Productivity Award and Maryland Quality Award. The evaluation team for these prestigious awards commented during its evaluation that "demonstrating its value on people, the company makes training available to employees, which includes tools for assessment of personal values and behavioral attitudes, techniques for developing a career plan. . . ." The evaluators also noted, "Training, education, and development programs are evaluated and improved by using the semi-annual MRR, the annual STRAP, and the AOP processes."

Individuals recognize AlliedSignal as an employer of choice. Scores in worldwide employee satisfaction surveys improved in 1998 in most areas. Allied is helping supervisors become better leaders, preparing managers to become better directors, and encouraging employees to learn on and off the job. In the past three years, AlliedSignal completed a $10-million, state-of-the-art learning center at its headquarters in Morristown, New Jersey, which provides an average of 31,000 student days of learning and more than 1,150 classes a year. The Learning Center and Learning Program is often benchmarked by Fortune 500 companies. Another similar center opened in March 1999 in Tempe, Arizona, to expand the West Coast employee population's accessibility to company learning programs.

No wonder AlliedSignal was named by *Forbes* Global Edition as the world's best diversified company; by *Fortune* as the world's most admired global aerospace company and—for the second consecutive year—as one of the 100 best companies to work for in America.

Investment firms recognize AlliedSignal as an organization with talent depth. In 1998, the equity research department of Legg Mason Wood Walker, Inc., reported, "AlliedSignal is managed by a strong management team with considerable depth" as part of its research in forming a "purchase recommendation." Legg Mason went on to state that CEO Lawrence Bossidy is "ably supported by a cadre of professional managers."

AlliedSignal is an organization that is thriving because of processes and tools that are easy to describe and not too difficult to use, but extremely valuable to the organization for the results produced.

Exhibit 2.1: Integrated Performance and Management Development Process Map

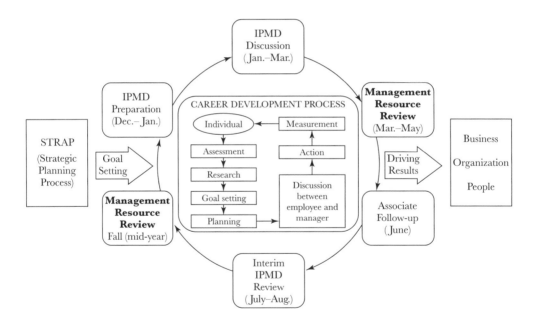

Linkage Inc.'s Best Practices in Leadership Development Handbook, edited by David Giber, Louis Carter, and Marshall Goldsmith. Copyright © 2000 by Linkage Press and Jossey-Bass/Pfeiffer, San Francisco, CA.

Exhibit 2.2: Allied Career Profile Form

AlliedSignal Career Profile

Name	**Title**	**Band**
	Business Unit	**Social Security**
Service Date	**Location**	**Citizenship**
Education		
Date	Degree	Major	School/Location

Training/Development
Dates
Awards/Patents/Recognition
Dates

Language/Proficiencies

Work Experience (Start with most recent—do not include current position)
Dates	Title	Business/Location

Career Interest:
Next	Longer Range	Relocation Preferences
		Interest in Foreign Assignment

Linkage Inc.'s Best Practices in Leadership Development Handbook, edited by David Giber, Louis Carter, and Marshall Goldsmith.
Copyright © 2000 by Linkage Press and Jossey-Bass/Pfeiffer, San Francisco, CA.

Exhibit 2.3: Continuous Improvement Summary Form

AlliedSignal Continuous Improvement Summary Form

Employee Name: S.S. No.:

Performance Highlights and Targets Missed (Results compared to objectives)	*Summarize Highlights & Development Needs*	*Code** (See Below)
	Business Acumen:	☐ ☐ ☐ ☐ ☐ ☐ ☐ ☐ ☐ ☐ ☐
	Customer Focus:	
	Vision and Purpose:	
	Values and Ethics:	
	Bias for Action:	
	Commitment:	
	Teamwork:	
	Innovation:	
	Developing People:	
	Performance:	
	Technical:	
	*EX=Exceeds Standard AS=At Standard ND=Needs Development	
	NA=Not applicable/Not Demonstrated	

Current Position	Future Position
	Development Actions and Timing

Potential Next Moves

Short Term—(0–2 Years)   Long Term—(2–5 Years)

Manager	Employee	Date	Second Level Review/Date

Employee signature indicates that a joint discussion with the manager has taken place and does not necessarily signify employee's agreement to the manager's assessment/evaluation. O indicates employee has made comments regarding objectives, discussion, etc., and comments are attached.

Linkage Inc.'s Best Practices in Leadership Development Handbook, edited by David Giber, Louis Carter, and Marshall Goldsmith. Copyright © 2000 by Linkage Press and Jossey-Bass/Pfeiffer, San Francisco, CA.

Exhibit 2.4: Performance Objectives Form

AlliedSignal Performance Objectives

Employee Name: _____   Supervisor: _____

_____
(Date and Year)

Social Security No.: _____

List the 4 to 5 most important financial and other business objectives for this period, assuring they are specific, measurable, achievable, and compatible with organization's goals and processes. Include milestones and timing. Use additional sheets as necessary.

Objectives—Milestones—Timing	Interim review	Results

Linkage Inc.'s Best Practices in Leadership Development Handbook, edited by David Giber, Louis Carter, and Marshall Goldsmith. Copyright © 2000 by Linkage Press and Jossey-Bass/Pfeiffer, San Francisco, CA.

Exhibit 2.5: Composite Summary Success Attributes and Behaviors

Spring 1997	Business Acumen	Customer Focus	Vision and Purpose	Values and Ethics	Bias for Action	Commit-ment	Teamwork	Innovation	Developing People	Performance	Technical
MORRIS	AS	EX	ND	AS	AS	AS	EX	AS	EX	EX	AS
ELLIS	AS	EX	AS	AS	ND	AS	EX	EX	ND	EX	AS
DENVER	AS	AS	ND	AS	AS	AS	AS	ND	AS	AS	EX
JOHNS	AS	ND	ND	AS	AS	AS	AS	AS	AS	AS	AS
CHARLES	AS	EX	AS	AS	AS	AS	EX	AS	ND	EX	AS
CONNOR	EX	AS	AS	AS	AS	AS	ND	AS	AS	EX	AS
BAKER	EX	ND	AS	AS	AS	EX	ND	EX	ND	AS	AS
ADAM	AS	EX	ND	AS	ND	EX	ND	AS	ND	AS	AS
SMITH											
FROST	AS	EX	AS	AS	EX	EX	ND	AS	ND	EX	AS
LAND	AS	EX	ND	AS	AS	EX	EX	AS	ND	AS	EX

Linkage Inc.'s Best Practices in Leadership Development Handbook, edited by David Giber, Louis Carter, and Marshall Goldsmith. Copyright © 2000 by Linkage Press and Jossey-Bass/Pfeiffer, San Francisco, CA.

Exhibit 2.6: Leadership Assessment Summary

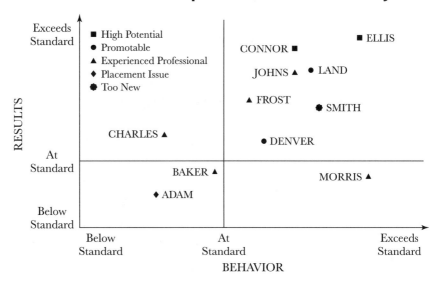

Linkage Inc.'s Best Practices in Leadership Development Handbook, edited by David Giber, Louis Carter, and Marshall Goldsmith. Copyright © 2000 by Linkage Press and Jossey-Bass/Pfeiffer, San Francisco, CA.

About the Contributor

Mimi O'Donnell (odonnem@clmmp001.atsc.allied.com) has over twenty-five years of experience providing organizational development consulting to individuals and groups in AlliedSignal units, primarily its service unit, AlliedSignal Technical Services Corporation. In addition, she has provided services to clients such as: the Department of Energy Transportation Safeguards Division; American Heart Association, Baltimore Regional Chapter; Potomac Home Health Inc.; and Federal Manufacturing and Technology Corporation. Specific services include: process reengineering; vision and mission development; employee satisfaction survey process management; succession planning; workforce planning; culture/climate survey development; and 360-degree multi-source feedback process design. Other consulting topics that she has covered include organization redesign; strategic planning; functional excellence; career development; middle management training and development; objective setting and priority; new employee orientation; and new manager assimilation.

She has been a speaker on the subject of 360-degree multi-source feedback process at national conferences including: The Best of 360-degree Assessment Conference (Linkage, Inc.); The Third Annual Leadership Development Conference (Linkage, Inc.); The 1998 Summit on Performance Measurement for Government Agencies (IQPC); and the Seventh Annual Assessment Measurement and Evaluation of Human Performance Conference and Expo. O'Donnell presented sessions on nonprofit board development at the 1993 and 1994 conferences of the National Association for Community Leadership (NACL) and presented an interactive session for NACL in 1999.

She holds a master's of business degree in management from Loyola College of Maryland and a bachelor's degree in psychology from the University of Maryland. She earned an Organizational Development Certificate at Columbia University and was certified as a Peer Coach and Facilitator for Total Quality Leadership and multiple corporate programs with AlliedSignal. O'Donnell is a member of the Board of Directors for the American Heart Association, Howard County (MD) Region and the Membership Committee of Leadership, Howard County (MD).

CHAPTER THREE

ARMY MANAGEMENT STAFF COLLEGE

This chapter outlines a technical, operational, assessment, and strategic-based leadership development program designed to develop high-potential civilian employees and military officers in a changing environment.

Introduction

Leaders and managers must know the skills of leading and managing, but most importantly, they must know their business and how its elements link together. If that business is as large as the Army and as wide as the world, how does the Army prepare functional experts to apply the executive knowledge, perspective, and skill critical to the success of their organization? It integrates content, context, organization, and experience in a learner-centered, practice-driven environment based on customer requirements for skilled, knowledgeable, and action-oriented leaders.

Defining the Need for the Army Management Staff College (AMSC)

In 1986, the Inspector General (IG) of the Army found civilians in or entering leadership positions ill-prepared for the challenges facing a new era of military leadership. Military leaders received regular leadership training, along with a position assignment to exercise their new skills; civilians did not. Before 1986, the Army hired civilians only for their functional expertise, which benefitted the long-term memory of the Army, especially as officers in leadership positions rotated. That began to change, however.

During the late 1980s, many governmental and economic changes began to affect the visibility of civilian leaders: (1) changes in government reform, technology, and the world economy; (2) the military's sustaining base (see definition of sustaining base that follows) came under increased Congressional scrutiny about effective use of resources; and (3) the fighting Army began to downsize. Two significant findings from the 1986 IG report on the state of the Army induced the creation of the Army Management Staff College (AMSC). The IG found that there was a lack of competent, confident, practiced civilian leaders within the sustaining base (about 65-percent civilian), and that a single place for learning and teaching about the sustaining base did not exist.

AMSC Definition of Sustaining Base

AMSC defines the sustaining base as that aggregation of people, guidance, systems, money, material, and facilities that prepare the soldier for action, get the soldier to action, sustain the soldier during action, return that soldier home, and take care of that soldier's family throughout. It encompasses headquarters, Department of the Army through installation, and even unit. It encompasses the environment and context within which the Army must accomplish its mission; functional areas such as financial, personnel, logistics, acquisition, and installation management; decision-making tools and practices; and creative, critical, and strategic thinking applied to problem solving. Within its broad educational mission, AMSC's Sustaining Base Leadership and Management Program (SBLMP) offers students the opportunity to be the literate of the future.[1]

Program Mission and Objectives

Intentionally broad, the AMSC mission allows full exploration of the sustaining base—from definition through execution, from design to change. That mission is *to educate and prepare selected Army civilian and military leaders to assume leadership and management responsibilities throughout the sustaining base* and *to provide consulting services and conduct research in support of the sustaining base.*

Strategic Fit with Other Army Programs

Because the AMSC already possessed a faculty broadly experienced with a "sustaining base focus and expertise," the vice chief of staff of the Army prompted AMSC to design and deliver courses in Garrison Command (for colonels serving in Garrison Commander roles and their executive assistants) and General Officer Installation Command. AMSC views these courses as highly significant contributors to its SBLMP. In 1997, AMSC produced a Garrison Sergeants Major Course.

Also in 1997, the Office of the Assistant Secretary of the Army, Manpower and Reserve Affairs, through its director of civilian personnel, added the fifty-four-year-old Personnel Management for Executives Program to the existing AMSC line-up. This leadership program focuses on the executive perspective of people issues and concerns of the organization.

With this addition AMSC now has the opportunity to develop the total command team—civilian and military. Faculty and students gain direct access to the perspective, experience, and skill of these other levels of organization.

Finally, the school and the SBLMP fit as the capstone learning experience within the larger Army Civilian Training, Education and Professional Development Plan (ACTEDS).[2] This plan details courses and steps to prepare for supervisory, managerial, and executive positions within the Army.

Selection into the Sustaining Base Leadership and Management Program (SBLMP)

AMSC draws SBLMP students from civilians in General Schedule Grades Twelve through Fourteen. Majors and lieutenant colonels who graduated from the Command and General Staff College—who are or are expected to be in sustaining base leadership positions such as directors of personnel, contracting, information management, logistics, plans, training, mobilization, and security—should also attend. An Army Central Selection Board selects students for the SBLMP, seeking the best and brightest from all functional areas, those open to exploring ideas, methods, responsibilities, organizations, and places—and those capable of graduate-level study. The Army selects military leaders for such schooling through a similar central selection process. Centrally selecting civilians for leadership education sends an important cultural message—the Army values the total team.

Offered in both a twelve-week resident and a twelve-month nonresident version, the SBLMP teaches the importance of linkages that make the sustaining base effective for the Army. The Army comprises a highly complex and sophisticated system of systems that works sequentially and simultaneously. Deriving the implications before acting on a decision is a matter of experience as well as education. The SBLMP uses educational principles to teach the experienced.

Tips and Tactics for Building the SBLMP

The first goal was to determine program requirements and ensure relevancy. Why? Because times and organizations change. To remain credible with Army leaders and students AMSC has to deliver something that matters.

AMSC developed a set of questions to help focus its study. The faculty wanted to know what was relevant to Army leaders, now and for the next five years. Was the curriculum valid in content, context, methods, and sequence? Was the program critical to the agency's mission? In simple terms, AMSC's task became to determine what skills, abilities, and knowledge are important to the people hiring SBLMP graduates.

AMSC saw the leaders who hired SBLMP graduates as *the customer.* Faculty and study designers assumed they had identified the correct customer pool, were going to interview the right customers, knew the customer's language, and were going to benchmark with the right organizations.

Validating SBLMP Requirements

The faculty developed a stratified random sample of the Army and Department of Defense (DOD). AMSC started with an eligible student population of 64,344, located organizations within the Army where the largest proportions of those eligible were to be found, and identified a sample size for proportions at a 95-percent confidence level Army-wide. AMSC sent a message over Army-wide communications systems requesting support throughout the organization. Support from the College's Army Chain of Command rounded out the preparations. Using an established organizational process to calibrate faculty scoring of examinations, AMSC instructed interviewing faculty on what questions to ask, how to ask openended questions, and collecting information—and sent the faculty out to interview. Together the faculty interviewed 169 executives of 187 originally identified. In addition, the faculty interviewed the Functional Chiefs' Representatives of the twenty-three Civilian Career Programs of the Army to gain their perspectives on developmental requirements. SBLMP faculty also interviewed a number of external-to-Army leaders, including those from the Offices of the Secretary of Defense and Joint Chiefs of Staff. Finally the faculty reviewed and analyzed student, graduate, and supervisor survey data available in AMSC's existing evaluation databases.

Before interviewing, the study designers established some ground rules: (1) look for what's needed—not what AMSC does, and (2) interview for what the customer wants—not what AMSC wants the customer to want.

Benchmarking Other Institutions

AMSC faculty benchmarked residence-based "business management" schools of private industry, colleges, universities, and other federal institutions. The faculty also benchmarked military senior service colleges and selected foreign military equivalents, as well as professional associations. As part of the curriculum development process, AMSC wanted to become knowledgeable of how others developed curriculum, how they viewed its production and delivery, as well as its successes, failures, and lessons learned. This information would be used to develop AMSC's curriculum materials, develop faculty, and develop ancillary systems and processes to support curriculum development and delivery.[3]

Benchmark Questions. AMSC's benchmark questions included the following:

1. How do they determine the training and educational needs or requirements?
2. How do they develop a curriculum to meet those needs or requirements?

3. What forms do their materials take?

4. How do they develop case studies, practical exercises, or role-playing exercises?

5. How do they integrate learning material across functional or topical lines?

6. How do they know they are succeeding at meeting the requirements?

7. How do they handle incremental process improvement (fine-tuning)?

8. How do they handle the evaluation of student learning?

9. How do they handle evaluation of faculty learning?

10. With whom do they benchmark?

The benchmarking visits occurred face-to-face. Analysis of data gathered pointed to one overwhelming fact—the most successful (attractive to students and students sought eagerly by the hiring community) looked for their learning material in the sort of jobs graduates might reasonably be expected to do after graduation.

Benchmark Findings. Most institutions AMSC visited showed great concern for the needs of the organizations hiring their graduates. They wanted their graduates to be instantly useful by not only having the foundation skills, but a knowledge of the organization for which they would work, and a view of the competitive needs of the organization as a high priority. They wanted their students to solve real problems and work with real teams to learn their business leadership and management skills. The long-term success of these institutions depended on the quality of their graduates' ability to meet ever-changing business needs. Analysis of SBLMP graduates' survey comments reinforced the benchmarked qualities—more real-time, practical exercises, more opportunity to do action research to solve existing problems, and more opportunity to work in teams with people diverse in background, experience, and interest.

Developing the Program's Core Skills

Next, faculty reviewed the analyzed information gathered from the requirements and relevancy study. Customers desired leaders with behaviors consistent with the following:

1. Those who can lead people, make decisions and solve problems, write clearly and concisely, and communicate orally.
2. Leaders who know their immediate organization and the "capital A" Army well; know how people, money, places, and things link up, and know the perspective and intent of the larger organization.
3. Finally, leaders who have vision and see connections, are mentally flexible, have a "can do" attitude, and have an organizational focus— selfless service.

The interviews also prompted refinements in curriculum delivery method— reinforcing the use of practical exercises, real-time problem solving, and student performance standards; and more intense levels of such learning opportunities.

The faculty also found several important subcomponents. Customers collectively want subordinate leaders able to reduce complex information to its essence—accurate and easily interpretable by bosses and peers. Subordinate leaders are those who are lower down the hierarchical ladder, comparable to "middle managers" in the private sector. They must be able to develop and promulgate useable written guidance, prepare decision papers for their bosses which clearly identify the problem, lay out alternatives and opposing perspectives, their advantages and detractors, consequences and implications, and recommend a course of action. They must express themselves clearly, concisely, and accurately by electronic mail. They must feel at home using a variety of electronic media—video-teleconference, satellite, Internet, and interactive computer systems. They must include relevant others in the development of communications— clearly formulate and explain vision, purpose, goals, and objectives, clearly task and check on the tasking of subordinates, listen to guidance and understand intent, and listen to subordinates to understand intent. They should be able to conduct clear, informative, persuasive briefings of bosses, peers, and subordinates.

Subordinate leaders should be able to establish a solid command climate, understand and use group dynamics to establish good environments for subordinates and peers. They should be able to motivate subordinates—create and use motivating forces to reward appropriate performance and create and use corrective measures to discipline inappropriate performance. They should be able to establish and reinforce effective teamwork and advise subordinates and their respective teams.

The ability to make decisions raised much interest among those interviewed. They wanted subordinate leaders who could identify the problem or issue at hand—apply critical thinking to problem identification and problem solving. They wanted leaders who could apply structured process to generate and evaluate alternative solutions, who could use quantitative tools when required, who could solve nonstandard problems—situations having no correct answer—and who would know when to decide, be decisive, and act.

Core Curriculum

The requirements and relevancy study contributed core skills that were important to Army leaders. Benchmarking contributed heavily to the highly practical and real-time problem-solving methods of education chosen for delivery. Instruction must be short, it must move into hands-on application; move to student and faculty discussion and critique with practical feedback, and allow student-processing time. Key skills must be repeated with each level of learning to ensure "unconscious application," or skills transfer.

Key Design Elements

Core curriculum in the SBLMP, therefore, must allow repeated opportunities to learn and practice the core skills identified by the customer, as well as opportunities to critique their application. In other words, students should research, write, brief, and otherwise practice the key communication skills by studying topics or themes identified as "to know" subjects. Students should practice the skills of decision making by applying them with "to know" subjects. Students also should practice by assuming classroom leadership roles of varying duration. In short, AMSC should integrate information, thinking skill, experience, problem solving, organization, and practice.

Curriculum Map

From the core skills AMSC established a curriculum structure (see Figure 3.1) and identified the goals of the curriculum. The curriculum finds expression in "terms": Pre-SBLMP; Leadership, Management and Decision Making; National Security Environment; Operational Army; Designing and Resourcing the Force; Sustaining and Projecting the Force; Sustaining Base Issues—Tracks; and Tracks and Capstone Exercises.

FIGURE 3.1. SUSTAINING BASE LEADERSHIP AND MANAGEMENT PROGRAM.

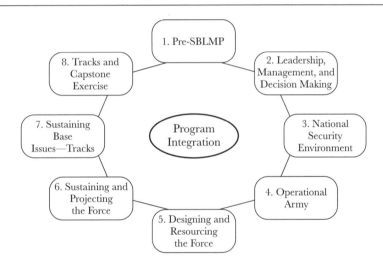

1. In the "Pre-SBLMP Term," faculty assist students in acclimating to the AMSC academic environment and curriculum, and they reinforce AMSC expectations. Within the pre-SBLMP package, students complete a battery of instruments assessing personality, leadership style, critical and creative thinking, and writing skills to aid in self-improvement. They also complete a self-paced learning workbook on decision-making tools as well as a workbook on the Army mission, roles, functions, and organization. Students take a diagnostic test for comprehension on both these workbooks during the resident phase. They write a short paper on their leadership philosophy. Finally students

bring information about their home organizations' vision, mission, functions, roles, and fit within the Army to the resident phase of SBLMP for discussion in their seminar.

2. "Leadership, Management, and Decision Making" guides student learning about organizational beginnings, growth, and change under a variety of conditions—including the influence of the individual upon the organization, impacts of change in external organizations and systems, and national change. Throughout the term, faculty members guide students and provide opportunities for oral and written communication on subjects of interest to leadership and national issues. The faculty teach Army values[4] here.

3. "National Security Environment" provides an introduction to the defense environment, both internationally and domestically, in order to establish the context within which the Army functions. This term exposes students to many of the Department of Defense's external factors, but especially those that impact an evolving national security environment. It also exposes students to the key documents and systems that involve national-level decision making in policy, strategy, mission, and resource allocation. Here is the foundation upon which faculty build further insights into Army responsibilities.

4. "The Operational Army" teaches the Army's legal purpose, as stated in Title 10 of U.S. Code, promulgated by Congress and U.S. legal process. The term helps students place into perspective the force's culture, history, missions, roles, and functions, including the roles of doctrine and the tenets of operations. It provides insight into how the Army trains, resources, and sustains its basic task of conducting land combat.

5. "Designing and Resourcing the Force" explores how the Army manages change today and tomorrow through Force Management and Integration. Army leaders and managers must have a knowledge of the systems and processes that organize, structure, man, equip, train, sustain, and resource the force in order to plan, program, and implement change. Resourcing the force refers to the literal resources required to, for example, equip, house, feed, and move the force. Of course, dollar resources are a large part of the process. The force refers to the whole Army: active, reserve, National Guard, and civilian components.

Force Integration is the management of change through the systemic introduction and incorporation into the force, and sustainment of new doctrine, new material, and new organizations. Here faculty expose students to the fundamentals, systems, and processes used to design, provide people, equipment, and other resources the Army needs to fulfill a mission. For example, after looking at other alternatives to fill a capability shortfall, students may determine as part of a practical exercise that a new piece of equipment is needed. Given only the military requirement, they design the equipment to meet the need. For example, if the requirement is for an anti-armor system, the result could be a $6-million tank, a $500-thousand missile, or a $100 mine. Students filling the roles of combat developer and material developer then collaborate to determine which system will offer the greatest flexibility in the future, and they then weigh these against affordability.

6. "Sustaining and Projecting the Force" provides the opportunity for analysis of the various elements of power projection to include mobilization, marshaling the force, transportation, logistics, strategic deployment, conflict termination, force reconstitution, redeployment, and demobilization. It further investigates the Army by looking at how installations sustain the force with emphasis on installation self-assessment and management.

7. Sustaining Base Issues—"Tracks and Capstone," the final terms consolidate the knowledge, leadership, and analytical skills acquired by the students throughout the SBLMP. The four-day tracks resemble electives. Track topics change as the contextual issues surrounding the Army change. Tracks allow a quick curriculum response to emerging DOD and Army issues. Current topics include Army Performance Improvement Criteria (based on the Baldrige Criteria for Performance Excellence), Congressional Impacts on DOD, and Joint Reform Initiatives. The Capstone exercise focuses on the conduct of military actions and the preparation for military operations—the business of the Army. It catalyzes student integration and synthesis of the sequential yet simultaneous Army sustaining base. See Figure 3.2 for a curriculum overview.

FIGURE 3.2. CURRICULUM OVERVIEW.

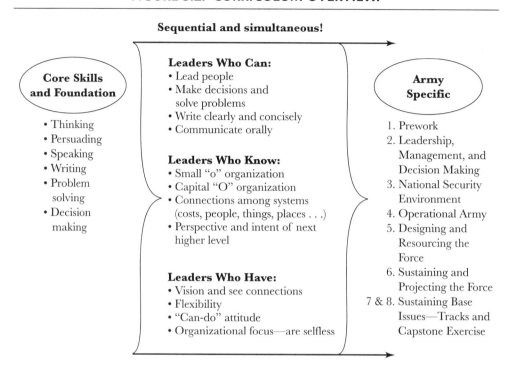

Key Features of the Program

Integration of Curriculum

Integration of curriculum is the single most-powerful feature of the Sustaining Base Leadership and Management Program (SBLMP). Learning integrates with organization and experience through a repetition of leadership, management, and decision making at increasingly higher and more sophisticated levels of organization, knowledge, analysis, synthesis, and evaluation. Integrated programs work on the premise that all people, places, and things are linked and that understanding and using these linkages can improve the organization's quality and performance. Integration uses the material inherent in the organization's business to teach. It spirals through the concepts, skills, themes, and topics that make up the organization and the environment in which it exists. It simultaneously explores the breadth and depth of the disciplines involved while it requires students to apply skills, themes, concepts, and topics. Continuous reinforcement is critical to learning. Integration anticipates a cumulative effect. AMSC's integrated curriculum counts on student and faculty team ability to exercise thinking skills—especially critical thinking. It assumes that both faculty and students learn from each other.

Most SBLMP work takes place in seminars of about fifteen students or less. The student teams in particular generate powerful lessons that graduates take away with them. Teams used for educational purposes come from the seminars,[5] the established learning units. Each seminar resembles a microcosm of the Army to the extent possible. Teams, whether across seminars or within, reinforce how to work with fast-changing requirements and memberships across a broad range of experiences and backgrounds. In a practical exercise, for instance, one team may make decisions based upon fielding something like a training system. Simultaneously, another team must make decisions about associated subjects like time sequencing, acquisition of equipment, budgets, and personnel. Both teams have time limits and must identify requirements, gather and reduce data, analyze information, develop and evaluate alternatives, and then make their decisions. The decisions, of course, will be better if thoroughly coordinated with everyone involved. Coordinated actions, along with the abilities to sort through large data sets, set priorities, and plan carefully, characterize the most successful teams. Ultimately, the most powerful and influential teams allow each individual to exercise critical thinking. By observation, the first sets of practical exercises maintain one characteristic in common—everyone ignores the experienced and informed team member. Team responses to practical exercises or to papers must always leave room for differing opinions. Often, it is the differing opinion that leads to the salient approach or answer. In class after class, students recognize only after reviewing their own behavior the amount of time lost to unimportant considerations. They also recognize their own discomfort in according the differing opinion.

A cornerstone to integrated learning, practical exercises allow the students to learn simultaneously about Army training, analysis, decision making, and the people and behavior roles that drive the process and lead to outcome. To reinforce the same view from different perspectives, the SBLMP regularly plans for and invites senior leaders to speak to and engage with students on emerging issues. In a strictly enforced, nonattribution environment, speakers encourage students to challenge the issues, the leaders, and themselves. As complex, large, and dispersed as the Army is, integration allows students to learn quickly in real-time examples, while reinforcing the daily concepts and skills they will have to apply as leaders, managers, and decision makers. Integration allows the faculty to teach several lifetimes' worth of experience to each student in a relatively short amount of time, at the same time teaching them about their organization.

Requirements for Integration

Integration requires exceptional faculty commitment to teaching complexity by finding the simple examples to gain understanding, linking theories to gain synthesis to improved practices, and constantly evaluating thinking skills. Integration remains an intense experience for faculty and students. Buy-in evolves through the successes the students and graduates report. Integration requires constant, almost daily, shoring up and, in the end, demonstrates varying levels of maturity. Students remain generally unaware of these concepts and events until after they graduate, when the first successful problem-solving session at work brings the experience home to many. In effect, the integrated learning environment rewires the brain, but the brain doesn't know it's been rewired until its environment normalizes. The graduate who previously was known to never take the initiative and treated the supervisor and team members poorly suddenly takes an interest in moving the organization forward and cooperates to accomplish the job at hand. The supervisor calls and wants to know what AMSC did to this individual. Other motivators there may be, but the simple effects of living under a strong process and influence for twelve weeks cannot be denied.

Assessment Instruments

Assessment instruments facilitate integrated learning by giving the students objective views of their perceived quality as leaders, managers, and decision makers. It is highly desirable for leaders, managers, and decision makers to analyze and synthesize that which drives them as people (personality), that which they have behaviorally demonstrated to others (360-degree assessment), and something about how they learn. Feedback occurs as part of the learning throughout the curriculum, especially in continued counseling and coaching.

AMSC uses its own faculty-developed 360-degree leadership assessment instrument (see Exhibit 3.1). The Army developed a view of leadership characteristics that grounds the instrument squarely in concepts important to the organization. These characteristics include (1) communication, (2) supervision, (3) teaching and counseling, (4) team development, (5) technical and tactical proficiency, (6) decision making, (7) planning, (8) uses of technology, and (9) professional ethics. Instrument results provide students with a working baseline as to how others may view them. Faculty assess work in the seminar and in teams in part on the exercise of these leadership criteria.

The Myers-Briggs Type Indicator, used to judge individuals' personality types, is applied to provide students insight as to why they may choose certain leadership paths, make certain management decisions, and why they are confronted with different viewpoints. Again, students assess their work as leaders and managers in part on how well they apply their preferences or knowledge of other preferences to achieve the desired end.

To help the individual learn most effectively, AMSC has found it helpful to show students something about their own style of learning by using Kolb's Learning Style Inventory. Based upon experiential learning theory, David Kolb's LSI measures learners' preferences for different kinds of educational experiences. Faculty use the results of the inventory across the seminar to find the best methods to help the students learn.

Students prepare as part of their prework a diagnostic paper so faculty may evaluate their writing. This helps faculty target students who may need tutorial assistance in thinking processes and writing. Additionally, AMSC's

ToolTime workbook reviews the fundamental quantitative and qualitative problem-solving and decision-making skills, which students should be prepared to exercise liberally during the program. In a similar workbook, faculty teach students the fundamentals of Army organization. Because the workbooks focus almost exclusively on knowledge, AMSC delivers them as part of a distance learning package. The SBLMP gives students six weeks prior to the start of classes to complete approximately forty hours of learning, including the assessment instruments. It is necessary to have all students begin with the same foundation.

Coaching

Faculty counseling and coaching remains the most meaningful program aspect to students individually. The counselor serves as a stabilizing influence throughout an intense experience, someone with whom more than curricular problems may be addressed. Faculty assignments include counseling and coaching five assigned students per seminar. The faculty member tracks the same students throughout the program even though the student moves on to other work teams and may work with other faculty.

To facilitate class entry and provide greater opportunity for learning, faculty identify students to serve in class leadership roles. Selection of class president and seminar presidents occurs before class arrival. Class leader orientation prepares the leaders to address questions about expectations, facilities, surrounding location services, and generally make the students feel welcome. Class leaders work closely with the AMSC management team during the program. The team continually asks students if selection of class leaders worked well or if they believe students should select their own leaders once classes begin. Students support prior selection of leaders because peer assistance comforts them at the beginning of the program and because they soon realize how infrequently they choose their leaders in their work environment. Class leaders, their selection, and their working styles create another integrated learning opportunity.

Most SBLMP students belong to an Army-wide career program that fosters development and education and identifies a variety of paths to promotion. Each class, AMSC invites the representatives of each career area to have lunch with interested students. In this way, the students share what they are learning, the career program managers can assess the benefits of the SBLMP firsthand, and everyone can exchange real-time lessons in building one's career.

Organizing Faculty

Faculty (about one-third each civilian, active military, and retired military) serve in one of three departments, supervised by one of three department chairs. The chain of command flexes for all other assignments. For curriculum development and seminar delivery teams, assignments mix and balance the resident experiences and skills among faculty. For development and delivery—across all program areas—mix criteria include gender, military experience, functional expertness, and general background. For special projects such as faculty awards review committees, academic boards, or grading equity committees, AMSC creates yet another balance of faculty to fit the situation. In short, AMSC has as many different views of organization as it has projects.

Faculty assignments change with each class although AMSC tries to maintain some stability for at least a year. Military officers moving through their three-year AMSC assignments catalyze many of the changes in faculty assignments—project requirements catalyze others. In short, AMSC maintains the maximum amount of flexibility among its faculty and assigns them accordingly.

The AMSC develops and maintains curriculum through a set of curriculum maintenance teams to which all faculty belong. Faculty organize teams based on the needs of AMSC's flagship program, SBLMP. Such an arrangement ensures faculty understand the content of other programs, keep the focus of each program in mind as they prepare their own lessons, and keep the level of education appropriate to each program. It is important to AMSC that programs do not unnecessarily duplicate each other. The teams ensure integration across curriculum. They also implement policy and resolve curricular issues. They provide their recommendations to the Curriculum Review Committee. The Curriculum Review Committee, comprising department chairs, dean, and commandant of the organization, sets policy, selects resourcing schemes, and reviews and approves the curriculum.

Technology

Technology binds together informational elements of the curriculum. AMSC's chief communication strategy to keep faculty and the varying development teams apprised immediately of delivery success and lessons learned centers on a "Discusware"[6] program available on the AMSC Intranet. Teaching direction set down in faculty guides does not necessarily fit the learning styles of each of ten delivering seminars. Through this decision board software forum, faculty who delivered the sessions share observations and methods that worked well in their seminar. In 1999, Students began sharing their observations with faculty using these same methods and technology. Of course, program syllabi, faculty guides, and visuals reside on an internal server, available in a latest version to all. And, of course, AMSC uses e-mail to apprise all of the changes. Varying faculty use technology to create in-seminar games to help students learn, and several of the practical exercises rely on technology to assist learning. Technology underpins the twelve-month nonresident version of the SBLMP program. While students must complete a one-week resident session at the beginning and ending of the program, all other work, including seminar meetings, takes place in a cyber-schoolhouse, conducted over the Internet. Using the cyber-schoolhouse gives nonresident students an opportunity to engage in seminar discussion with other students worldwide; access to a library to upload and download literature, supplementary readings, interview transcripts, and student surveys; and the ability to leave messages and receive answers in a variety of time zones. AMSC does not believe one can learn leadership without people to lead. However, since the nonresident SBLMP fulfills a legal requirement to make the SBLMP available to all eligible employees, faculty learn from this program how people learn and lead work groups at a distance.

Evaluation and Measurement

Students must pass the SBLMP standards before they graduate—these include participation in seminars, practical exercises, and class leadership roles. The SBLMP focuses primarily on evaluated briefings, performance in practical exercises, team projects, and research papers. Grading blends the parts and intellectual standards of critical thinking as outlined by Dr. Richard Paul[7] with the subject matter inherent in the briefing, team project, or paper. Dr. Paul is the director of research at the Center for Critical Thinking and Moral Critique. As an internationally recognized authority on critical thinking, he has written six books on the subject and more than 100 articles focusing on every educational level. While grading the SBLMP, faculty seek evidence of the student's or team's thought processes and the clarity, accuracy, precision, relevance, depth, breadth, and logic with which those processes come forth. AMSC's probationary procedures allow students to have the opportunity to make up and pass graduation requirements. The faculty developed a learning matrix that delineates all required work in one column, then requires students to self-assess (see Exhibit 3.2). Students evaluate their own performance and summarize that assessment in light of five major elements: (1) communicate; (2) lead; (3) decide; (4) see the big picture; and (5) apply critical thinking. An "initial expectations" section of the matrix sets the mark for each student for areas of performance and knowledge they would like to improve during their studies. This matrix helps faculty counsel students and assess their progress throughout the twelve resident weeks. Survey feedback from graduates tell program leaders that the standards give value to the diploma—a value they treasure and want the program to continue safeguarding.

The American Council on Education, College Credit Recommendation Service (ACE CREDIT) evaluated the college levels of the SBLMP, both resident and nonresident versions. Serving to validate the level of delivery to Army reviewers and fostering credibility with students who would like to apply their diplomas to degree programs, the ACE CREDIT review netted the SBLMP fifteen graduate-level credit equivalencies and nine upper-level undergraduate equivalencies.

AMSC's front-line customers evaluate the program, so that faculty may adjust the program mid-course or the curriculum for the next class. Graduates evaluate the program at six months, one year, and five years. At the same time, their supervisors evaluate the differences they remark in the graduate's performance since returning from the Army Management Staff

College's SBLMP. Supervisors and graduates report that confidence and competence have increased in all areas.

AMSC sponsored a longitudinal study to assess program impact on the Army and reviewed the key results of matched groups. Coming out ahead in promotion, geographic mobility, organizational mobility, and retention by the Army were SBLMP graduates. Much literature is available detailing the costs of training and educating new employees. AMSC saves those costs for the Army. It also continues to follow the longitudinal study population, now into its thirteenth year. With each year, promotion, mobility, and retention rates continue to be higher for graduates than nongraduates of the AMSC SBLMP. Graduates' published comments on the experience also point to value:

School gives challenge on return

Have you ever been faced with a mountain so steep that it seemed impossible to climb, but challenged you to the extent that you wouldn't dare let yourself give up?

Pentagram

College offers look at Army's big picture

. . . safe, yet rigorous environment for taking leadership risks and expanding your professional perspective . . .

Engineer Update

Novices get a Lesson in Washington's Ways

You're a GS-13 crunching the budget for Bradley tanks when you begin having some deeper thoughts . . .

DOD News

Exhibit 3.1: Leadership Assessment Instrument

Army Management Staff College

Leadership Assessment Instrument—Executive Summary

AMSC uses this instrument to counsel students and help them improve their leadership skill. We adhere to the Code of Ethics and the Standards of Practice American Counseling Association. Please express interest to the Army Management Staff College, ATTN SFCP CPC, 5500 21st Street STE 3111, Fort Belvoir, VA 22060-5934.

The student, the supervisor, peers, and subordinates respond to the instrument. Students distribute a total of six instruments along with a return envelope for direct return to the AMSC. AMSC faculty advisors compile the results just before classes begin. As a part of the counseling process throughout the program, the faculty present the results and discuss these with students.

Part I

My relationship to the participant is

A. Self (the student)
B. Current Immediate Supervisor (of the student)
C. Peer
D. Subordinate (of the student)

Use the following rating scale to indicate how you rate the student in each of the thirty-five questions:

A. A major weakness
B. Needs some development
C. About average for a person in the position
D. Relatively strong
E. Outstanding strength

1. Communication

   Questions cover the effectiveness of the exchange of information and ideas from one person to another, thinking through a problem to its consequences, and translating its ideas in a clear, concise, appropriate fashion.

2. Supervision

   Questions cover the control, direction, evaluation, coordination, and planning of subordinates' efforts. They include consideration of the competence, motivation, and commitment to perform a task.

3. Teaching and Counseling

   Questions cover teaching employees or team members new ways to succeed, professional and personal development, and the use of a problem-solving rather than an advice-driven approach.

4. Team Development

   Questions cover the effectiveness and cohesiveness of the team, the confidence displayed for leaders, and helping team members become committed participants.

5. Technical and Tactical Proficiency

   Questions cover knowing your job and teaching others to know theirs, as well as knowing your leaders' intent so you can meet organizational goals.

6. Decision Making

   Questions cover how to make decisions, include subordinates in the decision-making process where appropriate, and produce high-quality decisions.

7. Planning

   Questions cover the forecasting, setting goals, establishing priorities, delegating, sequencing, timing, organizing, budgeting, and standardization of procedures.

8. Uses of Technology

   Questions cover the techniques, methods, and tools—computers, analytical techniques, knowledge of process and system, and other modern technological means available to manage information.

9. Professional Ethics

   Questions cover duty, selfless service, and integrity—in general, how the leader behaves in a way consistent with Army doctrine on leadership, FM 22-100 which defines army leadership and is used on the teaching points in the program. The doctrine, available in most public libraries, is currently under revision, but covers these leadership principles and behaviors: leadership, duty, respect, selfless service, honor, integrity, and courage.

Part II

Questions allow the responder to describe the student's leadership style, philosophy, and what skills might most benefit from improvement.

Exhibit 3.2: Learning Matrix for Class 99-1

This matrix is intended for student use in recording a summary of faculty feedback and grades assigned to student work. It is also used as a permanent record of student requirement satisfaction. As such, it will be jointly signed and dated at the end of the twelve-week program by both the student and faculty advisor.

Students are responsible for using this matrix to keep their own accurate record of satisfaction of requirements, grades, and/or feedback. Fill in the matrix either by hand or by computer, using Microsoft® Word software.

The two left-hand columns of the matrix list lesson numbers, tentative dates (based on the draft schedule for Class 99-1), lesson titles, and required products. Where the products are *graded*, the two left-hand cells of the matrix are *shaded*.

The large cell to the right of the lesson identification cells is for recording feedback (and grade, if appropriate). Above the feedback column (at the top of each page) are five cells that list the four major elements in the Core Curriculum Template and an additional criterion—*critical thinking*—that is considered an elemental ingredient of the AMSC curriculum. These elements are placed here to remind students and faculty of the key elements that should be addressed in feedback. It is not necessary to include comments on all five elements in every feedback record, but through the course of the resident program all five elements should be the subject of frequent comments. At the end of each week, students also will comment on their overall performance (and improvement). These comments will be used by faculty advisors as the source of discussion topics during student counseling.

Students' records of feedback should include comments on the major elements, including strengths and weaknesses. The expectation is that, as students progress through the resident program, the feedback will reflect improvement. Faculty advisors will review and discuss the record of feedback with students during each scheduled counseling session and will use the feedback to support recommendations for performance improvement. It is not necessary, however, for students to wait until a scheduled counseling session to discuss feedback and performance. This can be done at any time mutually acceptable to the student and faculty advisor.

The last row of cells in the matrix will be used for a self-assessment across the entire twelve weeks of the resident program. Before the final counseling session, students will evaluate their own performance and summarize that assessment in the last block of the matrix. That self-assessment should address all five of the major elements listed at the top of the matrix.

The following abbreviated definitions may be of help in framing notes about feedback and the end-of-course self-assessment.

Communicate: Oral or written. Concentrate information. Lay out information logically. Express oneself clearly. Include relevant others. Understand and apply intent.

Lead: Healthy command climate. Apply group dynamics. Use motivational tools. Build teamwork. Direct, advise, coach, counsel, and mentor. Be flexible.

Decide: Identify the problem accurately. Evaluate possible solutions. Use appropriate analytical tools. Decide, act, and monitor.

See The Big Picture: Understand context. See the vision and its implications. Understand connections. Be accountable.

Apply Critical Thinking: Look for the underlying issues. Question everything. Make rational assumptions. Objectively assess strengths and weaknesses. Look at all views—both supporting and opposing. Check all data before use. Consider implications and consequences. Key words are clarity, accuracy, precision, relevance, depth, breadth, and logic.

6/10/99 Edition

In order for students to have a better frame of reference in which to assess their progress as they move through the twelve-week AMSC program, it seems reasonable that:

1. There should be an initial "mark on the wall" that shows areas of performance or knowledge that students desire to improve during their studies.
2. It would be helpful to include those expectations in the learning matrix so that they may be used as a reference point each week as students evaluate their progress.
3. Students and their faculty advisors would use those expectations as the basis for assessing progress during scheduled counseling sessions.

In the following matrix block, record your initial expectations and/or those areas of your performance and/or knowledge that you would like to improve during your AMSC studies. Feel free to add to them as you progress through the program, but do not delete any that you have previously entered. You should try to phrase performance objectives in a way that relates to the five major elements of performance shown at the top of the Learning Matrix.

Refer to these initial thoughts each week as you do your "roll-up" progress report and try to comment on whether you are closer to your objective than you were when you began your studies at the college.

Exhibit 3.2: *(continued)*

AMSC LEARNING MATRIX

Session Number and Date	Title	COMMUNICATE	LEAD	DECIDE	SEE THE BIG PICTURE	APPLY CRITICAL THINKING
2-9	Goals and expectations	*Record your expectations for performance/knowledge improvement during your AMSC studies. The five categories in the above boxes may help you focus your thinking.* **Bring these comments with you to your initial counseling session with your faculty advisor.** *(If you need more space, add a blank piece of paper between this and the following page of the learning matrix.)* *If appropriate, add comments here that result from the initial counseling session.*				
Initial Counseling: 1/13						

AMSC Activity and Deliverables

Learning Requirements, Feedback, and Grade

	AMSC Activity and Deliverables	Learning Requirements, Feedback, and Grade
2-32 Due: Various dates	Information Briefing: 20-min briefing once during the 12-week program	
1-3 Pre-Arrival Mail-In	Leadership Philosophy: *Written "Think Piece"*	
2-13 1/14	Personal Assessment and Leadership: *Self-Asessment*	
2-16 1/14	Army Diagnostic Test: *In-class Evaluation*	
2-17 1/15	Leaders and Learning Styles: *Self-Assessment*	
2-19 1/15	Organizational Analysis: *Discussion of Home Station O&F*	
Week #1 1/15	*Summary and Self-Assessment*	*Evaluate how you did this week in each category. Look back over previous weeks and comment on how your performance may have improved.*

2-30 1/21	Information Analysis Applications: *Data Analysis*	

(continued)

Exhibit 3.2: (continued)

AMSC Activity and Deliverables	Learning Requirements, Feedback, and Grade
2-25 1/21	Critical Thinking and Informal Logic: *Small Group Discussion*
Week #2 1/22	*Summary and Self-Assessment* — *Evaluate how you did this week in each category. Look back over previous weeks and comment on how your performance may have improved.*

AMSC Activity and Deliverables	Learning Requirements, Feedback, and Grade
2-35 1/25	Problem Solving Using Models: *Case Studies and Discussions*
2-27 1/26	Leaders, Organizations, and Teams: *In-Progress Review*
2-38 1/26	Pro Interpersonal Communications: *Case Studies and Role Play*
2-40 1/27	Effective Speaking and Briefing Techniques: *Extemp. Speeches*
2-27 1/27	LOT Panel: *Intra-Seminar, Small Group Panel Discussion*
2-42 1/28	Team-Leader Development: *Experiential Activities*
2-45 1/29	The OILEX: *Practical Exercise in Operational Planning*

Week #3 1/29	Summary and Self-Assessment	Evaluate how you did this week in each category. Look back over previous weeks and comment on how your performance may have improved.
2-46 2/01	Assessing Your Health Risk: Personal Health Assessment	
2-49 2/02	Decision Making in Action: Group Project and Briefing	
2-50 2/02	Multi-Rater Assessment (MRA): Automated MRA Instrument	
Term 2 Due: 2/03	**Term 2 Evaluation**	
Week #4 2/05	Summary and Self-Assessment	Evaluate how you did this week in each category. Look back over previous weeks and comment on how your performance may have improved.
3-10 2/09	Intermediate Counseling: One-on-One with Faculty Advisor	
Term 3 Due: 2/11	**Term 3 Evaluation**	

(continued)

Exhibit 3.2: (continued)

	AMSC Activity and Deliverables	Learning Requirements, Feedback, and Grade
4-2 2/11	Force Composition and Structure: *Small Group PE and Briefing*	
4-3 2/12	Reserve Components: *Guest Speaker Synthesis*	
4-4 2/12	Army Operations: *Seminar Discussion*	
Week #5 2/12	*Summary and Self-Assessment*	*Evaluate how you did this week in each category. Look back over previous weeks and comment on how your performance may have improved.*

	AMSC Activity and Deliverables	Learning Requirements, Feedback, and Grade
4-6 2/16	Operational Case Study: *Case Study and Discussion*	
4-7.2 2/17	Gettysburg: Setting the Stage: *Seminar Discussion*	
4-7.3 2/19	Gettysburg: Staff Ride *Field Trip and Discussion*	
4-74 2/19	Gettyburg: Analysis-Synthesis *Seminar Discussion*	

5-3 / 2/19	PPBES: *Small Group Briefing*	
Week #6 / 2/19	Summary and Self-Assessment	*Evaluate how you did this week in each category. Look back over previous weeks and comment on how your performance may have improved.*

5-5 / 2/22	Battlefield Requirements: *Small Group Briefing*	
Term 4 Due: 2/23	**Term 4 Evaluation**	
2-23 Due 2/23	Leadership Paper: *Personal Assessment*	
5-7 / 2/23	Developing Material for the Force: *Small Group Briefing*	
5-13 / 2/26	Unit Training: *Small Group Briefing*	
5-14 / 2/26	Force Readiness: *Small Group Briefing*	
Week #7 / 2/26	Summary and Self-Assessment	*Evaluate how you did this week in each category. Look back over previous weeks and comment on how your performance may have improved.*

5-16 / 3/01	Force Design PE: *Practical Exercise and Small Group Briefing*

(continued)

Exhibit 3.2: (continued)

AMSC Activity and Deliverables

Term 5 (5-17) Due: 3/02	RM Article— Research and Evaluate: Written Review for Grade	Learning Requirements, Feedback, and Grade
3/01-02	*Briefing on article Analysis for Feedback*	
6-3 3/03	Installation Operations Exercises: *Practical Exercise*	
6-5 3/04	Mid-Term Counseling: *One-on-One with Faculty Advisor*	
6-8.1 3/05	Intro to APIC: *Quiz*	
6-8.3 3/05	Fort Carson: How Did They Do? *Synthesis*	
Week #8 3/05	*Summary and Self-Assessment*	*Evaluate how you did this week in each category. Look back over previous weeks and comment on how your performance may have improved.*

6-11 3/08	Contracting for Services: *Practical Exercise*	
6-13 3/09	Managerial Costing = Activity Based Costing: *Practical Exercise*	
2-31 Due: 3/12	**Professional Article or Special Project Deliverable**	
TRACK 3/12	**Individual Track Topics: Paper and/or Briefing and/or Briefing Book**	
Week #9 3/12	*Summary and Self-Assessment*	*Evaluate how you did this week in each category. Look back over previous weeks and comment on how your performance may have improved.*

6-16 3/15	Force Projection Overview: *Quiz*
6-17 3/15	Focused Logistics: *Quiz*
6-20 3/16	Levels of Mobilization: *Game-Quiz*

(continued)

Exhibit 3.2: (continued)

	AMSC Activity and Deliverables	Learning Requirements, Feedback, and Grade
6-21 3/16	Role of the Installation in Mobilization: *Game-Quiz*	
6-29 3/19	Operation Vigilant Impact: *Practical Exercise*	
Week #10 3/19	*Summary and Self-Assessment*	*Evaluate how you did this week in each category. Look back over previous weeks and comment on how your performance may have improved.*
6-33 3/23	The Snow Blower Case: *Practical Exercise*	
6-35 3/24	The Army Strategic Logistics Plan: *Practical Exercise*	
Term 6 Due: 3/25	**Term 6 Evaluation**	
6-38 3/25-26	Operation Vigilant Benefactor: *Practical Exercise*	

7-1 3/26	Army Diagnostic Test (Post-Test): *In-Class Evaluation*	
Week #11 3/26	*Summary and Self-Assessment*	*Evaluate how you did this week in each category. Look back over previous weeks and comment on how your performance may have improved.*

7-2 3/26–31	Capstone Exercise: *Linked Practical Exercises*	
Program Summary	*Cumulative Self-Assessment*	*Evaluate your **OVERALL** performance in each category. Look back over previous weeks and comment on how your performance may have improved.*
Final Counseling: 3/31–4/1		

(continued)

Exhibit 3.2: (*continued*)

Student and Faculty Advisor certify all requirements are completed; graded requirements with a minimum of "pass or satisfactory."

Student Signature:_____   Date:_____

Faculty Signature:_____   Date:_____

Faculty route through DEPARTMENT CHAIR and DEAN to REGISTRAR, ARMY MANAGEMENT STAFF COLLEGE

References

Kolb, D. (1976). *Learning Style Inventory, Self-Scoring Test and Interpretation Booklet.* Boston: McBerard Company.

McCall, M. W. Jr. (1997). *High Flyers.* Cambridge, Mass.: Harvard Business School Publishing.

Notes

1 Toffler, A. and H. Toffler, (1994). *Creating a New Civilization: The Politics of the Third Wave.* Atlanta: Turner Publishing, Inc.

2 For more details, access http://cpol.army.mil/ and click on Training and Development.

3 A good source of information about other programs is: Schwartz, M. K., Axtman, K. M., Freeman, F. H. (Eds.) (1998). *Leadership Education: A Source Book of Courses and Programs.* (7th ed.). Greensboro, N.C.: Center for Creative Leadership.

4 Field Manual 22-100, Army Leadership.

5 Seminars are learning groups or units of fifteen students each. Typical classes have ten seminars, each comprised of as much diversity as the total class demographics represent.

6 AMSC Faculty Feedback is a moderated discussion board based on the Discus program from Hope College in Holland, Michigan. All Discus scripts and static files were authored by Kevin W. Paulisse with design ideas and implementation advice from William F. Polik. All files associated with Discus are copyright © 1997–98 by Kevin W. Paulisse and William F. Polik, all rights reserved. Discus is free and can be downloaded immediately. To learn more about the Discus program, or to download your own free copy, visit the Discus home page: http://www.chem.hope.edu/discus/

7 Paul, R. (1992). *Critical Thinking: What Every Person Needs to Survive in a Rapidly Changing World.* Sonoma, Calif.: Foundation for Critical Thinking.

About the Contributor

Dr. Ursula G. Lohmann (lohmannu@amsc.belvoir.army.mil) is dean of academics at the Army Management Staff College. Prior to joining the AMSC, Lohmann directed training activities for the National Institutes of Health, including a fee-for-service training center. She facilitated organizational development interventions and taught courses in all areas of leadership, management, and career development. At the same time, she actively worked with federal advisory committees in the area of training and development. Lohmann has developed and managed research grants and taught German at American University. She most enjoys working with professional groups interested in human behavior, change, and the workplace.

Lohmann earned her Ph.D. in organizational development and higher education from American University and holds degrees in languages and linguistics from both American University and Georgetown University. She has a solid foundation in the hard sciences, which has sparked an interest in her in how the laws of nature affect leadership and management of the workplace.

Much of her work centers on her experiences at the AMSC. Her article, "Leadership Education Lessons Learned" (*Public Manager,* Summer 1994) focuses on the value of linking curriculum closely to organization. Linkage's 1996 Leadership Development Conference Proceedings, "Integrating Content, Context, Organization, and Experience to Develop Leaders," chronicles the research and benchmarking processes for the core curriculum. In 1998, she presented "Integrated Education for Organizational Benefit" to a conference on career development in government. Other papers, workbooks, and presentations cover linguistics and technology, critical thinking in decision making, and the use of psychological type in leadership and management development. Her current work in progress is entitled, "Leadership Challenges for the Millennium and Beyond."

CHAPTER FOUR

BARCLAYS GLOBAL INVESTORS (BGI)

This chapter outlines a strategic initiative based on assessment, action learning, and coaching that is designed to develop and sustain a global leadership culture.

Context and Challenge

Barclays Global Investors (BGI) is one of the leading institutional investment management firms in the world. Headquartered in the United States, the firm has offices in Australia, Europe, Canada, Hong Kong, and Japan. Its clients include corporate multinationals and government retirement plans, universities, foundations, financial planning advisors, mutual fund distributors, and central banks. Its far-reaching vision is to create financial freedom and security for millions of individuals and thousands of organizations around the world.

In 1971, as Wells Fargo Investment Advisors, the firm introduced the concept of indexing, and over the next twenty years expanded its offerings of highly structured asset management strategies. In 1990, the firm joined with Nikko Securities Company, Ltd. and began global expansion. In 1996, the firm was acquired by Barclays, PLC, which then reorganized its business units in 1998, creating BGI as its Asset Management entity. BGI was going global and going there fast. An increasing share of revenues was coming from non-U.S. business.

The company's business requirements could not be met with a disparate collection of independently operating offices around the world. "Because of the tremendous growth of BGI over the last several years, we had been crying out for management training and a greater sense of clarity and common purpose," said Garrett Bouton, head of global human resources and CEO of the Americas. Some intervention was needed to answer the cry. Going into the next millennium, the company has 1,900 people in six countries, a mix of nationals and expatriates. A leadership development program was needed to answer questions regarding BGI's future leadership needs.

Building the Business Case for Leadership Development

Based on this very general request for management training, a needs assessment was in order. In an intense four-week effort, more than 100 people were interviewed or participated in needs assessment focus groups.

Needs Assessment

The initial step in the needs assessment was to query senior executives about the business challenges and the management skills needed to meet them. Individual meetings with twenty five of the top fifty senior executives, including the co-chairmen, drew out specifics for the analysis. Executives were asked the following:

- What are the critical activities of your business or function?
- What are your challenges?
- What is not happening that should be? Why?
- How well-equipped are your people to meet these challenges?
- On a scale of one to ten, where would you put your people? Describe the gap.
- What skills need to be improved immediately?
- What other skills will be needed in the future?
- What skills are completely missing?

Next, meetings with individuals and small groups at all other levels provided a perspective from mid-level managers and associates. This two-tiered process captured both the training needs and organizational issues that BGI could reasonably expect to address in its program. A useful by-product of these meetings was educating the organization about how a training and development function could address the day-to-day needs of the business.

The needs assessment revealed key abilities BGI needed to develop in its managers. They were:

- Working in a global organization
- Merging corporate cultures
- Managing and communicating with geographically dispersed groups
- Functioning effectively in a constantly changing environment
- Thinking strategically
- Setting expectations and delegating
- Effectively making decisions

- Managing in a matrixed organization
- Coaching, developing, and evaluating people

However, what became crystal clear from the needs assessment was that the management development program had to go far beyond improving individual skills. It had to develop leaders who could meet the unique and longer-term needs of the business. BGI's leaders should be able to "think and act globally" and leverage the capabilities of colleagues in other functions and offices. BGI needed to improve the flow of communication vertically, horizontally, and globally to increase the speed of knowledge transfer for its clients. The simple request for a management development program had turned into a strategic wall-to-wall organizational development initiative.

Viewing this project more strategically presented the unique and immediate opportunity to positively impact organizational change and bridge communication among leaders.

Program Objectives

The program objectives emerging from the needs assessment allowed simultaneous individual development and organizational development:

- *Begin transformation of BGI into a truly global firm.* To truly capitalize on global opportunities, people at BGI needed to work across time zones, with multiple computer systems, using various stock exchanges and currencies—moving synchronously with people whom they may have never met. BGI's business strategy calls for alignment across geographies, functions, and individuals.
- *Improve communication and connections between senior executives and managers around the globe.* One of the consistent messages in the needs assessment was that people had incredible regard for the expertise of BGI's senior managers. However, they did not feel that they had access to them. The consensus was that senior executives have critical information to teach and that they could provide a broad repertoire of lessons learned. As it was, however, there were not enough forums for substantive dialogue.

- *Revitalize and retain top talent.* BGI is in the challenging position of being on the leading edge of its business. It can continue to hold that enviable place only by attracting and inspiring the best people in the industry.

- *Differentiate through a leadership culture.* Historically, the investment management business is not known for developing management and leadership skills. Its workforce has been comprised of very technically competent individual contributors. BGI was no different. Its leaders had been valued and rewarded on the basis of their technical expertise, rather than their management skills. To create the significant shift that would differentiate BGI from its competitors, the company needed to make sure its leaders understood the bottom-line impact of leading effectively. They wanted leaders to focus on their people as intently as they focus on their clients and/or the functions they lead, but hadn't yet committed the time or attention to it.

- *Create common understanding, practices, and vocabulary for leaders around the world.* BGI needed to support the creation of a truly global firm while allowing and respecting individual and local differences. BGI wanted to create a common experience of leadership, regardless of which office or function people led. That shared understanding would lead to greater agility in meeting client needs.

Gathering the Resources

In an effort to quantify resources needed for the program, experts, time and money, and executive sponsorships were identified.

Expertise

Facilitators were carefully chosen for their group process skills as well as knowledge of BGI's needed course content. The requirement went far beyond the classic "classroom trainer." Facilitators would have to conduct one-on-one coaching both in the sessions and on request afterwards. They also needed to provide perspective based on work with other corporate clients, constructively lead discussions of organizational issues, and produce skill development with immediate application to real business issues.

Although training implementation was on a fast track, BGI undertook an extensive research process to identify the most suitable consulting firm with the needed expertise. After careful consideration, two finalist firms were brought in for half-day "showcases" to present an overview of their proposed program and a brief demonstration of a module. Executives from five different areas of the business and two senior human resource generalists evaluated the presentations.

Personnel Decisions International (PDI) was selected to develop and deliver Global Leadership Essentials (GLE), the assessment-based development program tailored to BGI. Potential consultant facilitators were frequently observed before the actual rollout of the training. They were screened for their track record with global companies. Academic background and cultural "fit" were also considered.

Time and Money

GLE was a huge cash investment, which included the cost of moving participants around the world for each offering and rotating the program to each of its global locations. The company also had to consider the opportunity cost of committing the time of its leaders. More than 150 leaders would participate in GLE in its first year. For each participant the business had to plan on two weeks out of the office, and that did not include time spent on prework and work between sessions. That represented a lot of productivity. Despite a campaign of expense reductions in running the business, BGI's Management Committee funded the global price tag of this program and made it a priority for people to attend.

Executive Sponsorship

Because business executives made the final vendor selection, buy-in and sponsorship began from the start. The executive viewpoint was incorporated in the program design, and executives from all locations were integral to the program delivery.

Program Design

This program was specifically designed to link BGI's business goals with the behaviors of its leaders (see Exhibit 4.1 for more details on GLE competencies).

Guiding Principles

The design of GLE was governed by a set of overarching guiding principles:

- Learning goes far beyond an actual training event. Participants must take ownership for their development and learn as much from each other as from the course facilitator.
- All those with current management responsibility—business managers and principal-level leaders—will benefit from attending, rather than a selected group of "high-potentials." The businesses have responsibility for prioritizing their people's enrollments.
- The program should show participants how to leverage their existing strengths as well as how to develop new ones.
- BGI's strategic business goals should be explicitly linked to the leadership training. The program will challenge the frequently held assumption that leadership and management training delivers primarily intangible results.

Target Audience

BGI is a flat organization with only three levels—executives, middle managers, and associates. The audience for this program was all mid-level managers and individual contributors with leadership roles. Executives nominated participants and gave priority to those who, in their view, would benefit most from GLE. The intention was to train a "critical mass" of people to affect change most quickly.

Size of Group

The relatively small group size—from fourteen to eighteen participants—encouraged interaction and networking. Participants were intentionally mixed by geography and function.

Training Focus

The training focus was on management and leadership competencies within the context of the business. People at BGI are bent on driving to business results. Part of the appeal of the GLE leadership model was the specific modules related to "business excellence." Participants could make the connection between the skills learned—such as influencing others, decision making, strategic thinking, client service—and what they knew to be effective for business outcomes. Other elements of the model focused on "personal excellence," "people excellence," and "work excellence."

Teaching Methodology

The program was fast-paced, content-rich, and utilized a range of classroom teaching methods, including lectures, exercises, learning partners, learning teams, and action planning. Other learning tools were used before, during, and after the sessions, including:

- 360-degree feedback and other assessment instruments
- Job-related assignments
- Exposure to senior executives
- Company specific data such as client satisfaction survey, people turnover reports, and five-year strategic plan

Following the guiding principles, both the company and the facilitators made clear that more than mere attendance would be required. Participants and learning teams held a great deal of the ownership for learning and change inside and outside the classroom.

Teaching Devices

The room was large, and was set up to facilitate interaction and create the optimal learning environment. People sat in table groups of five or six. When necessary, the tables were moved around to create a fresh perspective or accommodate an activity. The table group set-up allowed the facilitator to stand at different points in the room, observing the interaction of the participants without imposing. It also helped the session flow between the content to be presented and the issues that emerged from group conversation. Various media were used both to deliver content and capture it. They included videos, electronic slide presentations, overhead projectors, flipcharts, and whiteboards.

Strategic Intent

The program's objective was to achieve BGI's vision of thinking and acting more globally. BGI's key asset and product is knowledge. Demanding workloads and the accelerating pace of change have been personally challenging to many key people. BGI realized that to succeed globally and leverage its intellectual capability for clients it needed a strategic shift. It had to turn inward a bit to support and develop its talented people through better leadership. GLE was designed to develop leadership capabilities throughout the organization, with a sophisticated, practical, action-oriented approach.

Program Overview

GLE is an integrated action learning approach to leadership development. The program addresses evaluating, building, and sustaining leadership excellence with regard to:

- "Personal" competencies—those that focused on individual characteristics and skills
- "People" competencies—targeting effectiveness in working with and influencing other people
- "Business" competencies—exploring areas of strategic effectiveness
- "Work" competencies—which focused on getting work done through others

Each program had two four-day sessions separated by six to eight weeks for application of learning. One session was always held in San Francisco, BGI's corporate headquarters, and the other session was held in Tokyo, London, or Sydney.

See Exhibit 4.2 for a day-by-day training agenda. Here is an overview:

Session 1, Day 1. This day established the tone and context for all that followed. Participants listened to senior executives giving personal presentations to begin their understanding of what leaders do. Senior executives gave presentations to share their personal guides to leadership effectiveness. They talked about competition in the marketplace, key elements of BGI'S strategic plan, change initiatives, globalization, and managing the people in their areas.

Participants asked some tough questions, and they received candid answers. They reflected on the leadership characteristics and corporate values that were demonstrated by the words and actions of the executives. Most began to make the connection that their own leadership behaviors also had an impact on BGI. After this classroom introduction to GLE, participants toured the hosting office and city, spending some relaxed time socializing with each other and the local BGI people.

Session 1, Day 2. This was the day to jump in to the core leadership skill-building content. Participants took a learning styles assessment so they could discover their learning preferences and strengths, and apply that self-knowledge throughout the program. Because they would be using the 360-degree feedback instrument continually, they spent time learning how to read and interpret those reports. They began creating a personal definition of leadership that included developing a mission and vision for their BGI team, an example of which was, "I will create a compelling vision of how great my team can be and communicate our strategies and tactics to key people in the organization."

They were also introduced to some specific tools and techniques for providing direction, establishing plans, and managing execution. For example, in the "providing direction" section, they created "SMART" (Specific, Measurable, Achievable, Regularly-reviewed, Time-bound) feedback for one of their direct reports. They then practiced and refined their goal with a learning partner to get ready to try their new approach at their workplace.

Session 1, Day 3. After working on the mission and vision for their team the day before, participants learned about change on Day 3—both individual and organizational. They discussed strategic versus tactical thinking, moving from managing in the present to managing for the future. They learned what it takes to champion change in an organization, and how to align and plan specific change initiatives. The day wrapped up with an executive panel, which helped anchor all the information in business reality. The executive panel consisted of three executives who fielded questions from the participants based on the skills content from the first three days. (The executive panel is described in more detail in the section called "Strengthening Communication.")

Session 1, Day 4. This part of the program shifted participants from an internal focus on themselves and their team to a view of clients and the marketplace. The concepts of internal and external clients—what they value, how their expectations may change over time, and defining quality from their point of view—were all thoroughly explored. The afternoon activities emphasized the importance of facilitation skills to foster teamwork, build relationships, and encourage open communication. Again, participants learned specific techniques for exercising these skills back in the workplace.

Session 2, Day 1. (*This session convened four to six weeks after participants completed Session 1.*) After trying out many of the concepts and skills between sessions, participants were full of questions and ready to take in more information. In a different venue, they heard again from local senior executives about personal and organizational leadership challenges. In Session 1, participants had already committed to growing in their leadership roles. On the opening day of Session 2, executives articulated what BGI needs from its emerging leaders and how they are expected to grow within the firm. As before, the end of the day program allowed for meeting, greeting, and touring.

Session 2, Day 2. The growing conceptual framework of leadership was tested by a discussion of successes and challenges. This day covered the disciplines of credibility, including acting with integrity, valuing diversity, and demonstrating adaptability. Participants learned a model of influencing others—getting agreement and managing disagreement. As on the other days, they worked on elements of their individual development plans that were relevant to the day's topics. Participants discussed the Thomas Kilman model of conflict (accommodate versus compete versus avoid) and identified their natural reactions to conflict. This two-dimensional model of conflict-handling behavior is adapted from "Conflict and Conflict Management" by Kenneth Thomas in the *Handbook of Industrial and Organizational Psychology* (1976). Participants learned how to move beyond an unconscious response to a more intentional approach based on real issues in their jobs, such as what happens when different functions are working on the same project, but have objectives and priorities that are misaligned.

Session 2, Day 3. Decision-making styles—being the "collaborator," the "detective," the "facilitator," and the "lone ranger"—led the day's program. Using a case study methodology, participants learned when to use which style. The most consistent theme was that, as a group, they over-collaborated with their peers, but under-facilitated, which reduced the effectiveness of getting their projects done and ensuring the buy-in of all the stakeholders.

Session 2, Day 4. This was the wrap-up day. Participants worked through a business simulation that required them to use all the concepts, tools, and skills they had covered in the entire program—both in and out of the classroom. In this simulation, participants formed into "companies" from different countries that tried to merge with a target company. As part of the exercise, the participants used skills such as strategic thinking, influence, and leading a team.

Participants shared their personal vision of leadership, just as the senior executives had done at the beginning of the program. Of course, GLE was only a beginning for these leaders. The final task was to commit to an action plan that integrated all they had been exposed to in the program, giving priority to steps that would help the participant make a difference as a leader. Each "company" had different advantages and disadvantages that were not known to the other "companies." As part of the exercise, the participants had to use skills such as strategic thinking, influence, and leading a team. Participants chose the skills they were particularly interested in working on and took on a specified role and character. The team then developed their best strategy for influencing the decision maker in the acquiring company.

Curriculum Highlights

Participants agreed on several highlights they experienced throughout the program.

Raising Anticipation

Eight weeks before each program, participants were brought together via videoconference for a global "kick-off session." The kick-offs covered the strategic reasons for the program; an overview of the content, intent, and key features; and the "prework" assignments, including a 360-degree assessment. They began to build excitement, and some anxious anticipation. A fair amount of time was spent during the "kick-off" sessions getting employee buy-in to the 360-degree feedback process and getting them prepared for the feedback. The program coordinator assured participants that the assessments measure perceptions but not necessarily truth.

Before the launch of GLE, BGI's global human resources director sent a letter to each of the managing directors explaining the background, strategic intent, and content of the program. This was followed with meetings and videoconferences to provide more specific information about the content, the senior manager's role in reinforcing the program, and a recommended strategy for nominating their people. BGI worked with PDI to design "coaching kits" for leaders. Material in the kits illustrated the role of coach, particularly in working with development planning. The kits were delivered to participants, their immediate managers, and senior management so all would hold similar expectations of what would happen once the participant returned to "the real world."

Strengthening Communication

Very quickly, the GLE objective of strengthening the connection between executives and middle managers was accomplished. And it was accomplished in a very public forum. In the first morning of each session some of the senior executives for that location—usually three—would discuss their own business and leadership challenges. This personalized the experience for participants and began to draw the business context for the session. The executives were selected to present based on how well they could articulate a vision of global leadership, their demonstrated global leadership perspective by virtue of their job, and their reputation in the firm. Participants took copious notes on the presentations, and later discussed among themselves the leadership characteristics and corporate values that the speakers demonstrated by their remarks and attitude.

The speakers also described:

- How BGI is going to be expected to lead differently as a global firm
- How they personally lead differently in a global environment
- The implications for BGI if it didn't become truly global
- What the biggest barriers are to becoming global
- How BGI's clients are pulling it towards being global

Later in the first session, participants were exposed to senior executives a second time, this time as an executive panel. The purpose of the executive panel was to provide a communication forum in which the participants could discuss leadership concepts they had already covered in the program and other organizational issues that surfaced in the context of the first day's training. These panels were held in the late afternoon, and the panel members would join the participants for drinks and refreshments immediately afterward. The sessions were lively and informative, though sometimes tense because extremely sensitive issues were discussed in a very candid manner. Participants asked executives about why communication seemed to stop at certain levels and how certain people got promoted, for example. The executives and participants learned a lot about each other and gained a better understanding of each other's roles and challenges.

BGI had tremendous support from its executives for the presentations and the panels. In fact, its co-chairmen presented at every one of the ten sessions BGI held in 1998. The participants reported they greatly appreciated the opportunity to meet and discuss key leadership and business issues, and the executives got a much broader perspective of the emerging leaders in the firm.

Building a Peer Network

The program also promoted and enhanced the development of an internal peer network. Networking activities outside of the classroom were woven into the program. For example, on the first afternoon of each four-day session, there was either a tour of the local office, the city, or both. This gave the participants a chance to recover from jet lag and get to know each in a more relaxed setting. Each office had a different flavor. In Sydney, the office tour was followed by an informal gathering with all the participants and office staff over pizza and beer.

On the first evening, BGI hosted a group dinner. After that, participants usually planned their evenings on their own, often with the locals leading the way to their favorite restaurants and drinking establishments. Out-of-towners got a good sense of the location from these "tours" to karaoke bars in Tokyo, Indian restaurants in London, and harbor cruises in Sydney and San Francisco.

Forging Business Partnerships

In addition to the network that participants built with each other, another highlight of the curriculum was the business partnerships forged in the hosting local offices. Participants leveraged their visits to address real-time business and client challenges as part of the action learning. Some participants visited clients while they were "in the neighborhood." Others worked on pressing issues with teams at the host offices, such as BGI's technology initiative or the European Monetary Unit conversion. BGI offices in Australia and Great Britain were both planning major relocations in the GLE timeframe. Those involved were able to share information face to face, and really learn from each other.

Inspiring Celebration

GLE gave BGI people a reason to celebrate. The non-U.S. offices used the leadership sessions as an opportunity to show their hospitality and give the visitors a closer view of their business and people. On the last day of the program, BGI held a "graduation" ceremony during which one of its executives would provide an inspirational message before people returned to the workplace. In Tokyo, the chief executive invited all his team leaders to attend the graduation ceremony, which made for a very large celebration.

At the end of the graduation program, each participant received a certificate and a memento that symbolized the global experience. They talked in turns about the most powerful learning for them and gave a parting message for the group. The participants committed out loud to one leadership behavior or tool that they planned to implement immediately. These parting ceremonies were very poignant and emotional for the group. They had spent a great deal of time together both inside and outside the classroom, establishing friendships and relationships with their global colleagues. They had communicated personal challenges and successes in modifying their leadership. In their parting messages, many of them pledged to keep in touch. Some had already started organizing informal and formal gatherings. Clearly, they were all excited about what they had learned and very sad to leave each other.

Key Features

The program emphasized several essential elements such as action learning, the use of multiple assessment instruments, and one-on-one coaching.

Action Learning

One of the elements that differentiated this program from others was the "action learning" component at all phases of the process—before, during, and after the training itself was completed. *Everything* had to have practical application for the business.

Extensive Prework Set the Stage for GLE. It was assigned at the kick-off with an eight-week lead time. Thus the program required the learner's commitment from the start. Prework included:

- Interviewing two people, either inside or outside the organization, whom the participant admired as leaders
- Completing two "client audits" with either internal or external clients to determine the client's overall satisfaction and what else was needed to meet the client's short-term and long-term goals
- Having a discussion with his or her manager to establish mutual expectations for developmental outcomes. The learner also discussed the manager's perception of BGI's newly articulated vision. Because the participants developed a vision and mission for their functional group in the context of the workshop, they needed it to be aligned with their manager's perception of "the big picture."

Company-Specific Business Data was Integrated in Every Learning Module. BGI is a data-driven organization. There was plenty of it in GLE. For example, BGI's biannual client satisfaction survey was used in three modules: "Thinking Strategically," "Focusing on Clients," and "Committing to Quality."

In the "Focusing on Clients" module, participants linked information from the client satisfaction survey to their own results from the prework. The content in the module focused on heightening awareness of the full circle of clients they serve and identifying products and services for both internal and external clients. Participants pulled out their prework client interviews and evaluated them to determine overall client satisfaction and identify short-term and long-term needs. They then analyzed whether they had the resources, authority, and so forth to meet the needs identified. They looked at their 360-degree feedback to see how they personally rated on the client-related items such as working to anticipate client needs, meeting commitments to clients, and continually searching for ways to improve client service. All of these information-sharing and analysis activities helped participants understand how clients define value and quality and how these expectations change in various contexts.

As the GLE sessions progressed throughout the year, results from the 360-degree feedback instruments were aggregated. One of the organizational strengths that came through is BGI's focus on clients. Part of the power of GLE is that the ability to leverage strengths is emphasized as much as the developmental activities. Using this concept of "focusing on clients," participants were asked to define how they would lead and manage differently if they treated their boss, peers, and most important, their direct reports as "clients." This concept resonated deeply with the participants and was very useful in helping them define actions for themselves that would be more favorably received by their people when they returned to their jobs.

Learning Teams Concentrated on Functional Areas. At various points during the program, global "learning teams" representing a variety of functional areas came together. They discussed leadership issues related to specific functional areas, such as information technology or operations. In this way, participants were able to hear about and develop solutions that could be implemented globally. The learning teams were created during the first training session, continued between sessions, and met again in the second session. The teams chose their own leader from within the group.

Between the two GLE sessions, participants had assignments related to their individual development goals and targeted activities with their "learning teams."

Insights Were Built Daily Into Individual Development Plans. After each module, participants were given time to reflect on the key insights in terms of what their 360-degree feedback told them, the content of the session, and the other participants' opinions and points of view. Participants also identified which of the many tools would be most useful to them, and finally, what actions they would take to improve their leadership skills, based on all of the above.

On the last day of the session, participants spent a significant amount of time fine-tuning their overall development plans and working with the other participants to get feedback on their intended actions.

Several weeks after the sessions, BGI followed up with the participants to determine which tools they had utilized or behaviors they had attempted to change. In this way, participants could try out new ways of leading, then get additional encouragement or coaching.

Multiple Assessments

The competencies evaluated in the 360-degree assessment instrument completed before the sessions were directly linked to the training modules. For example, in the "Credibility" module, important supporting behaviors such as having the confidence and trust of others, showing consistency between words and actions, living up to commitments, and protecting confidential information had all been evaluated in the 360-degree feedback instrument.

Participants referred to their feedback in virtually every module. This created relevance and buy-in for all the modules, whether people were learning how to leverage a strength or improve an area of development. Seeing how they were perceived in black and white made it more real. This was the first opportunity for many to get this kind of assessment on themselves. The 360-degree feedback gave people an opportunity to start thinking about their leadership skills to get a preview of the content of the program.

The emphasis of this assessment—and the others used in GLE—was individual development, not actual evaluation of performance. Participants were advised to expect a few "surprises," because it is always difficult to be completely accurate about the perceptions others may have of you. Although participants were not required to share their results with anyone, most did. They used the opportunity to get more feedback on their results from their learning partners and the course facilitator during the sessions and their managers, direct reports, and peers when they returned to the workplace.

During the course of the training, a number of other assessments were used. On the first day of the program, there was a "pre-test" so that participants could assess their understanding of their role as a global leader, their strengths and development needs, their ability to improve their skills, and their perceived level of support from their immediate manager and the organization. BGI also asked if they had an individual development plan. On the last day, BGI conducted a "post-test" asking the same questions. These self-assessments showed dramatic improvement in most areas, particularly in the areas of understanding their development needs and creating a development plan for themselves.

The participants completed a "Learning Styles Inventory" during the first morning of the session before they established their learning teams. Participants also used assessment instruments to determine their decision-making and conflict resolution styles. Taken altogether, the assessments increased individual awareness and, more important, taught participants how to recognize differences and how to work with differences in their direct reports. They also provided fodder for some very rich discussions about BGI's organization and culture.

One-on-One Coaching and Development Planning Around Assessment Results

Individual development planning focused heavily on the assessments, both from the perspective of leveraging strengths and meeting development needs. Feedback did not end with the assessments. Participants were encouraged to seek clarification from the people who rated them—especially their bosses. Because there were usually a number of possible areas for improving skills, participants were asked to limit the areas they planned to address on the basis of what would have the greatest impact for their business. The facilitators coached many of the participants individually.

During the initial meetings with BGI senior managers, some expressed concerns about their role as coaches and the insights that they may or may not have about leadership capabilities. As a result, BGI implemented a 360-degree feedback process for the managing directors (MDs), using an instrument called "Executive Success Profile" that evaluated executive competencies. The MDs then received one-on-one coaching from an executive coach and worked with this coach on their own individual development plan—an added benefit of the program.

Evaluation

The program was affirmed by the positive reactions of participants and achievement of organizational objectives.

Participant Reaction

Reports generated from multiple assessments indicated that the facilitators were excellent at tying the curriculum with real-life issues and experiences at BGI, allowing for honest debate. One manager observed, "The facilitator didn't come across as knowing more than we did, and he led the discussion in ways that helped us all find practical solutions."

Participants recorded substantial percentage improvements in pre- and post-session survey results. Answers indicated a growing confidence in their role, their strengths, and their ability to develop their skills.

Follow-up evaluations sent several weeks after the program asked which leadership behavior or tool participants had implemented. The key trends in the responses were better delegation, holding more meetings with staff, closer contact with their people (for example, fewer e-mails, more direct contact), better upward communication, giving people more accurate and timely feedback, and more involvement by their teams in the decision-making process.

Positive reactions were felt around the world. "It has been interesting working in Tokyo because the environment is so vastly different, with the language and the cultural implications," said Hector Rualo, head of information technology for BGI Tokyo. "But knowing that we have so much in common and that our basic human motivations are so much the same is helping me to become a better communicator."

Objectives Met or In-Progress

Begin Transformation of BGI into a Truly Global Firm. In a 1999 company-wide People Opinion Survey, results confirmed that people understood that globalization is the right strategy for the firm. "Three years ago people were experiencing globalization for the first time and it didn't feel good," said Pattie Dunn, BGI chairman. "We have created a sense of why globalization is important to BGI and that's a huge accomplishment," she notes. In one of the first issues of *b.global,* BGI's worldwide newsletter, Dunn attributes the change in part to GLE. BGI also benefits from a growing number of global conferences and task forces now that people are presented with a different model of how to work and communicate. Besides the survey dimension entitled "The Global Company," other dimensions such as leadership, organizational culture, teamwork, and performance management were assessed.

"This is a really powerful effort that has given us a great awareness that we all are wrestling with the same problems," said Esmond Jenkins, client service and marketing manager in London. "GLE brought life to the whole idea of working globally."

Improve Communication and Connection Between Senior Executives and Managers Around the Globe. The executive presentations and panels quickly became one of the most popular features of GLE. Word quickly got around that BGI's senior executives were anxious and willing to hear managers' concerns and address their issues when they could. After these presentations, participants reported they are proud be part of an organization that had this calibre of leadership. The sessions naturally made it easier to pick up the phone to connect with someone, even an executive, you had already met.

Because BGI is a relatively new and ever-expanding global organization, it is challenging to keep up with its rate of change. The program facilitated learning on how to navigate the formal and informal organizational structures, and helped participants clarify roles and responsibilities of individuals and groups.

BGI also developed other communication vehicles and forums to address the ongoing challenge of communicating in a global firm. In various parts of the business there are now regular leadership briefings, business specific newsletters, and multilevel communication sessions on important topics. BGI also hired an experienced communications manager to push this effort.

Revitalize and Retain Top Talent. BGI's global turnover rate has remained stable throughout its leadership development program. BGI has attracted some top players in the industry for key roles in its strategic plan. "BGI's strengths are reflected in its image, goals, and values. That confirms part of the reason I came here," said its newly recruited chief administrative officer for the United States. "It's the big strong hook into what is pulling us forward." Interviews with employees about the impact of BGI's leadership development program on their feeling of "fitting" in the organization is one variable that might impact its stable retention rate.

Differentiate Through a Leadership Culture. BGI needed an accelerated roll-out of GLE which would touch a critical mass of its leaders to get the maximum impact. Chairman Pattie Dunn wants a legacy of developing a strong leadership and management culture. Perhaps the most significant result of the program was that it transformed the organization by developing more than 50 percent of the target population (through GLE) in one calendar year. The post-program surveys confirm that new leadership skills are being used.

Create Common Understanding, Practices, and Vocabulary for Leaders Around the World. All managers and individual contributor leaders are expected to go through the program at some time. The curriculum was expanded in both directions this year—to the executive population and the entry-level managers to ensure that everyone is well-versed in the same models and behaviors. From the aggregated 360-degree assessment results, BGI developed themes of coaching, delegating, and decision making for the near future. The aggregated results will continue to be analyzed on an ongoing basis and themes revised, as appropriate.

Critical Success Factors and Lessons Learned

Value-added

Opening remarks by BGI co-chairmen at each session emphasized the importance of aligning leadership development with the strategic business objectives of the company. A clear connection between these objectives and the leadership skills greatly increased the likelihood of buy-in and support for the program from executive sponsors and participants. This was especially critical when facing intense competitive pressure and cost-controls. Without a clear value-added in the eyes of the participants and senior executives, the program would have lost impact and sponsorship.

Action Learning

Learning and doing business were treated as the same activity. Each element of GLE had practical application. From the learning teams to the individual development plans, it all centered on real-time work.

Executive Involvement

Executive presence at its programs was one of the most powerful and popular features of the program. Both the participants and the executives learned a great deal and gained a different perspective. Participants directly stated that interacting with the executives increased their confidence that BGI could meet its very ambitious strategic goals. Essentially, it increased the credibility of its executive team.

Continuous Improvement

All elements of the program are continually adjusted throughout the year to meet the needs of the participants and the business. Often a seemingly good concept can, in reality, be impractical. For example, the action learning component of GLE changed as the year progressed. When the program was first designed, BGI asked its co-chairmen to identify several key global initiatives in which the participants could add value as global working groups tackling these issues between and after the two sessions. What BGI found, however, was that what might have been a good concept in its normally fast-moving environment was anxiety producing in an extremely accelerated work environment. Consequently, BGI took a more streamlined practical approach to participants' action learning, and had them identify work in their own area that they hoped to impact from their participation in the program.

As the year progressed, BGI provided a "group" assessment—an aggregate of the 360-degrees—of the key strengths and developments areas of all the participants so that BGI could discuss the implications for the organization. This allowed the design of the program to be revised as the year progressed and drove the key themes and design for future sessions.

Have Fun

Having pizza and just "hanging out" in Sydney, Australia, was a very important part of the program. It's important to build some fun into the programs. BGI has a very hard-working, dedicated employee population, and they do not get many opportunities to spend time together in a more informal setting.

360-degree Feedback

The 360-degree feedback process was one of the most well-received, albeit sometimes anxiety-producing, features of the program. BGI is a quantitative, data-driven organization, and people were much more attuned to the content knowing their personal survey feedback. Also, the briefing before the process gave them a chance to be educated about the process and view it more positively. Clarity in communicating the process and intent is essential to the success of a 360-degree process, particularly if this is a new initiative. The emphasis on feedback for development rather than evaluation was critical. Using actual performance feedback related to each skill made the learning journey personally compelling.

Summary

An initial request "to implement management training, firm-wide" expanded to a global program for surfacing organizational issues and transforming the organization. Needs assessment steered the program design toward developing individual and *global* organizational leadership capability simultaneously. A rigorous vendor selection process led BGI to Personnel Decisions International for program design and delivery. Executive sponsorship went beyond providing resources for the program. Executives were involved in networking during sessions, presenting, supporting participant development plans, and inspiring GLE graduates in their send-off back to the workplace. Action learning grounded the course content in practical application. Use of extensive prework, company-specific business data, learning teams, and development plans assured the relevance of the GLE experience. Participant reactions and business results have reinforced the value of the Global Leadership Essentials program.

Follow-up

In 1999, BGI focused the content based on the development areas identified in the aggregated group results from the 360-degree feedback. The specificity of the skills and organizational application becomes more refined each year. There is continued commitment to the "baseline" GLE program, which will be offered to all managers who have been in their position for at least three months. Additionally, follow-up sessions will be organized on an ongoing basis to bring GLE graduates back together in a new forum to examine their progress on their leadership journey, and another joint offering is being provided for executives and mid-level managers who lead large and complex functions.

To address the needs of the new manager, courses are being developed internally that cover basic management concepts and skills such as what it means to go from being an individual contributor to a manager, how to manage the performance of others, dealing constructively with conflict, and managing your time.

Following the precedent and model of GLE, a Global Council was established with representation by all the global businesses, and local task forces have been charged with addressing the issues on the opinion survey. This will continue this process of globally leveraging knowledge of successes and best practices.

Exhibit 4.1: Topic Overview

Below are essential competencies for each area of leadership.

GLOBAL LEADERSHIP ESSENTIALS™ COMPETENCIES

CLIENTS
- Commit to quality
- Focus on client needs

STRATEGY
- Think strategically
- Champion change

FACILITATION
- Foster teamwork
- Build relationships
- Foster open communication

INFLUENCE
- Manage disagreements
- Influence others

CREDIBILITY
- Act with integrity
- Value diversity
- Demonstrate adaptabil

JUDGMENT
- Use sound judgment

RESULTS
- Provide direction
- Establish plans
- Manage execution

CAPABILITY
- Coach and develop
- Motivate others

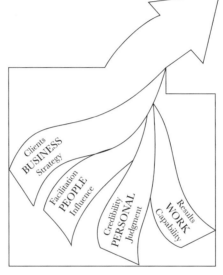

Business excellence is the ***goal*** of leadership.
Personal excellence is the ***foundation*** of leadership.
Work excellence is the ***proof*** of leadership.
People excellence is the ***power*** of leadership.

Exhibit 4.2: Day-by-Day Training Agenda

SESSION ONE

Day One	Day Two	Day Three	Day Four
• A Look at BGI's Future (presented by BGI senior executives) • Where BGI Is Going • Leadership Expectations—Now and in the Future • Leading in a Global Firm • Building a Global Network of Relationships • Geographic Overview—Wins, Strengths, and Challenges • Networking Activity	• Introduction: Creating a Personal Definition of Leadership • Leadership Definition • Program Overview • Learning Styles Inventory • 360-degree Feedback—Interpreting the Ratings • Results: Provide Direction, Establish Plans, Manage Execution • From Mission to Roles • Leadership Tools • Using Tools to Address Leadership Challenges	• Strategy: Think Strategically, Champion Change • What Is Strategic Thinking? • Change: Organizations and Individuals • Visioning and Aligning for Change • Linking Strategic Capabilities with Individual Competencies • Executive Panel	• Clients: Commit to Quality, Focus on Client Needs • Introduction to Business Excellence • Who Are Its Clients? • What Do Clients Value? • Defining and Planning for Quality Facilitation: Foster Teamwork, Build Relationships, Foster Open Communication • Mapping Group Communication • Leader Facilitation and Techniques • Promotion Decision

SESSION TWO: (4–6 WEEKS AFTER PARTICIPANTS COMPLETE SESSION ONE)

Day One	Day Two	Day Three	Day Four
• Expectations for Emerging Leaders (presented by BGI senior executives) • What BGI Needs from Its Emerging Leaders • How BGI Expects Them to Grow with Us • Building a Global Network of Relationships • Geographic Overview—Wins, Strengths, Challenges • Networking Activity	• Credibility: Act with Integrity, Value Diversity, Demonstrate Adaptability • Successes and Challenges • Acting with Integrity • Credibility Skill-Building • Influence: Manage Disagreements, Influence Others • Increasing Leadership Influence • Managing Disagreements • Development Options	• Judgment: Use of Sound Judgment • Individual Decision Analysis • Making Decisions • Business Decision Case Studies • Capability: Coach and Development, Motivate Others • Leader as Coach • Coaching Practice	• Integration, Development Planning, and Close • Business Simulation • Personal Vision • Contracting for Action • Program Closing—BGI senior executive

Linkage Inc.'s Best Practices in Leadership Development Handbook, edited by David Giber, Louis Carter, and Marshall Goldsmith. Copyright © 2000 by Linkage Press and Jossey-Bass/Pfeiffer, San Francisco, CA.

About the Contributors

Margaret Latif (margaret.latif@barclaysglobal.com) is the director of global training and development for Barclays Global Investors. Before working at BGI, she was the training director at a multistate retail consumer electronics firm and a vice president in the training department of a major financial institution.

Brian Anderson (briana@pdi-corp.com) is the vice president and general manager of the San Francisco office for Personnel Decisions International (PDI). Anderson's career includes consulting for a variety of Global 1000 companies. Before working at PDI, he held line management and human resources leadership positions at Dayton Hudson and General Electric.

CHAPTER FIVE

THE BOSE CORPORATION

This chapter outlines a competency-based leadership development
system for first line, middle, and senior-level managers
that is designed to develop a leadership pipeline.

Company Description

Bose Corporation was founded in 1964 by Dr. Amar G. Bose, professor of electrical engineering at the Massachusetts Institute of Technology. While doing graduate work at MIT in the 1950s, he began a research project into psychoacoustics. His investigation of the relationship between reproduced sound as perceived by people and sound as measured by electronic instruments led to the development of new audio technologies that he patented. Bose Corporation creates products that combine high technology with simplicity and small size to create the best possible sound systems that are easy to use and accessible to all consumers.

Since its entrepreneurial beginnings thirty-five years ago, Bose Corporation has demonstrated product and market leadership best exemplified in its strong brand image. Millions of consumers associate Bose with innovation and excellence, two of its founding values. But like most companies that grow rapidly in size and complexity, Bose has entered a new threshold of growth and opportunity that holds many new challenges. Organizations that wish to retain their competitive edge realize they cannot continue to rely solely on doing the same things that made them successful yesterday. Bose recognizes that it, too, must continue to build on its past by reaffirming its founding values, renewing its core competencies, and developing new skills and practices to take advantage of emerging business opportunities.

Building a Business Case for Leadership Development

Transitions are not new to Bose; the company has successfully navigated its way through many changes in technology, markets, and customer expectations to deliver innovative products through novel channels. But the new challenges that growing companies face are not always a larger version of what happened yesterday; scaling it up to size is simply too facile a response. There comes a time when a company enters a totally new threshold of development that requires it to examine the way it fundamentally runs its business in order to sustain its edge. By and large, companies faced with this form of transition find themselves faced also with emerging challenges that current management cannot adequately handle when relying on the skills and knowledge of the present. The future is no longer just about new products or markets, but about the depth and breadth of leadership within the company. The quality, mix, and availability of leaders at all levels become a critical success factor for the long-term future of the company.

Bose management came to the realization that transitioning from a medium to a large company would demand an equally sizeable shift in leadership requirements. Several studies reinforced this perception. Technical leadership has always been broad and deep at Bose and for many years this has carried the company successfully forward. But with growth and complexity and a new set of market challenges came the need to generate leadership in all areas of the business.

> "Bose has been built on technology and innovation . . . but the greatest challenge ahead is for leaders to step forward from all corners of the organization and take advantage of the opportunities that lie in front of us."
>
> Sherwin Greenblatt, President

For most companies, acquiring leaders from other companies is a gamble, and for organizations like Bose with strong, rich cultures, filling leadership needs from outside is not an easy proposition. It takes time for new employees to adapt to the distinct norms and practices of the work environment. In consequence, the development of leaders from within becomes a strategic imperative. It was in this context that the Center for Organization Development and Education (CODE) was conceived and given responsibility for engineering this leadership initiative.

Leadership Development System

In response to this new leadership initiative, CODE designed a development system that would deliver and support three competency-based education programs for frontline, middle, and senior-level talent. The strategic framework below and Figure 5.1 overview the elements involved in this three-year initiative.

1. Several organizational audits have revealed the need to broaden the bench depth of the company to take advantage of future opportunities.
2. Successful leadership must be founded on the core values that are embedded in the company's culture.
3. Leadership competency models reflect the attributes and results required of the company's future leaders.
4. Identification of leadership talent at all levels should be undertaken.

FIGURE 5.1.   STRATEGIC LEADERSHIP DEVELOPMENT SYSTEM.

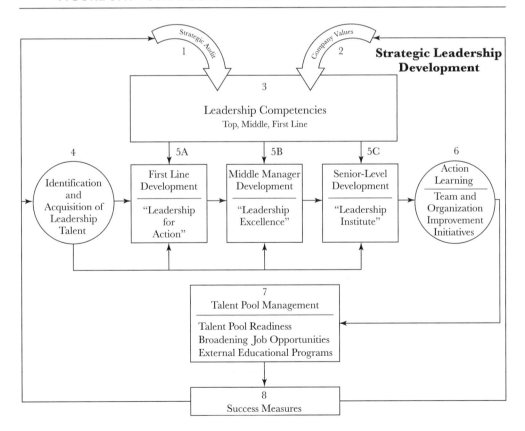

5. Competency-based leadership development programs for multiple stages:

    A. First line manager program: "Leadership for Action"

    B. Middle manager program: "Leadership Excellence"

    C. Senior-level program: "Leadership Institute"

6. Team and organization development initiatives transfer learnings from educational programs to work area or business challenges.

7. Succession planning processes review senior-level talent and match ready candidates for broadening opportunities.

8. Process for measuring the success of the program defines its value, resells supporters, and creates demand among candidates.

1. Organizational Audit Identifies Leadership Needs

The need for leadership development came from several studies, as mentioned above. The overall objective that ran throughout all these audits was the need to have the right people ready for new leadership roles at the right time. CODE translated these needs into more specific goals such as:

- Agree on desired leadership competencies for all levels in company.
- Identify high-caliber people early and get them into the pipeline.
- Accelerate readiness for future roles.
- Replenish critical skill gaps as promising leaders move forward.
- Implement competency-based education programs for first line, middle, and senior-level talent.
- Match high-potential candidates with appropriate assignments that will more fully prepare them for key leadership roles in the future.

2. Bose Values

Foundational to all leadership requirements are the values that have stood the test of time at Bose. They are interwoven into the culture and have been embodied in all business practices. Values are the foundation of the character of a company. They represent the ideal behaviors that an organization wishes to pursue even though it does not achieve all of them all of the time. When they are known, behaviorally described, and consistently practiced, core values link co-workers together as a community and develop a consensus about what is important. Leadership development in any organization with a strong culture must be grounded on the core values of the company. At Bose a great deal of time was spent reviewing the presiding values as an essential part of the curriculum.

3. Leadership Competencies

Bose has three sets of leadership models for the first line, middle, and senior management levels. The leadership competencies were derived from a combination of behavioral event interviews, focus groups, and benchmarking with other companies of a similar profile. There is, as should be expected, great similarity across all models; yet, each represents a skill set that differentiates the various levels of responsibility. Two models are contrasted; first, the senior leadership model (Figure 5.2), and then, the first line set of leadership requirements.

Individual Leadership. One can observe that the inner circle of competencies represent the qualities of being a champion at Bose at all levels. This is the fundamental set of leadership requirements, reminiscent of the entrepreneurial style that has propelled the organization through its earlier stages of growth and helped shaped its unique culture. These remain critical competencies for the future and must constantly be replenished. In fact, these are fundamental requirements that are expected among the high-potential pool.

Business Leadership. The middle ring of the competency model reflects the key qualities descriptive of the best business leaders at Bose. Again, these were derived from senior management through a fairly rigorous data collection and analysis process. These competencies have become central design criteria for the senior leadership development curriculum.

FIGURE 5.2. SENIOR LEADERSHIP COMPETENCY MODEL DIAGRAM.

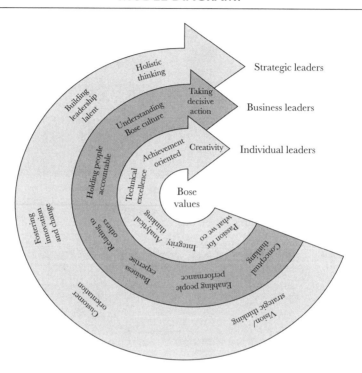

Strategic Leadership. The outer ring of the competency model addresses the key requirements of the executive members of the company. These particular competencies were seen as critical for remaining competitive in a changing marketplace. They help shape the future of Bose and as such become vital design criteria for the senior program.

In contrast to the senior competency model, the first line model as shown below (Fig. 5.3) focuses on primary leadership skills. The competencies are divided into three clusters: Managing Self, Leading Others, and Building the Team. The competencies have been translated into a 360-degree instrument for use in the Leadership for Action program. As you will see later, the modules in the first line leadership program are designed to match these clusters.

FIGURE 5.3.   FIRST LINE COMPETENCY MODEL DIAGRAM.

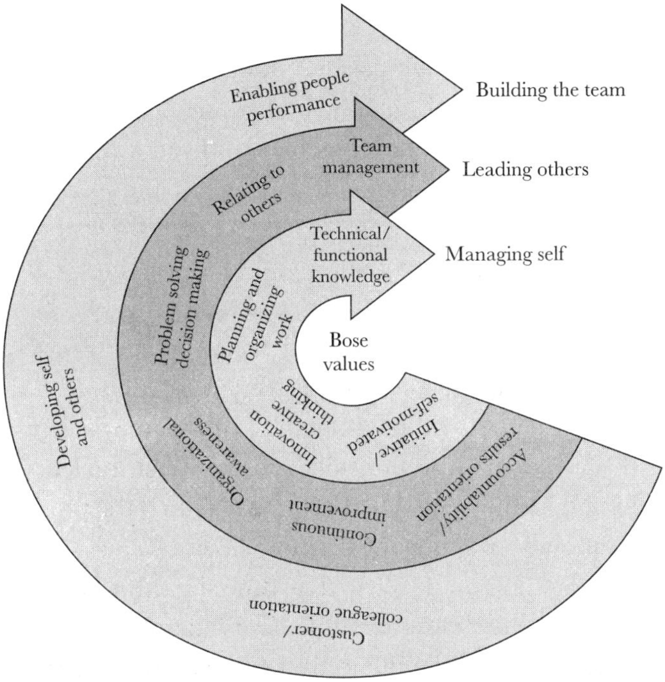

Building the team

Leading others

Managing self

Enabling people performance

Team management

Technical/ functional knowledge

Relating to others

Problem solving decision making

Planning and organizing work

Bose values

Developing self and others

Organizational awareness

Innovation creative thinking

Initiative/ self-motivated

Accountability/ results orientation

Continuous improvement

Customer/ colleague orientation

4. Identifying Leadership Talent

More Than One Audience. The first decision in leadership development is to choose the right audience. Neither leadership nor talent
is locked in at one level. Most companies now subscribe to the belief
that leadership does not solely reside at the top of the organization;
leadership potential can thrive at all levels and development programs
are best designed when they actualize leadership talent at the first
line, middle, and senior manager levels. While there may be core
leadership requirements across all these levels, there is a quantum leap
in responsibility and complexity among them. The result is that managers experience greater relevancy being trained with peers rather than
subordinates.

Establishing Who Would Benefit Most from the Program. Within each audience there are members who are ready and willing to take advantage of the developmental opportunities that the particular program offers. These people will often develop into role models for others. It is the contention within CODE that the best educators in the company are those we admire and emulate—develop them and you will develop most of the company in turn. In actuality, this was one of the easiest propositions in the whole development process. Senior managers accepted it because it rang with logic and matched their own best developmental experiences in our culture. However, when it comes to delivering the best candidates, logic seems to evaporate in a melee of louder needs. Program managers must prepare to advocate for—and in some cases against—the priority participation of each individual thought to be a potential leader. Not every leadership development session will have these natural leaders occupying every seat, but hopefully enough of them will enrich the pipeline and set the standards of leadership for those who follow.

It should be made clear that Bose does not believe in educating only those who are the most talented. Every member of Bose has opportunities for development. The dilemma here is about leveraging your education dollar to its fullest right at the start so you can achieve improved business results faster and create a successful track record that encourages others to seek participation.

Selection Criteria. To fill the programs with talented people, CODE uses the matrix shown in Figure 5.4 as a useful guide to selection. This performance-potential matrix is an adaptation of similar matrices used by several other companies.

The matrix axes of Performance Impact and Potential for Growth and Increased Contribution are each divided into three levels, resulting in a nine-way grid. The top third in performance and the top third in potential for increased contribution to the company are *Stars* (9), who are the highest role models for leadership. They are usually few and far between. The bottom third in both categories are the *Derailed* (1), who need the most help but are more in line for corrective and hands-on improvement than development of leadership talent. *High Potentials* (8) are those individuals

FIGURE 5.4.   CODE PERFORMANCE-POTENTIAL MATRIX.

Outstanding	**5** High Professional	**7** High Potential	**9** Star
Performance Impact	**4** Tried and True	**6** Utility Player	**8** High Potential
Modest	**1** Derailed	**2** Misspent Talent	**3** Past Credit
	Unproven	Potential for Growth and Increased Contribution	High

who are outstanding performers but need more broadening to reach star performance or who have capabilities but are not yet up the experience curve. A *Utility Player* (6) is a flexible, talented individual who likes variety and change and can adapt to many different positions and do a reasonably good job (or hold down the fort until the right candidate is available). *High Professionals* (5) are those outstanding performers in a particular discipline who have a singular interest in their functional area only and who wish to deepen, not broaden, their skill portfolio.

The ideal goal of a leadership development program is to enroll those people ranking highest against the matrix for the following reasons:

- With limited funds, time, and resources, most training and education departments must go for the biggest payoff for the company. Educating talented individuals has a far more beneficial impact on the company than training individuals who are mediocre or marginal.
- If high-caliber participants (matrix numbers 5–9) are put into a learning environment with like-minded individuals, their ability to expand their leadership potential is more highly assured than for those in the lower categories.

• High-caliber role models teach the rest of the organization the skills they have learned. In the end you are teaching leaders and potential leaders to thereafter be teachers of others on the job.

While concentrating first on the high-impact players may be the ideal approach, it is not always a matter of form. First, there may not be as many potential stars as you would like in some areas to draw from, and second, not every manager agrees with this "best go first" philosophy. Some are more interested in getting their toughest group members into some type of corrective therapy rather than training for the future. The diagram in Figure 5.5 paints the issue in a few clear strokes. It portrays the decision that program managers and company executives face between a tactical and a strategic development opportunity, and their related impacts.

FIGURE 5.5.   DEVELOPMENTAL SPECTRUM DIAGRAM.

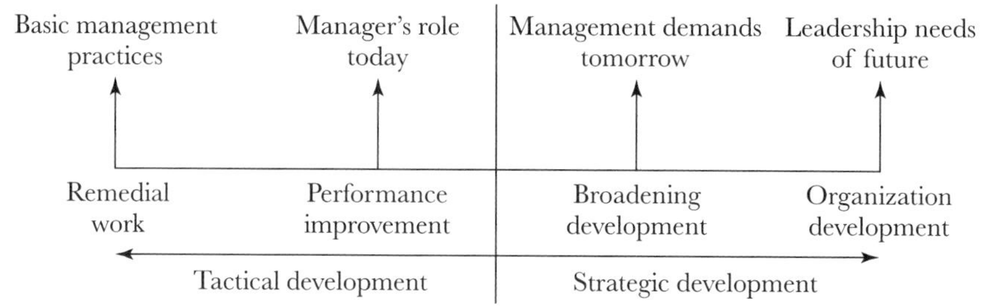

Basic management practices	Manager's role today	Management demands tomorrow	Leadership needs of future
↑	↑	↑	↑
Remedial work	Performance improvement	Broadening development	Organization development
← Tactical development		Strategic development →	

Ideally, leadership development is focused on broadening the role of the leader for tomorrow. Many managers, however, are faced with the more immediate and tactical need to get average performers up to speed or marginal performers to acceptable levels of ability. So, asking managers to release good people for future development while they are hemorrhaging from maleficent supervision today is like asking them to invest their salary in a promising stock and skip the mortgage payment for a month or two. Those who have extra reserves are more willing than those who have thin resources. It isn't always an easy decision; you better have an attractive program with promising results, and sometimes you have to help the manager at both ends and accept other than top performers. And then, sometimes, you need to draw on your last resort and carry a mandate down from above. This is not the cleanest approach, but the right one when you are kicking off a new program. In our senior leadership program the first crop of candidates were selected by the chairman, president, and executive vice president from a longer list of sterling performers. In this case the selection became an honor, with accompanying messages intended to offset the burden of added time and workload.

5. Competency-Based Development Programs

One Size Does Not Fit All. When it comes to program design, one approach does not fit all. Organizations have their own particular collage of leadership needs, training biases, educational standards, and distinctive cultural beliefs as to who should be trained, in what manner, for how long, and by whom. And all of this has to be sold over and over again to multiple audiences to build their understanding, respond to their objections, and gain their approval to launch and, in the best cases, actively support the program.

At Bose, the leadership development design did not emerge easily. The leadership system had to fit the Bose culture, which meant it must be innovative, unique in that it could not be imported from somewhere else, demonstrate measurable improvements, and attract participants through the quality and results of the program itself. In setting the standard, one executive advanced a rule of thumb for designing the new program:

> "If you think you have done a reasonably good job, then it's time to go back to the drawing board and see what more you've got to do to make it better."
>
> John Coleman, Executive Vice President

It is widely thought that leadership development should begin at the top first and then be implemented down the line with knowledge and support from above. While that may be optimum, circumstances and opportunities do not always comply. CODE decided to begin with the first line managers during the first year because the talented individuals at this level were more eager to learn and be coached in the fundamentals. This program was named "Leadership for Action" to project the message that what the participants learned, they had to apply. With this program firmly in place, the senior management level would be targeted for year two, and finally, in year three, the middle-level management population. Currently in the second year, CODE has firmly established the first line program and now has selected the high-potential members from among the senior management ranks and initiated the first phase of the program.

Although leadership development is treated as a series of distinct programs, CODE actually thinks of them fitting together into a process (see Figure 5.6). The programs are not event-driven; most of the learning takes place outside the training sessions, through coaching, personal application, and both team and organization development sessions. In addition, the development programs are designed to provide ongoing opportunities for learning, application, and community-building among that leadership level. Participants stay with a particular group for more than a year, taking follow-up training modules and attending quarterly reunion meetings to explore a topic of interest. It is hoped that our leaders-in-training will progress from one segment of the leadership pipeline and enter the next stage of their learning.

FIGURE 5.6.   LEADERSHIP PIPELINE DIAGRAM.

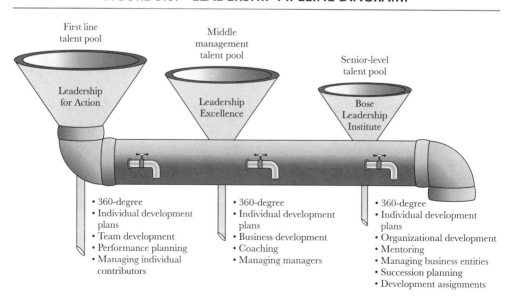

Leadership for Action Program. The Leadership for Action (LFA) program is aimed at managers who have received little or no formal training in leadership. The participants can be new to management or have been in the role for several years. The overall goal is to search for leadership talent and promote it through ongoing developmental opportunities.

Leadership for Action Objectives

- Communicate company values as well as the roles, responsibilities, and required leadership competencies to those who manage work units.
- Provide the requisite skills and individual coaching to assume a stronger leadership role within one's respective work unit.
- Create a developmental path for motivated participants who demonstrate the talent for higher leadership contributions to the company.
- Provide the requisite skills and exercises to develop higher performing teams within one's work unit.
- Build a climate of continuous individual development among participants.
- Pass these learnings down the line by expecting all participants to use the concepts they have learned and teach them to others.

The LFA program is divided into three phases echoing the three rings of the first-level competency model. The first three-day phase focuses on learning what it takes to be a leader at Bose, with an emphasis on values, personal style, and primary interpersonal skills. The second part of the course is focused on team development activities. In this phase, the participants sign up to work with their own teams on group effectiveness issues. The third module is focused on managing performance and the skills associated with planning, evaluating, and rewarding performance. The Leadership for Action program has seven full days of formal education that is core for all participants followed by a series of one- to three-day electives every quarter. Table 5.1 shows an outline of the sequence of activities within the program.

Key Success Factors for LFA. The LFA program is designed to give the participants a variety of learning formats. It seeks a blending of lectures, simulation, survey feedback, action learning, and personal coaching. It

TABLE 5.1. LFA PROGRAM OUTLINE.

Pre-Workshop

8:30 to 10:00 a.m. Participant Kickoff **Introduce coaches** **Prework survey instruments**	10 to 11:00 a.m. Manager Kickoff **Expectations**

Workshops

DAY 1	DAY 2	DAY 3
• Introduction to Leadership at Bose® • Leadership Development Success Factors	• Leadership Case • Motivation • Leadership Style and Skills	• Commitment to Action • Prepare for 360-degree Leadership Assessment

Group Assignment	Group Assignment

Development Planning with Coach and Manager

DAY 4	DAY 5
• Review of Development Plans • ACTION Model of high performing	• Chartering the Team • Teambuilding team characteristics
DAY 6	**DAY 7**
• Performance Management Skills and Practices • Role Play Scenarios	• Performance Management Meetings • Individual and Team Development Planning Meetings (with managers)

Post-Workshop

Measurement **Post-Assessments** • Leadership Development • Team Development • Pre-/Post-Test Analysis of Competencies	**Continuing Development programs** • Developing an Employee Profit and Loss • Project Management • Creative Thinking • Fundamentals of Financial Management • Communications • Delighting the Customer

involves the participants' managers, coaches, and staff members. The pace is fast, the homework deliverables are mandated, and participants who fail to attend any workshop session forfeit their membership.

In essence, there are five factors that make the program successful.

1. The *curriculum* is designed to be interactive and engaging in order to keep the participants' interest and energy level high. The content must be on target and fit the leadership competency model. See the section entitled "Curriculum Design" for an example of how the curriculum is formulated to engage the whole person.

2. *Coaching* has turned out to be a more important success factor than previously believed. In fact, coaches help participants translate their learnings back into their natural work area. Coaches work with the participants on development plans for self and work unit. The best coaches do more for the participant than the classroom experience itself. It is a longer-term commitment, with regular meetings, counseling sessions, group facilitation, and work area interventions. Coaches also work with the participant's boss and staff to make sure that the development path forward is on terra firma.

3. *Action learning* is another winning strategy for this program. See the discussion on "Team Development" in section 6 for an explanation of how the learning is put into action. In brief, participants are required to work with their staffs to develop a more effective and efficient work unit by applying the "high-performing teams" model that they learn in class together.

4. Having a *leadership competency model* that has been derived from organizational members at this level is a central pillar supporting multiple program features. The 360-degree feedback, based on these competencies, becomes a key component of the participants' learning (see "Curriculum Design"). Also, the ability to test the participants' behavior before and several months after their participation in the program is a great tool for measuring success and determining which competency areas need further development.

5. *Organizational support* is critical to any leadership development process. In this program there are many demonstrations of support from several

corners of the organization. First, the president and other executives play a role in presenting their ideas, values, and expectations for future leaders at one of the sessions. They accept this role as an important part of their position in the company and they give generously of their time and preparation. This support is strongly appreciated by the participants who acknowledge it as a forceful message as to the seriousness of the leadership initiative.

Curriculum Design. Designing a leadership curriculum that will be on target for a diverse set of participants is rarely achieved in a first attempt. It is usually a work in constant revision—a little more application here, a little fine tuning there—even though the fundamentals are rarely changed. The objective is to get the learning objectives across in the most powerful way. One approach, the teaching of first-line leadership competencies through a court case, is a good example of trying to match interest with learning.

The story of a manager turned down for promotion due to competency gaps is transferred to a mock courtroom scene in which two groups of participants, one representing the defense and the other the prosecution, put forward their arguments. Through this exercise the participants review in depth the leadership competencies for their level of responsibility by applying them to the central character in the case study. They learn the importance of each competency and also the hard fact that a major gap in even one competency can harm one's career. And they have a lot of fun in the courtroom drama comprising a judge and several jury members who were participants of previous programs and are now willing to support and enrich others' learning. Perhaps the most important learning comes from the fact that the central character in the case has attributes or issues not too far removed from what many of the participants experience personally. This compels the participants to take their development more seriously and their appraisal of others more thoughtfully.

360-degree and Individual Development Plan. The competencies were not only identified for curriculum design purposes, but for feedback to the leadership development participants. This practice is pretty routine in many companies and with most development programs. In the LFA program the participant's manager and an assigned coach work through the 360-degree feedback results with the individual participant. Based on the skill or knowledge gaps as well as other behavioral or interaction problems, an aggressive development plan is identified to improve the competency limitations. Participants are encouraged to work closely with their managers and work groups to get the support and ongoing progress feedback they need to keep moving forward.

It is not easy to stay on top of our development action plans. Unless improvement is visible, all good intentions to shore up one's leadership failings fall by the wayside, much like being on a new physical exercise or weight reduction program. It is as much for this reason as some others that CODE has decided to spread out the leadership development programs to keep the participants locked into a support system for several months until real progress is noted, and the commitment to sustain the new behaviors is strong enough to stand alone.

Bose Leadership Institute. At the higher end of the leadership pipeline is the senior level program, the Bose Leadership Institute. Institute members are proposed by their department head, but the final selection and invitation is by the chairman of the company in association with the president and executive vice president. The Institute invites those who have been selected to broaden their perspectives and develop new ways of thinking. While the first line program is about building foundations, and the middle manager program will be aimed at reinforcing better business practices, the Institute is about innovation, building work relationships across the company, and strategy. It is about pushing participants to look outside the box, forming them into broader peer networks and cross-functional alliances that will eventually reduce silo mentalities (thinking only within your division) and enrich teamwork, trust, and holistic thinking.

Bose Leadership Institute Objectives

- Communicate company values, goals, management philosophy, and required leadership competencies of senior-level members.
- Enhance understanding of the fundamentals of running the business.

- Provide the requisite skills and insights to become a well-rounded professional/senior manager.
- Provide senior management with a forum to enhance key corporate priorities and messages.
- Transfer knowledge and learning across and within business units.
- Build associations and networks that participants can use to build support for company-wide strategies and initiatives.
- Cascade the Institute learnings down the line by expecting all participants to use the concepts they have learned and, more important, to teach them to others.

The Institute runs for two years with five formal sessions lasting approximately three days every four months. The group size is limited to twenty-five participants or less to ensure individualized coaching and focused team development. Between sessions there are substantial business projects that make considerable time commitments on participants. Once the first group has completed its Institute work, another list of high potentials will be forwarded for the second wave. Those completing the Institute move from active membership to internal faculty, project sponsorship, and mentor roles for the next wave of active members.

Overview of Bose Leadership Institute. Figure 5.7 gives an overview of the four major elements of the Institute program. The column on the far left represents the leadership symposia. These are the five residential seminars, which are a combination of lectures by noted experts in a particular leadership area and work sessions on a particular business challenge.

The experts come from academia, other recognized companies, or consulting firms, and also from within the ranks of Bose Corporation. The five symposia are built around specific themes that have been derived from the senior leadership competency model.

The first symposia, "Built to Last," relates the work of authors James Collins and Jerry Parras to Bose. It focuses on the core values of the company and, in particular, the value of innovation. Outside experts give the participants a perspective from other organizational settings while internal sources review the import of these values within the context of Bose's past,

FIGURE 5.7.   BOSE LEADERSHIP INSTITUTE OVERVIEW DIAGRAM.

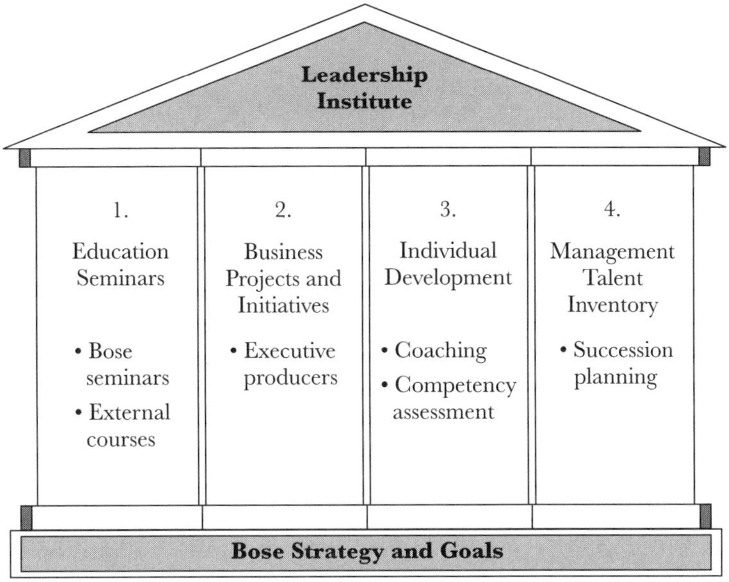

present, and future. Because innovation is both a primary value and leadership competency, the objective is to ensure that senior leaders examine how they personally relate to it, how they can deploy it down to others, and how they, as an Institute group, can retain and reinforce innovation throughout the organization, particularly in the face of constantly changing market opportunities and technology advances.

The other symposia focus on competencies such as "Delighting the Customer," "Business Expertise," "Enabling People Performance," and "Strategic Thinking." The objective is to assist this special talent pool in examining, confronting, and sharing their views in relation to these themes. This significant, sometimes trying work transforms concepts into action that will impact not simply their own individual leadership, but the direction, performance, and future success of the company.

The second column in the Bose Leadership Institute diagram addresses the Business Project element of the program. Because this group is being groomed to think as entrepreneurs and innovators, they are asked to apply their skills and knowledge toward a business opportunity within the company. The participants are divided into two teams, each responsible for a different business proposition. The projects are real and significant and require real and significant effort from the participants over several months. The teams have an executive sponsor, and a facilitator, and are requested to deliver their final plan and recommendations before an executive panel.

The third column in the figure signals the individual learning and coaching that each participant receives over the lifetime of the program. Personal coaches review 360-degree data, assist on individual development plans, and offer or find specific support for developmental needs. In addition, the participants are divided into learning pods consisting of five or six members. These pods are responsible for helping one another, giving and receiving feedback on performance, and in general holding each other accountable for their contribution to the Institute proceedings.

The final column in the model refers to the talent pool management process more commonly known as succession planning. It is examined in more detail further on, but suffice it to say that the Bose Leadership Institute is the front-end of an ongoing development process that continues after the participants have completed the Institute seminar portion of their development.

Key Success Factors of Leadership Institute.   The Institute has six key success factors.

1. *Choice of candidates* is vital. Without high-caliber members, the Institute would lose its appeal, its significance, and its ability to tackle important business projects.
2. Like other development programs, the *content, presentation,* and *relevance of the seminar themes* is crucial. High-potential senior managers will not waste their time and talent with nice but irrelevant topics. They want on-target, useful, fast-paced, enlightening information that will make time away from their jobs worthwhile. Naturally, it is almost impossible to satisfy all of the members all of the time, but in aggregate there must be a reasonable sense of having spent beneficial time together.

3. *Executive support* is a sine qua non for this type of program. Fortunately, the top-ranking officers in the company are fully on board. In fact, the Bose Leadership Institute Board consists of the chairman, president, and executive vice president, all of whom play active roles in the success of the program. Other executives give of their time and expertise to support the objectives of the program.

4. *Action learning* in the form of significant business projects is another key success area. It takes the Institute out of the realm of pure education and places it squarely in the context of organization development.

5. The *longevity of the program* is seen as another success factor. Too often leadership development programs end up as bursts of activity over a two-week or three-month period. Great things happen, but they fizzle out due to lack of continuity. This program keeps the participants together formally for two years, allowing the trust, alliances, and friendships to nurture and mature.

6. Finally, the alignment of the *succession planning system* with the program recognizes the need for navigating this pool of talent into the key leadership positions that will arise due to growth, new business opportunities, and turnover.

6. Improvement Initiatives

These outputs address the action learning that arises from the leadership development programs. They allow the participants to apply their skills and make improvements in their work units or the organization as a whole. Profiled below is the team development activities that arise from Leadership for Action.

Team Development. A unique feature of the Leadership for Action program is in the action learning phase. Participants are expected to diagnose and improve the functioning of the work groups for which they are responsible. The assumption is that if you help these talented individuals increase the effectiveness of their own teams, the learning will be significant, meaningful, and lasting. This phase of the program (see days 4 and 5 in the LFA outline[Table 5.1]) utilizes the ACTION model which represents the six characteristics of higher performing work groups:

1. *Alignment:*   The group is aligned around a performance challenge.
2. *Clarity:*   Members are clear about what they have to do to succeed.
3. *Teamwork:*   Trust and collaboration bring a sense of teamwork.
4. *Initiative:*   Group members feel empowered in decisions and action.
5. *Organization:*   The group is organized and disciplined.
6. *Norms of Action:* A sense of urgency and can-do spirit invades the culture.

Each participant and his or her work unit first diagnose the effectiveness level of each of these characteristics. Participants then work in several improvement sessions with their coach and manager, if necessary, to bring the effectiveness of the group to a higher level of performance. The belief is that teaching individual skills without correspondingly changing the work climate or group functioning amounts to nothing but frustration in most cases. Individual coaches help participants work with their groups on whatever performance characteristic is out of sync with desired results. For some it is a one-day team development session; for others it requires several team initiatives. The advantage in this program is the upfront "buy-in" from the participant's manager and team members that they, too, share a responsibility for the participant's success, even though it is mostly in his or her hands. Once work groups get into their own team building, they mostly find it a beneficial and, at times, enlightening experience. After repeated programs, this particular module has been discovered as vital for building that type of team leadership experience that enhances the credibility and self-confidence of leaders in development. Along with the customized coaching process, this team development module is a unique success-forging experience.

7. Talent Pool Management/Succession Planning

As we mentioned earlier, development is a process, not an event. Even by stretching out the Bose Leadership Institute forum across several months, there are no guarantees that new learning and new leadership behaviors will be enough to give participants the broadening experiences they may need for higher level roles. This is where "talent pool management" or succession planning come into play. It is the contention at Bose, particularly for the senior leadership program, that those participants who have stood out among their peers in leadership abilities should be afforded further broadening opportunities that will enhance their preparation and readiness for important business roles. The objective is to use succession planning only at the senior level and with a manageable set of people and positions.

While a formal leadership program can work on core leadership requirements, preparing people for important organizational roles may require broadening in certain functional or technical areas that goes beyond the charter of the formal leadership program. In this sense, succession planning helps link development to business needs and, more specifically, to key organizational positions that, with strong leadership, can have a major impact on the company.

Inadequate succession planning ranked second only to poor leadership training as a barrier to leadership development, as reported in the Watson Wyatt survey report entitled "Global Management Study" (1997). The pivotal factor in the success of succession planning is how well the review process is managed. Matching candidates and their development with future roles only bears fruit when the review process is earnestly managed, just like any other important business operations meeting.

This requires that each candidate's file have accurate and timely data, including reeducation and experience, performance data, assessment of potential, competency strengths and developmental areas, interests, contributions, broadening opportunities, and other helpful data. There should just be enough information to make a quality decision and no more. In tandem, any key roles must be equally well-profiled with clear requirements, status of incumbents, if any, and a listing of potential replacements with their degree of suitability and level of readiness. Because of constant changes, many companies find it overkill to focus on targeted positions; matching people to broader band roles and levels of responsibility is a more helpful and pragmatic approach.

8. Measuring Success

This is the last and perhaps the most difficult element in the leadership development system. There is a great deal of face validity when it comes to asserting why a leadership program should be considered successful. Most of it is anecdotal. The harder evidence requires research that in turn requires time and effort; yet without it, success remains nothing less than a list of nice but debatable testimonials.

For the Leadership for Action program it was decided to test behaviors before and after the program. The behaviors were associated with the leadership competencies and scored in the 360-degree survey feedback process. Pre- and post-tests (six months after the program) were administered, and in almost every case the raw scores showed improvements. A test of paired comparisons was made to discern if there were significant differences in these scores and early results show a positive profile.

For the Leadership Institute program, the measures were established beforehand. While pre- and post-testing for changes in leadership competencies is an obvious interim measure, the goal of having 70 percent of all new positions filled by "ready," internal candidates by year 2002 was adopted as a much more pragmatic metric. CODE is currently examining other measures of success in order to quantitatively demonstrate a true return on the leadership development investment.

Learnings

Strong Mandate From Above

Typically, most companies would acknowledge leadership development as an ongoing and vital requirement for success. Developing leaders, however, does not yet take place in "Internet time"; it takes effort and patience. Without a strong mandate from above, weak priorities tend to wilt and fade. Without support from the executive vice president at Bose, leadership development may never have gotten off the ground. He clearly realized the need for leadership development after sponsoring a fairly comprehensive study and decided to champion the cause. Eventually other executives came on board and gave support. If you don't have a burning platform, then you better find a strong champion who can draw the management support necessary to create action.

Overcoming Initial Resistance

Traditional leadership programs were mostly off-the-shelf, static packages with a one-size-fits-all design. This left a sour taste with a number of managers. But trying something entirely new is bound to meet with skepticism and resistance. People with leadership talent are busy people who want to see results or get guarantees before they commit themselves to anything that will take them away from their jobs. They put up lots of barriers to entry, with the most common mantra being "no time." Of course time is a valuable commodity for talented people, but when you get a "no time" excuse, you are being politely told that the person does not believe the program adds value. You must have a persuasive argument that either demonstrates the clear need for action or shows how an investment in leadership development can reap beneficial returns. You must talk the language of tangible results, not some lofty prospects that snap from reality. The initial attempts to kick off any new program require tremendous marketing, endless persuasion, and more than a healthy dose of patience.

Seek Out the Best Talent

It is vital to go after the best talent and turn them into role models, teachers to the company, and advertisements for others. One must always be careful not to overlook the hidden talent; future stars are not always obvious, and they are not always found in the major trade routes in the company.

Readiness and Pacing

If you wish to develop a leadership pipeline then you have to be careful not to try it all at once. CODE learned that the company could not focus on or absorb all three developmental programs together. It is best to begin where you think there is the most likely opportunity of success, not necessarily where the biggest potential, or most serious need, lies. Success is much-awaited, and once proven, tends to breed success.

Building Support Systems

Many development programs fail because they do not have the requisite support systems to keep them buoyant. CODE developed its infrastructure before launching the development programs. A competency model was developed internally, the 360-degree survey capability was put on-line, coaches were trained, a new performance management system was designed to support development practices, individual development plans were designed to match with the requisite competencies, succession planning procedures were mapped out, and success measures were crafted. Designing the program is one thing, but fitting it into a support infrastructure is equally important for continued success.

Action Learning Is Vital

Leaders are not developed in a classroom. They may be stimulated by discussion, but the real learning comes from applying new tools and techniques. Developing leaders is best achieved when they are given projects or jobs in which their leadership mettle is tested. Good leadership development programs must work at constantly applying learnings and giving the participants task-specific and constructive feedback on the results of their efforts.

Aggressive Individual Development Plans

Individual Development Plans (IDPs) tend to be paper commitments unless they are real, meaningful, and aggressive. To be aggressive they must have clear, measurable, corrective actions that are monitored by coaches or managers on a regular basis. An IDP should be seen as a contract between the participant and his or her boss that has the same value as the other aspects of one's performance. It cannot be treated as an add-on.

Development Is an Ongoing Process

When development is viewed as an event, it often lasts just about as long as the event. One of the most important learnings in developing others is to get them to see their own development as an ongoing process. At Bose Corporation the development programs may last several months, but it is important to attract people to follow-up activities. CODE tries to activate former participants' interest in their development through invitations to additional training programs inside and outside the company, as well as occasional lunch talks and quarterly meetings for graduates. Finally, coaches are asked to periodically touch base with their former internal clients to make sure that the graduates are moving forward.

Postscript

Designing and implementing a leadership development system places visible long-term demands upon the organization and many, if not most, of its major contributors. Such a course cannot be charted unless it maps directly to the company's strategic business issues. The way cannot be paved without the public commitment and effort of the company's senior executives. The steps taken along that way must tie directly to the desired leadership competencies, and the people asked to make the journey should be the organization's best. The experience at Bose includes all of the above, but centers on the fact that the vision, ideas, and dedication of talented people throughout the organization allows participants to constantly check the course of their leadership efforts.

About the Contributor

John C. Ferrie (john-ferrie@bose.com) is the director of the Center for Organization Development and Education at Bose Corporation. He is responsible for leadership development, succession planning, organizational design, and change management practices. In addition, Ferrie teaches business research and analysis to M.B.A students.

CHAPTER SIX

BP AMOCO

This chapter outlines an integrated leadership development system based on leadership competencies that leverages assessment and a worldwide, high-potential development program as the cornerstone for developing future top leaders.

Company Description

BP Amoco is a recently merged $143-billion petrochemical company with annual revenues of $108 billion and earnings of $6.4 billion. The workforce numbers 85,000 in 100 countries on six continents. More than 70 percent of profits are generated in the United States and Europe. In mid-1999, BP Amoco announced the planned acquisition of the $27-billion American oil company, Arco. Subject to shareholder and regulatory approval, this acquisition will make BP Amoco the second-largest oil company in the world by the end of the millennium.

Introduction

The case study begins with the leadership competencies that were launched in 1992, concurrent with a record-low share price of £1.84 and the departure of the company's chairman/CEO. While BP Amoco was a company in crisis, these competencies contributed to the foundations of a turnaround. Over the last seven years, the leadership competencies have provided the cornerstone for an integrated management development system that has developed world-class international leaders who have delivered a £10-share price. This chapter will describe the design and implementation of BP Amoco's competency-based management development system including:

- The nine leadership competencies
- A 360-degree feedback tool that measures the leadership competencies for developmental purposes
- A state-of-the-art, senior-level assessment center that measures the leadership competencies and is linked to action plans after returning to the workplace
- A groupwide high-potential program that develops people viewed to have the potential to achieve the top 120 posts

The Development of the Leadership Competencies

"Project 1990" was a massive culture change initiative that introduced and encouraged a more open and empowered style of leadership throughout the organization. However, it soon became clear that there was a need to identify and communicate a common set of leadership expectations and the key characteristics and behaviors required for success within the organization. Most people understood what was necessary for success in the "old culture," but the rules and expectations were changing rapidly and it was not clear what would be required for success in the new and evolving culture.

Nine leadership competencies emerged from an eighteen-month in-depth study of the top 120 leaders. Behavioral events interviewing targeted two selected control groups: fifteen "superior" leaders (for example, those most likely to be managing director successors) and fifteen "average" leaders (or, those who had essentially plateaued). Analysis revealed the unique characteristics that distinguished superior leadership performance from average leadership performance at the top of the organization.

These unique characteristics or competencies were reviewed at a two-day "concept formation meeting" attended by a worldwide group of a dozen people, including three industrial/organizational psychologists. The purpose of the meeting deliverable was to ensure that the leadership competencies were aligned with the strategic direction and aspirations of the organization (for example, leadership behaviors that would be required for a dynamic and highly competitive future). In addition, the competencies were articulated in the BP language and context while maintaining the technical integrity of the model. Strategic alignment and positioning in the BP language were critical success factors for management buy-in and for the longevity of the model. Without these key successes, progressing the model would have been like "pushing a boulder uphill." The final model (illustrated in Table 6.1) defined the behavioral framework in which outstanding performance was delivered at the top of the organization.

These nine competencies each contain three "underlying behavioral indicators" for a cumulative total of twenty-seven behavioral characteristics

TABLE 6.1.   LEADERSHIP COMPETENCIES.

Respected player	Acts wisely and decisively	Leads change
Strategic influencer	Builds best teams	Shapes performance
Strategic conceptualizer	Environmentally astute	Ensures alignment

or competencies. For simplicity and to ensure management buy-in, only the nine core competencies were displayed or profiled, rather than all twenty-seven underlying competencies. However, all twenty-seven behaviors are measured in generating the final profile of these nine leadership competencies.

In 1992, Roy Williams (then head of group learning and development and currently advisor to BP Amoco) gained the full endorsement and championship of both the company's CEO at that time, Sir David Simon, and the managing directors. With visible and active support at the top, use of the leadership competencies model was cascaded downward throughout the top 3000 leaders and individual contributors in the organization. (A more appropriate competency model is utilized at junior professional levels.)

360-degree Feedback Tool

While the leadership competencies provided critical information about leadership behaviors required for success in the organization, the model alone was not sufficient. People needed a user-friendly method to measure their strengths, development needs, and weaknesses against the leadership competencies. Following some professional technical work in 1993, a forty-five-item questionnaire (including five items per competency, covering each of the three underlying behavioral characteristics) was designed and piloted. Each item is evaluated on a ten-point scale with the guidance of several behavioral anchors.

To initiate the process, an individual sends an e-mail package to their line manager, peers, team (their direct reports), and self. Questionnaires are completed on the computer screen and e-mailed anonymously to an internal human resources professional (rater categorization is provided, but sender's name is removed). Questionnaire responses are automatically aggregated and a quantitative report, an overall leadership competency profile or "snowflake" (Figure 6.1), and the nine individual competency profiles are generated.

A human resources development specialist analyzes the participant's package of results and provides approximately two hours of feedback and coaching on strengths and development areas, as well as guidance in prioritizing development needs to construct an action plan to be shared with the participant's line manager and team.

The 360-degree feedback process is a critical ingredient in the development of people; however, it has four key limitations. First, it is unlikely that every individual will have the opportunity to demonstrate all nine

FIGURE 6.1. LEADERSHIP COMPETENCY "SNOWFLAKE."

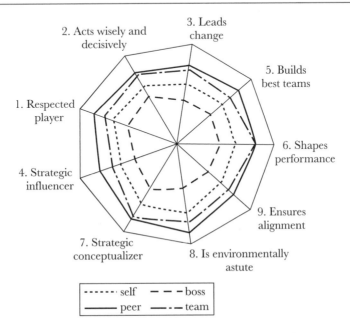

leadership competencies in his or her role. Second, it is unlikely that every "rater" will have the opportunity to view and properly evaluate all nine leadership competencies. Third, the results from the 360-degree questionnaire cannot be used to compare or rank different individuals' talents, as each individual will have a different job with different challenges and a different set of raters with different internal metrics. It would be like comparing apples and oranges. Lastly, the results from 360-degree questionnaires cannot be aggregated for strategic interpretation for the same reason. Analyses will be meaningless at best and misleading at worst. This assertion was tested by aggregating the results of the top 500 leaders' 360-degree profiles, only to discover 20/1000 of a difference between the three "strongest" leadership competencies and the three "weakest" leadership competencies. The difference was meaningless. However, the development of a senior level assessment center addressed all of these issues and progressed the company's competency-based management development system a significant step forward.

The LEAD Program: Senior Level Assessment Center

The LEAD (Leadership Enhancement through Assessment and Development) program is a state-of-the-art, senior-level assessment center that was designed in 1993–1994 to measure the nine leadership competencies and provide a blueprint for development, as well as establish a standardized process and metric to measure leadership talent across the organization.

Participants

Participants are nominated by their business (for example, Upstream, Downstream, Chemicals, and the Global Business Center) from the top 450 to 1600 leaders within the organization, based on performance history and perceived potential. A key feature is that people can self-nominate to their Business HR Committee for consideration, which ensures a level playing field of opportunity. Observers are selected from the top 275 senior leaders within the organization and are complemented by a HR observer who brings a development perspective.

The program has been recognized as a development opportunity for observers to:

- Sharpen observation and documentation skills (which can also be applied during the annual performance management process)
- Learn to more objectively gather data and information about an individual's leadership skills and behaviors and translate it into feedback (enabling them to make fairer and more accurate judgments, both at the program and afterwards)
- Learn to provide constructive developmental feedback in a ninety-minute, one-on-one coaching and feedback session
- Gain a personal understanding of the meaning, application, and value of the leadership competencies, as well as the LEAD reports

Program Overview

LEAD is a week-long program (see Table 6.2) which starts on Monday morning with a full-day interactive training program that prepares observers for their role and a two-hour unobserved icebreaker exercise for participants on Monday evening. The icebreaker exercise essentially enables participants to practice before the observed business simulation begins

TABLE 6.2.   LEAD SCHEDULE.

	Monday	Tuesday	Wednesday	Thursday	Friday
OBSERVERS	Training introduction (evening)	Business simulation	Business simulation	Integration	Feedback (morning)
PARTICIPANTS	Introduction (evening) Unobserved activity (pm)	Business simulation	Business simulation	Leadership day	Feedback (morning)

on Tuesday morning (in other words, they experience a business simulation and learn about the leadership styles of their five peers). This creates a win-win situation; participants feel more comfortable about the process and it does not effect the validity of the subsequent observations or assessment.

Tuesday begins with the integrated two-day business simulation set in a worldwide beverage corporation in the year 2008. The simulation was designed outside of the petrochemical industry and into the future to ensure a level playing field that measured leadership behaviors, rather than experience within BP Amoco, current events, or political knowledge. Participants assume one of six equivalent but different senior business line roles (all regional director roles in Resources, Bottling, or Recycling for either Asia Pacific or Europe and North America). They are faced with a variety of people, operational, and strategic business challenges. Participants have the opportunity to work individually, in small groups of two or three people, or large groups of six people, with the CEO of the beverage corporation (role-played by a top-275 observer) and one of their subordinates (role-played by a London West End actor) in a variety of integrated exercises and activities over a thirty-six-hour period.

On Thursday, participants attend Leadership Day where two external speakers engage them in two interactive sessions on leadership. In the morning, a London Business School professor talks about leadership from an academic and applied perspective. In the afternoon, a leader from a nonbusiness background challenges the participants to think about leadership. These leaders could be from the world of sports, achievement, music, or military.

Concurrently, on Thursday, observers from two integration teams spend between fourteen and sixteen hours to review and discuss the observations and development needs of each of the six participants they observed over the preceding two days (combined twelve participants). Both integration teams are comprised of three observers and an internal industrial or organizational psychologist who leads the integration. The integration team reviews each of the observation reports, makes individual ratings on a five-point behaviorally anchored scale, shares their individual ratings with the integration team, discusses the behavioral patterns and themes that have emerged, and then categorizes each of the nine leadership competencies as a strength (for example, powerful asset), development need (expected performance for current grade level), or a weakness (priority for development and barrier to performance). Actual performance definitions are given below.

- *Strengths and Potential Strengths* (color-coded as green)
  Clear indication that the individual demonstrates real power in this competency, which enhances his or her performance. May need rounding at higher levels of responsibility, however, overall impact for current level of responsibility was powerful.
- *Development Zone* (color-coded as blue)
  Level of competence probably sufficient for current level of responsibility, however, will need to be strengthened for higher levels of responsibility. Strengthening this competency would also enhance performance in his or her current role.
- *Potential Weaknesses* (color-coded as red)
  Indications that the individual has limitations in this area which are/or could have a significant impact on his or her performance, particularly at higher levels of responsibility. Development will be key to removing this potential barrier to performance.

Discussion is finalized with key development priorities and recommendations for next steps.

Competency Profile

On Friday, participants receive ninety minutes of feedback and coaching from a senior observer on their leadership competency profile; leadership style, interpersonal skills, key messages for development, and next steps.

Following the program, participants will receive a four-page written report displaying a color-coded leadership competencies profile (see Table 6.1) and one to two paragraphs on each of the nine competencies articulating key challenges and priorities for development, as well as strengths to build on and leverage. Key themes and development recommendations are highlighted.

Linking Competency Assessment to Development Action Plans

Once participants have received their LEAD reports, they are strongly encouraged to form a "Development Group" including their line manager, HR development professional, and a mentor (and if the individual does not have a mentor, this provides an excellent opportunity and foundation to build a mentoring relationship). While HR development professionals are very keen to be invited to participate and/or facilitate the process (as well as provide coaching and support for implementing the development plan thereafter), the participant takes full responsibility for selecting and organizing his or her Development Group. The Group will meet and review the LEAD report and other performance information (for example, recent performance appraisals, personal development plans, 360-degree feedback, and upward feedback) to check the accuracy of the LEAD report, as well as generate a clear action plan for development. A written summary of this meeting is agreed upon and signed-off by members of the Development Group and then permanently attached to the LEAD report to ensure a fair and balanced

FIGURE 6.2.   LEAD COMPETENCY ASSESSMENT AND DEVELOPMENT PROCESS.

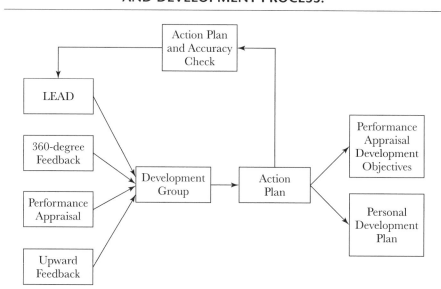

assessment of the individual (see Figure 6.2). As development progresses, the individual is encouraged to meet with their Development Group, who can submit updated comments. In essence, while the LEAD report is in "stone," the individual, working with their Development Group, has the opportunity to make it a "living report." Reports are available to the Group, business high-potential programs, and hiring line managers.

Through the Development Group process, LEAD has accomplished what very few assessment centers have ever achieved in the past. That is, the Development Groups have validated the accuracy of the LEAD program (for example, 90 percent of all Development Groups have characterized the report as a "fair and accurate" portrayal of the individual's performance on the job and have thereby validated the accuracy of the program).

Competency Fit with Critical Business Situations

Following the Development Group meeting, the line manager and participants are encouraged to work in partnership on their action plan for development. To create a framework to facilitate career development discussions, meetings were individually arranged with forty senior line managers to establish what competencies would be most important in various business roles. The responses were aggregated to create "finger-prints" (see Figure 6.3) for four business challenges. (The shaded boxes represent the aggregate views of senior leaders of the four most critical competencies required for certain business challenges.) See Table 6.1 for specific competencies.

One of the pivotal successes in launching LEAD was gaining the support of the chairman of the Group's high-potential committee to attend the first LEAD program as an observer (he is currently an executive director of the BP Amoco Group). After attending, he felt that it was an "excellent developmental experience" and at the next Group high-potential committee meeting, he strongly encouraged the committee members that "attending would strengthen their ability to perform their roles" on the committee. While the iron was hot, arrangements were made to confirm every committee member on a program over the subsequent eighteen months. Their attendance in the program significantly raised the credibility and profile of the program, strengthened their interpretation of the

FIGURE 6.3. COMPETENCY FIT WITH CRITICAL BUSINESS SITUATIONS.

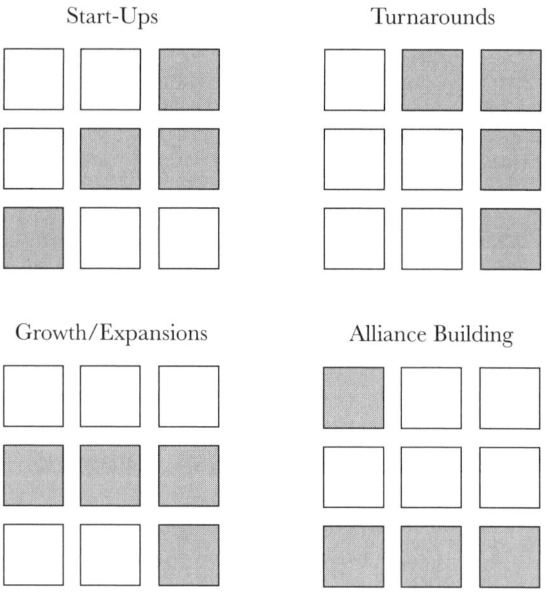

Start-Ups

Turnarounds

Growth/Expansions

Alliance Building

LEAD reports, built momentum and endorsement at the most senior levels, and facilitated the procurement of other senior observers.

Aggregating LEAD Performance for Strategic Advantage

Over the last five years, the LEAD program has evolved into an incredibly powerful tool within the organization. It has gained the championship of the deputy chief executive officer and provided a common metric and language to discuss and compare leadership talent across the organization. On the individual level, it enables the organization to review multiple candidates for posts or opportunities (for example, acceptance on the high potential program) with at least one common yardstick or reference point. LEAD will be particularly critical in enabling BP Amoco to fairly and efficiently calibrate the BP and Amoco talent pools (and the Arco talent pool—subject to shareholder and regulatory approvals of the proposed acquisition).

On the aggregate level, it enables an organization to understand key messages about the strength and depth of their leadership talent pool. That is, one can aggregate the LEAD competency profiles of all prior participants and create a chart that highlights the number of strengths, development needs, and weaknesses for each of the nine competencies (see Figure 6.4). This can be statistically analyzed for significant patterns and trends and utilized for strategic purposes (for example, focus program development, frequency of training programs, development initiatives, and senior recruitment to fill gaps). No other tool can provide an organization with this high-quality critical insight. Picture walking into a boardroom with anecdotes to justify the need for £10 million for the development and delivery of several specific leadership development programs. Now picture walking in the boardroom with these analyses (which were generated and owned by the top 275 senior leaders, including two of the current managing directors sitting around the table). This provides a very powerful opportunity for the human resources function to demonstrate a quantitative

FIGURE 6.4. HYPOTHETICAL AGGREGATE LEAD PERFORMANCE DIAGRAM.

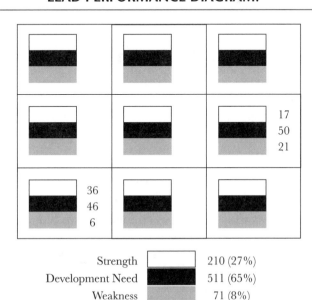

and professional sophistication that plays extremely well to managing directors accustomed to dealing with quantifiable business issues.

Furthermore, the LEAD program has also enabled the identification of "missed" talent (fifteen to twenty years' experience), which has created a more level playing field and sent a very motivating message to people later in their careers throughout the organization. A senior level program is particularly important because the company's junior level assessment center program (ALP—Assessment of Leadership Potential) was designed to assess people for potential after approximately four to ten years of technical or entry-level experience. While leadership talent can be spotted at this early stage of career development, some undeveloped talent will clearly be missed—that is, assessed before they have had the opportunity to gain leadership and business experience (operational, strategic, people, and bottom-line management). Others may be "late bloomers" or shift the balance of their personal priorities later in their careers. LEAD has enabled the identification of talent regardless of their current stage of career development. Specifically, the program has identified ten high potentials with twenty years' experience who were missed through earlier high-potential identification processes. High-quality senior talent is rare and an organization cannot afford to miss anyone who might possess that potential.

Integrated Group High-Potential Program

There has been a Group high-potential program for almost thirty years; however, it has evolved from a "list in the Chairman's desk" in the early 1970s into a very sophisticated development and deployment process during the 1990s. This process is managed by a Group-level committee of the top fifteen leaders and an industrial/organizational psychologist, who meet once a month for a full-day meeting. Three hundred people in the top 23,000 posts worldwide (the top four sections in Figure 6.5) have been identified to have the potential to achieve the top 120 posts within BP Amoco.

The cornerstone of this program has been the creation of a framework to strategically understand the distribution and potential gaps of leadership talent over the next twenty years. High potentials are categorized

FIGURE 6.5.   ORGANIZATIONAL LEVELS.

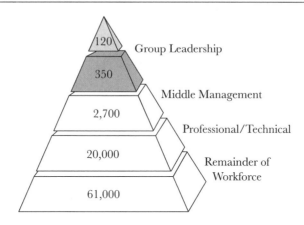

every December into one of four cohorts based on current grade level, historical rate of progression (average length of time in post), and longer-term potential (top 120, twenty-five, or seven posts within the organization). For example, individuals assigned to Cohort 1 are viewed to be within five years of the top 120 posts, whereas those assigned to Cohort 4 are viewed to be within sixteen to twenty years of the top 120 posts (see Table 6.3).

TABLE 6.3.   COHORT CATEGORIZATION.

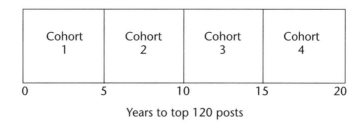

Development criteria are communicated to guide high potentials on the key development priorities at different stages of their careers, essentially providing a developmental road map for a senior general management career within BP Amoco (see Table 6.4). For example, high potentials within Cohort 2 would seek to attend an international business school and a LEAD program, while high potentials within Cohort 3 would seek to gain people management, cross-business, and international experience. These

TABLE 6.4. DEVELOPMENT AND EXPERIENCE FOCUS.

Mentoring/ coaching/assessor Group leadership meeting Final development reviews	International business school LEAD program	International Bottom-line (responsibility for financial targets and output) People management Cross-business Stage II (week-long program highlighting group and strategic issues)	Cross-functional ALP program (junior-level assessment program Stage I (week-long program highlighting group and strategic issues)
1	2	3	4

Cohorts

development priorities are then highlighted by an individual in their Personal Development Plan.

Progress against these development objectives is tracked by the Development Group high-potential committee and utilized as a tool to sharply focus development discussions and action plans. Progress is recorded on the Cohort Development Checklist (see Table 6.5 with hypothetical data).

While each row provides a powerful, succinct summary about an individual, each column enables the committee to track their own performance over time. These checklists are generated for each cohort annually and then analyzed for percentage of developmental gaps. These percentages can be tracked over time to assess the performance delivery of the committee (for example, delivering jobs that fill these development gaps). This provides a powerful motivator to ensure that the long-term developmental needs of the high potentials and the strengthening of the talent pool take priority over the short-term needs of a business.

The committee reviews the development of all high-potential individuals at least once every eighteen months. This Cohort Review process (Figure 6.6) is supported by an efficiently organized and colorfully displayed package of information held on an integrated database, including: education/career/grade history; performance appraisal; 360-degree feedback

TABLE 6.5.   HYPOTHETICAL COHORT DEVELOPMENT CHECKLIST.

Downstream
Upstreams
Chemicals

Cohort 2 Development Checklist—1997

	Cohort 4	Cohort 3					Cohort 2		Cohort 1	
	Cross-Functional	Bottom-Line	Inter-national	People Man-agement	Cross-business	Corporate	International Business School	LEAD Attendance	Mentor/Coach	Group Leadership Meeting
Pierre Michelin	✓	✓	✓	✓	Chem		Insead AMP 2000 Insead Int Exec 98			✓
Steve Cox	✓	✓	✓	✓		✓		✓		✓
Vincent Graham			✓	✓			Stanford Sloan 95	✓	LEAD 7/97	✓
James Brown	✓	✓	✓	✓						✓
Wendy Palmer	✓	✓	✓	✓	Ex	✓	MBA Rochester/ Erasmus	✓	ALP 6/96	✓
David Macdonald	✓		✓	✓		✓		✓		
Richard Goldberg	✓	✓	✓	✓		✓	MBA Witwatersrand / Harvard PMD 99		Leader as Coach 4/97	✓
Helen Smithers	✓	✓	✓	✓	Ex		Cornell Exec Prog			✓
Alex Christensen	✓	✓		✓			Stanford Exec 97	✓		✓
Elsa Forero	✓	✓	✓	✓	Oil & Chems			✓		
Peter Adams	✓		✓	✓		✓		✓	LEAD 10/96	✓
Howard Rowland	✓		✓	✓			Insead AMP 98			✓
David Thomas	✓		✓	✓			Global Prog. Mgt. Dev—Michigan	✓		✓

FIGURE 6.6. COHORT REVIEW PROCESS.

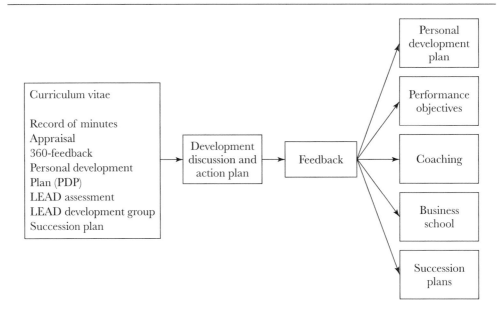

results and action plan; LEAD report with Development Group comments; summary of succession plans; and a personal development plan (written by the individual and checked for accuracy by the line manager, HR development specialist, and mentor who represents them on the committee). These materials, together with the Cohort Development Checklist, focus the development discussion around the key priorities for development.

Following a ten-minute discussion focusing on performance, key issues, and development priorities, an action plan is agreed on by the committee and minuted. High potentials are provided with feedback from the meeting by their mentor (a committee member who represents them at the meeting) and they are encouraged to reflect this feedback in their personal development plans and performance appraisal objectives. The secretariat ensures inclusion on appropriate succession plans, attendance at an international business school, as well as attendance on internal leadership development programs that best meet their specific needs. Ongoing executive coaching and guidance is provided by the line manager, mentor, and/or the secretariat who is an industrial/organizational psychologist.

Evaluation

LEAD has emerged as a powerful assessment and development tool within BP Amoco over the last few years. The program had eight original objectives and has successfully delivered on all of them, including providing:

1. An objective assessment of the nine leadership competencies
2. A standardized process or yardstick to fairly measure and calibrate talent across the organization
3. An opportunity for participants to receive indepth developmental feedback from an observer before they depart the program
4. A complement to existing performance data rather than a replacement of existing performance data
5. A framework to develop action plans linked to and owned by the line (and in partnership with the participants' Development Group)
6. An opportunity to identify high-potential talent later in an individual's career
7. A development opportunity for observers (such as, observation and coaching skills, as well as a deeper appreciation of the leadership competencies)
8. An opportunity to aggregate data that could be used for strategic advantage

While LEAD met and exceeded its original objectives, the real test of success has been that 90 percent of the Development Groups (which includes the line manager) have validated the LEAD program reports by checking, in writing, the fairness and accuracy of the assessments. This endorsement by the line has strengthened the reputation of the program throughout the organization.

However, continuous improvement is critical for LEAD to keep its edge (for example, training materials, creating user-friendly guides for observers and participants, simulation instructions and background, administration processes and delivery, participant and observer nominating process). Over the last five years of programs, an hour-long session has been held with the participants on Wednesday evening to encourage candid feedback on the program. Following the program, participants and observers are requested to provide written feedback on numerous aspects of the program. All feedback is aggregated, reviewed, and addressed. The four members of the LEAD team meet annually for a two-day strategy and brainstorming meeting to consider key issues in continuously improving the program.

Critical Success Factors

The keys to BP Amoco's leadership development success are:

- CEO and senior management championship, as well as direct involvement and ownership in delivery
- The emergence of a "development culture" that embraces these processes (in other words, a culture that encourages the commitment of time and resources to the development, coaching, and mentoring of people)
- An ability to provide meaningful strategic insight from analysis of these processes (for example, it creates an opportunity for HR to contribute to the strategic agenda)
- Access and opportunity to influence senior executive decision makers on the value of these leadership development processes
- High-quality user-friendly processes (for example, summarization of large quantities of information into succinct and visually powerful charts and materials)
- Maintaining buy-in through evaluation and continuous improvement processes
- The view that these processes create a more level playing field for opportunity and progression within the organization
- Creating a fully integrated competency driven model with a measurement bias
- Internal professional/technical support and delivery of the processes

About the Contributor

Candy Albertsson (cka@albertsson.demon.co.uk) is an industrial/organizational psychologist with twelve years of experience in the strategic, design, and operational phases of various management development systems, including competency development, competency-based 360-degree feedback, assessment centers, high-potential development programs, executive succession planning, and survey processes, as well as executive coaching in BP Amoco. She has been an invited keynote and presentation speaker at twenty-five European and American conferences, workshops, and professional meetings. She has been based in London since 1992.

Albertsson's last role with BP Amoco was as manager of high-potential development, where she provided managing directors with strategic support on a variety of issues including a review of BP's leadership talent pool, supply and demand for top twenty-five succession, and the supporting infrastructure to develop world-class leadership. Previously, she worked for American Telephone and Telegraph in their selection and assessment center division in Basking Ridge, New Jersey. Albertsson has recently established Albertsson Consulting, a leadership development consultancy based in London.

CHAPTER SEVEN

COLGATE-PALMOLIVE

This chapter outlines a global training program for sales executives that develops business leadership capabilities through training seminars, partnerships with senior managers, and action learning.

Training Colgate-Palmolive's Global Sales Leaders

The Colgate-Palmolive Company recently developed a global training program for sales executives who are responsible for managing the company's most strategic retail business accounts. This proprietary program, *Key Accountability: Managing the Account as a Business,* develops the business leadership abilities needed to meet the challenges faced by the company and its customers in a complex and rapidly changing global marketplace. It serves as the cornerstone of a worldwide sales curriculum designed to transform key account managers from their old role as salespeople to their new roles as business leaders for Colgate-Palmolive and business consultants for key customers.

Company Background

The 38,000 people of the Colgate-Palmolive Company generate more than $9 billion in annual sales, serving 5.7 billion people in over 200 countries and territories in every area of the world with high-quality consumer products for oral care, personal care, household surface care, fabric care, and pet nutrition. Colgate is striving to become the best global consumer products company while making important contributions as a fully responsible member of the global community.

Strategic Reasons for This Program

The Key Accountability program is strongly aligned with Colgate-Palmolive's global business strategies. Four strategic issues have been especially important in prompting the company to undertake this leadership training initiative:

1. Colgate-Palmolive faces many new business challenges in common with its customers.
2. Important trends are emerging in the global retail marketplace in response to these common challenges.

3. New business risks are arising from these trends.

4. Colgate-Palmolive has adopted a challenging global sales strategy to respond to these challenges, trends, and risks.

New Challenges Shared with Its Customers. Colgate Palmolive and its customers around the globe share many of the same challenges that are forcing companies to implement improved practices at an ever-increasing pace.

Globalization. Regional and global trade agreements, communications, and logistics networks are making geographic borders less and less important.

New political pressures. Changes in currencies, new employment regulations, ever-changing tax laws, and evolving environmental standards are just a few of the challenges that are faced today.

More active consumerism. More educated consumers are demanding products and services that are more responsive to their changing tastes and lifestyles.

Slow economic growth in some markets. Recessions and high unemployment in many economies around the world have reduced disposable income and resulted in low growth, or even shrinkage, of some consumer markets.

Implementation of new information technology. An accelerating flow of information must be distributed among internal operations, suppliers, and customers in order to remain competitive.

Increased competitive pressures. Retailers—and their suppliers—who cannot improve operational efficiency and respond more quickly to their customers cannot survive against competitors who are more agile.

Emerging Trends in the Global Retail Marketplace. A number of important trends are emerging in response to the challenges in the global retail marketplace served by Colgate-Palmolive.

Emerging Trends

From:	To:
Focus on volume	Focus on profit
Focus on brand	Focus on category
Focus on trade	Focus on consumer
Fragmented trade (smaller accounts)	Trade concentration (larger accounts)
Adversarial relationship	Collaborative relationship
Only financial support for customers	Consulting support for customers
Reluctance to share information	Open sharing of information

New Business Risks. These trends present new business risks for consumer product suppliers such as Colgate-Palmolive. For example, 55 percent of Colgate-Palmolive's worldwide business will be concentrated in "modern trade" key accounts by the year 2000. This makes key accounts even more important to Colgate's success than they were in the past—and any problems with these accounts put the overall business goals and targets at greater risk. Key account managers have the greatest impact on the ability to turn these challenges into opportunities. They are the ones who must manage Colgate's investment and profitability in these key accounts. They must respond to an ever-increasing demand for support in such areas as customer service, marketing, category management, and supply chain management. They play the most powerful frontline role in helping Colgate-Palmolive differentiate itself and thrive in this marketplace. The board of directors has established a high strategic priority for providing them with the competencies they will need to lead Colgate-Palmolive and its customers to success in this new and ever-changing environment.

A Challenging Global Sales Strategy. Colgate-Palmolive's board of directors has approved a worldwide initiative to maximize profitable sales growth and to become the "preferred supplier" for the company's most strategic key accounts that are competing in a global consumer products marketplace that is diverse, complex, and rapidly changing.

To carry out this strategy, funding was budgeted in late 1996 and a strategy was prepared to build a program that would combine the best practices from around the world, placing Colgate-Palmolive on the leading edge in responding to the emerging trends in the marketplace.

Audience for the Program

The primary targets for the program are those key account managers and trade marketing managers serving Colgate-Palmolive's largest and most strategically important global, regional, or national key accounts that represent approximately 50 percent of the company's revenues. The global task force found that these key managers must succeed in several important roles in order for Colgate-Palmolive to succeed in its new approach to key accounts. They must:

- Establish professional and personal relationships with account functions such as buying, merchandising, logistics, marketing, and management.
- Understand how the account makes money.
- Develop an annual business strategy and plan for each Colgate-Palmolive product or category.
- Negotiate account agreements.
- Oversee retail execution of the plan and agreement for each account.
- Manage each account to meet Colgate-Palmolive's profit and loss objectives.
- Generate business-building ideas with customers based on consumer insights and expertise regarding products, category management, and supply chain management.

Designing and Developing the Program

Substantial resources were committed to this initiative, and the development process proceeded in accordance with Colgate-Palmolive's global process.

Determining a Need for Training

Colgate's senior management determined that a global training program would be required to help key account managers acquire the knowledge, skills, and tools to integrate this process into their ongoing business practice and to make the transition from salespeople to business consultants and partners for key accounts. Because the need was urgent, the program had to be developed and implemented globally within a year.

In addition, the training had to be consistent with Colgate-Palmolive's basic principles for training:

- Be Colgate specific
- Share best practices worldwide
- Provide practical work application
- "Colgate Leaders Teach"

Program Design: A Global Task Force

In accordance with Colgate-Palmolive's general principles of leadership development, a task force was formed to design a comprehensive leadership development program that met the needs of the end users. The task force included all levels of experience and a broad geographic range within the company. Sales directors representing a cross section of countries and marketplace dynamics participated in the task force. High potential key account managers from a number of countries—the people who must provide leadership to help Colgate-Palmolive and its customers meet the new marketplace challenges—also served on the task force.

Task force members were required to commit 15 percent of their time for a period of nine months leading to the launch of the program. Intense cooperation among task force members resulted in the identification and documentation of best practices in a number of business areas that have a great impact for Colgate-Palmolive and its customers. Some of these areas include category management, supply chain management, business planning, and evaluation processes, which form the core of the program. The task force also contributed to developments in information technology practices to support the sales force.

Members of the task force continued to network with each other, relying on relationships forged during program development to broaden knowledge and understanding of business practices in other subsidiaries (countries). Participation has helped members succeed to the next level of professional development within Colgate-Palmolive.

Colgate-Palmolive's core design and development team consisted of the project leader, the task force leader, and two key representatives from the training supplier (The Forum Corporation). The project leader led the design and development effort full-time for nine months, optimizing the flow of technical support and communication among all members of the development team, and overseeing the ongoing implementation process. The task force leaders provided a consistent view of the core content and "big picture," and they resolved questions relating to the technical content of the program.

The broader design and development team from Colgate-Palmolive included a global task force of eight subject matter experts from as many countries. They brought their experience of business challenges, best practices, and leading edge ideas to the project. They were supported in their work by a broad web of subject matter experts from across Colgate-Palmolive.

Training Objectives Based on Best Practices

The global task force explored best practices around the world and redefined a common strategic approach to key accounts that is responsive to customers, adaptable to local conditions, and up to the task of meeting the challenges faced by the company. This new approach requires that key account managers develop or strengthen leadership competencies, understand key issues affecting the company and its customers, and ensure alignment with Colgate-Palmolive's global strategy.

Develop Key Sales Leadership Competencies to Meet New Challenges.
The global task force identified three important competency clusters that

serve as the basis of the learning objectives for the Key Accountability program.

1. Strategic thinking and planning:
   - Recognize and respond to strategic trends in the global marketplace—both Colgate's and its customers'. Adapt strategies to respond to differences that will continue to exist among local or regional markets.
   - Understand and become champions for Colgate-Palmolive's strategic goals and initiatives and at the same time be sensitive to customers' strategic goals. Recognize and respond to the financial, operational, and competitive trends that Colgate—and its customers—must respond to today and in the future.
2. Taking responsibility for results:
   - Manage key accounts as a business; become the CEOs of this business.
   - Take responsibility for everything that happens with these accounts. Implement business plans, evaluate them continuously, and make adjustments as needed to improve bottom-line results, both for Colgate and its trade customers.
3. Partnering:
   - Break down barriers and form partnerships with Colgate-Palmolive geographic areas and business functions, suppliers, and customers.
   - Work collaboratively to improve the efficiency and effectiveness of the company's planning, production, and distribution systems across geographic borders around the world.
   - Collaborate more closely with outside suppliers and distribution resources.
   - Work with customers to help them improve the overall profitability of various lines of products in their stores (*category management*) and to improve their processes for getting to consumers the right products at the right time and at the right price (*supply chain management*).

Understand Key Issues Facing Colgate-Palmolive and Its Customers.

The Key Accountability program was designed to establish a common language and set of business practices, skills, and tools that enable key account managers to address the issues facing Colgate-Palmolive and its customers in a more strategic and profitable manner. A common skill set also allows sales professionals to move more easily into leadership roles both locally and cross-border, consistent with Colgate's global strategy for sales leadership development. The six core modules of the resulting program address these issues:

1. *Economic and Retail Environment* explores the external pressures to which Colgate-Palmolive and its customers are exposed, and it looks at ways in which trade customers are responding to pressures in the economic environment. Presentations by each country on their unique trade conditions result in identification of differences and similarities in the retail environment. This provides a common understanding of global business issues.

2. *Retailer's Perspective* examines the key drivers that influence retailer decisions. Through a case study and simulation in which participants take on the role of the retailer's board of directors, they make strategic decisions relating to finance, marketing, and retail operations, thereby learning the retailer's perspective on decisions that affect Colgate's business outcomes.

3. *Supply Chain Management* investigates how to advise trade customers on improvements in their supply chain (the business activities starting from sourcing of raw materials to final deliveries of products to customers). A video illustrating supply chain management best practice is followed by an exercise in which managers analyze the supply chain for their key account and identify opportunities for improvements and efficiencies.

4. *Category Management* explores the business prerequisites for managing product groups as profit centers and supplies a tool for key account managers to use in determining their readiness level, and that of their accounts, for category management solutions.

5. *Account Strategy* applies tools for quantitative analysis of the investment in an account. It also evaluates the relationship, as part of the overall process for developing account plans that fit into the marketing and

business strategy for the Colgate-Palmolive subsidiary. Strengths, weaknesses, opportunities, and threats (SWOTs), macro investment analyses, a relationship grid, and an account strategy template are among the tools used in developing a strategy that aligns Colgate and the retailer's business objectives.

6. *Business and Promotional Planning* applies a spreadsheet process for planning, implementing, and evaluating the investment in key accounts in line with corporate- and account-specific goals. Promotional planning takes into consideration all activities that might impact the outcome of the account business plan: marketing, account-sponsored, seasonal, media, and promotional activities are all factored into the business planning process.

Ensure Strategic Alignment. The overall global training and development strategy is linked to the marketplace and the long-term strategic goals of Colgate-Palmolive. This alignment has been developed and communicated for this initiative at all levels, from the board of directors to divisional presidents to general managers of subsidiaries to sales directors and finally to participants in the program. Each level clearly understands the significant competitive advantage that the success of this program can bring, and views it as a priority in terms of allocation of resources.

The Key Accountability program is also fully integrated with Colgate-Palmolive's global sales training strategy as developed by division presidents and sales directors. This strategy reflects the variety of trade practices and competencies required to meet the diverse business needs of markets ranging from emerging to developed. Strategic alignment cannot be achieved purely through a "top down" cascade. There also needs to be a process for building momentum and buy-in from the bottom up. Quality learning is assured when there is a true partnership between line and training functions. Therefore, those who benefit from training need to be part of the creation process. By including those who were to benefit in the design and creation process, Colgate-Palmolive ensures that the content is totally appropriate and that the buy-in from target audiences was generated from the earliest opportunity. Bringing together key account managers from different countries has also helped to establish the ongoing learning network that has been incorporated as a permanent feature of the program.

The program has been designed to be appropriate to all the participating countries and to address the issues that local key account managers see as most relevant and important to their changing role. Best practices were researched and the findings formed the basis for a new approach to account strategy and business and promotional planning. The program serves the interest of both Colgate-Palmolive and its employees by creating a common account management process for all divisions and practical planning tools that are applicable locally on the job.

Ensure Actionable Learning. Underscoring Colgate's commitment that training must be an enabler of business (rather than an interruption of business), their use of actionable learning methods ensures key account managers maintain a focus on their business development activities even as they attend the four-day training program. The structure for actionable learning begins prior to the program when participants meet with their sales director to agree which of their own key accounts they will focus on during the training program. Once they begin the training program, participants complete an indepth "Account Application" journal in which they plan and commit to use the specific new concepts and tools that they have acquired in training.

Another key component of actionable learning at Colgate is feedback and coaching (received from one's sales director prior to attending the training, from the course instructors; and from learning partners in the seminar). Because of this, the Key Accountability training program provides numerous opportunities for discussion and feedback to the individuals on the quality of their Account Application plans. At the end of each module, participants complete the Account Application, review it with their learning partners or instructors, obtain feedback, and refine their account strategies. This structure ensures a direct link between concepts and tools acquired in the training program and application back on the job. In this way, the methodology of actionable learning is one of the most important factors that has contributed to key account managers' being able to transfer their learnings in the classroom to specific behaviors and actions on the job that achieve improved business results.

Methods and Media

The design and development team decided on the following methods and media to facilitate actionable learning and development for the Key Accountability program:

- *Pre-seminar meetings with managers* provide an opportunity to
  Agree on personal learning objectives with each participant
  Direct each participant to focus on key issues in the program
  Assign pre-seminar case-study work
- *Four days of seminar sessions include*
  Instructor-led presentations of key points
  Small-group learning activities (discussions, exercises, and games) to acquire and apply key concepts and skills
  Case studies and role-play simulations based on actual Colgate-Palmolive customers and marketplace challenges to provide a realistic global reference in which to apply business consulting skills
  Seminars ideally include twenty-four participants to provide broad representation across boundaries and to allow maximum flexibility for small group activities.
- *An account application journal* translates program learning and experiences into concrete, high pay-off actions for each participant, who selects a key account to work on during the program. These actions include immediate applications to specific key accounts. For example, during the program, a participant is required to do a supply chain analysis for his or her account; assess the key account's readiness for category management; conduct a relationship analysis; and review the account profitability. Based on this work, key account managers develop strategies specific to their accounts that they implement immediately after training. Actions may also include medium-term applications to subsidiaries and longer-term applications to Colgate-Palmolive.

- *Learning partnerships* ensure that participants continue to receive collaborative support from one another both during and after the training sessions. For example, key account managers who have met face to face with their counterparts serving the same account in another country or region have continued the partnership after the training sessions with e-mail correspondence and follow-up visits to other subsidiaries.
- *An active worldwide learning network* has led to timely communication of state-of-the-art practices and technologies throughout Colgate-Palmolive's global organization, enabling speedy transfer of real-world learning in such areas as account management, business planning, promotion, and evaluation of results. It has also contributed to the development of a sales information system to support Colgate's global sales strategy.
- *Direct communication between participants and senior management* in Colgate-Palmolive provides immediate input from participants on business issues to be addressed by the top of the organization. Sales directors serve as hosts or sponsors of sessions in an ongoing upward communication process called "Recommendations to Senior Management." These sessions capture the commitments of key account managers and provide a vehicle for the periodic communication of their ideas to Colgate-Palmolive's senior sales management team.
- *Post-seminar meetings with managers* continue the structure for actionable learning. These meetings are used to review key concepts and tools from the seminar, discuss issues and ideas which have come to light, and jointly decide how to implement the Account Application plan that was put together during the training seminar.

Introducing the Program

Colgate-Palmolive's core team members were responsible for communicating, understanding, and building commitment to the program within the company, as well as supporting the design, development, and implementation of the program. The vice president of worldwide sales and division sales directors serve as ongoing sponsors, generating support from all levels. The vital work of building momentum and buy-in prior to implementation was also cascaded from divisional presidents to general managers of subsidiaries, all of whom dedicated significant resources to supporting the programs.

Implementing the Program

Colgate-Palmolive has set a goal for all key account managers and trade marketing managers to complete this and additional follow-up programs in the Global Sales Curriculum by the year 2000.

Global Partnerships

The partnerships for the Key Accountability program extend across all of Colgate-Palmolive's geographic boundaries. The design team's implementation strategy stresses the importance of having representatives from multiple divisions in each seminar. This helps foster organizational learning and team building by exposing participants to their colleagues from diverse parts of the world. Representatives from all divisions participated in the piloting and initial rollout of this global initiative. Implementation began in Europe in June 1997 and has since been initiated in all other divisions—central Europe and Russia, Latin America, Asia, Africa and Middle East, and North America.

Implementation Phases

The implementation phases outlined below reflect Colgate-Palmolive's global training strategy of "cascading" a program:

1. Senior management briefing sessions are sponsored by division presidents (senior-most levels of the organization) and are attended by division sales directors, subsidiary general managers, and subsidiary sales directors.
2. Participants are selected and prepared based on their managers' assessments of their high potential for leadership.

3. Trainers are selected based on:
- Strong interpersonal communication skills; the ability to:
  Express ideas and concepts
  Listen
  Encourage others to express ideas
- Credibility
  Knowledge of Colgate-Palmolive culture and operations
  Expert knowledge of the subject matter
  Respect of seniors, peers, and subordinates
  Recognition as a leader
- Advocacy for the project—understanding and belief in its content and purpose
- High leadership potential
  In accordance with its principles of leadership development, Colgate teams less experienced high-potential contributors with more experienced leaders as co-instructors for global training programs. This provides both with excellent development opportunities.

4. Trainers are trained in the following manner:
- By attending the program wearing two hats:
  As participants they gain full experience of the program content, learn the concepts, embrace and align them with their own beliefs and practices, and become a content champion.
  As future trainers they observe and take notes on how the model instructors deliver the program, how they interact with participants, how they handle questions, and so on.
- By attending a three-day instructor certification seminar:
  Drill and practice general presentation and facilitation skills
  Review and further master and commit to course content
  Practice conducting the program with video-based feedback from master instructors
  Review techniques, roles, and responsibilities of team teaching in a global environment that includes people from different cultures
- By spending one to two days of preparation and rehearsal with co-instructor immediately preceding delivery of the first program.

- By delivering first program with observation, feedback, and coaching by master instructor.
- By undergoing evaluation by participants—evaluation data goes into global database of instructor evaluation scores for benchmarking and quality management.

    Note: Instructors are certified at two different levels:

    Global instructors are certified to deliver program to multinational audience via pan-division or global sessions.

    Local instructors are certified to deliver program to local audience in local language.

5. Global and/or pan-division seminar sessions are conducted quarterly.
6. Six-month follow-up evaluations are conducted with results and recommendations reported to senior management to serve as basis for future business planning.

The implementation process is ongoing, with global and local instructor opportunities "back-filled" annually. To date, 550 participants from sixty-two countries in Europe, Central Europe and Russia, Latin America, Asia, Africa and Middle East, North America, and the Caribbean have taken part in *Key Accountability: Managing the Account as a Business*. Additionally, forty-two experienced and high-potential company sales executives have been certified as instructors.

The Delivery Team

Delivery of the program is being carried out by a world-class cadre of ten Colgate-Palmolive sales directors and key account managers, including some members of the development task force, who were selected and intensely prepared as the initial delivery faculty. Twenty-five additional instructors were certified to cascade the learning in situations where local languages are required. Teams of two or three instructors, to provide diversity of experiences and cultural perspectives, deliver program sessions.

Evaluation

Four levels of evaluation are being used to assess the program:

Level 1

Participant's reactions regarding how well the program meets their needs and expectations are recorded using the standard course and instructor evaluation questionnaires (Exhibits 7.2 and 7.3). Results are compared to average scores for all programs in Colgate-Palmolive's Global Curriculum Evaluation Database.

Feedback from participants completing Level 1 evaluation is consistently excellent. The quantitative results from the company's standard global evaluation format (see Exhibits 7.4 and 7.5) on three key attributes, measured on a scale of 1–5 (with 5 being the highest), were:

(a) Course contribution to competence   4.5
(b) Recommend peers to take this course   4.6
(c) Overall course average score   4.4

The majority of course participants agreed that the course had achieved all of its main objectives. For example, nearly all participants agreed that the course helped them to understand their roles as business leaders for Colgate's most important accounts (96 percent), and to better understand the business from the trade customer's perspective (96 percent). Most participants said that the course helped them achieve improved business results (83 percent) and build stronger relationships with key customers.

Sales directors whose people attended the program reported that as a result of attending the course their key account managers now:

- Took a more thoughtful approach to developing their accounts
- Took a broader commercial approach to managing the account
- Acted more like business managers than salespeople

Level 2

Learning (participants' increase in knowledge and skills) is demonstrated by participants successfully solving realistic business case simulation and developing practical action plans with a high impact for their own accounts.

Level 3

On-the-job behavioral improvements are assessed through anecdotal data and follow-up questionnaires completed by all participants and their Sales Directors.

The questionnaire is administered four to six months after the training and identifies the degree to which participants and their sales directors estimate that:

- Key Accountability has resulted in further professional development
- Tools and concepts taught in the program have been applied in the workplace
- A positive impact on business results is based on participation in the program

Additional reactions from the questionnaires show that other behavioral changes are taking place. Participants indicated that the most highly valued components of the experience were:

- An ability to interact with others from other country subsidiaries
- Access to information, resources beyond day-to-day experience, and exposure
- Tools and concepts that were presented clearly, in a user-friendly, understandable framework that allowed for individual adaptation and application
- Opportunity to view the business from a broader perspective from the retailer and the supplier viewpoint and within the context of the broader business environment

- Senior management's embrace of the concepts, tools, and processes in their subsidiaries, which contributed to improved performance and motivation of salespeople

Level 4

Business results are also being tracked by specific business and financial measures which include the efficiency with which key account managers are meeting their account profitability targets and results of direct promotional ideas.

Evidence of business results can be found in the responses in the six-month follow-up survey to this question: *"Overall, what would you say have been the business results of attending this training program?"*

Participants

"Greater profitability of promotions through systematic pre- and post-evaluation."

"Significantly improved the return on investment in our key accounts in 1998."

"Increased understanding of the business; increased use of data; increased sales."

Sales Directors

"Increased sales by 20 percent in modern accounts and increased margin by 2 percent in all customers."

"Systematic approach to developing account strategies has given the team clear direction."

"[Participant] exceeded budget targets by 11.4 percent."

In summary, 83 percent of key account managers and 100 percent of the sales directors stated that the "course helped to improve business results."

A follow-up evaluation was conducted in Europe in 1998 to determine how much key account managers' performance had improved as a result of the program. The results, shown in Table 7.1, were impressive and showed a strong correlation between the evaluations of key account managers and their sales directors.

TABLE 7.1.   FOLLOW-UP EVALUATION OF KEY ACCOUNT MANAGERS' PERFORMANCE.

	Key Account Managers' Estimate (average)	Sales Directors' Estimate (average)
Performance on course objectives	+29 percent	+29 percent
Use of skills and knowledge learned in the course	60 percent reported they had used	60 percent reported their participants had used
Improvement in overall job performance	+20 percent	+18 percent

Ongoing Support and Development

In addition to the positive effect on sales behaviors and bottom-line results, the Key Accountability program has produced additional leadership and organization development benefits for the company's overall leadership development strategy.

Colgate-Palmolive's Basic Principles of Leadership Development

1. Identify high-potentials early
2. Assign sequence of challenging work
3. Provide constructive feedback and coaching
4. Offer continuous learning opportunities

At Colgate-Palmolive, global sales training is an important vehicle for identifying the best talent and future leaders within the sales function. Sales directors nominate participants for the Key Accountability program based on their high potential for leadership. Sales directors also serve as coaches before and after the training.

During training, high-potential contributors are identified and subsequently given additional opportunities to develop their leadership competencies, for example, serving on global task forces or coinstructing training programs with experienced Colgate-Palmolive leaders. Thus, Colgate-Palmolive constantly improves its ability to identify experienced role models, improve the coaching skills of its managers, and groom high-potential contributors for leadership positions. In addition to providing a continuous learning opportunity, Key Accountability and other Colgate global sales training programs link closely to the leadership development and succession planning processes of the company.

A Catalyst for Culture Change and Shared Learning

Cross-border participation in this program has acted as a catalyst for fundamental culture change, including the development of a global mindset, establishment of peer networks, and the ongoing exchange of customer information and best practices.

Several of the innovative methodologies that contributed to the successful development and implementation of this program are transferable to other situations that require a global approach under a wide range of market conditions.

This program has also driven the demand for globalization of business information systems to support the account management process. *The Business and Promotional Planning Process* (Exhibits 7.6 and 7.7) developed for the program has contributed significantly to the clarification of information-technology needs and is driving the formation of a worldwide information system for Colgate-Palmolive.

Key Success Factors

Several factors have contributed greatly to the success of the Key Accountability program:

- Strategic alignment
  Driven by business need
  Supported from above and below
- Line participation in design, development, and delivery
  Real-world needs
  Real-world applications
  Real-world best practices
- Multi-country representation in development and implementation
  Global approach and exposure
  Local application
- Investment in instructors
  Identification of high-potential candidates
  Careful selection
  Team teaching (experienced with high potentials)
  Rigorous preparation and coaching

These factors provide guidance for similar projects requiring complex, strategic program development, multinational or global application, and a vehicle for accelerating the learning of future leadership talent at Colgate-Palmolive.

Exhibit 7.1: Seminar Session Overview

MANAGING THE ACCOUNT AS A BUSINESS COURSE AT A GLANCE

	Day 1	Day 2	Day 3	Day 4
AM		• Supply chain management • Category management	Account strategy, (continued) Retailer SWOT analysis	• Business and promotional planning
PM	• *Start 12:00* • Introduction • Economic and retail environment • Retailer's perspective	• Category management (continued) • Developing an account strategy: information gathering	Account strategy, (continued) Macro-investment analysis relationship grid	• Action planning • *End 3:30*
	• Evening assignment	• Evening assignment	• Evening assignment	

(KAM1) © February, 1998 Colgate-Palmolive

Exhibit 7.2: Course Evaluation Form

COLGATE-PALMOLIVE GLOBAL EDUCATION AND TRAINING
COURSE EVALUATION FORM

Course Title _____ Completion Date: _____

Course Feedback: Upon completing this course, read the following statements and circle the number which best represents the extent to which you agree or disagree with each. **Return this form to Global Education and Training, 300 Park Avenue, New York, NY 10022. Thank you.**

	Strongly Disagree				Strongly Agree	Not Applicable
1. Course objectives were clearly communicated.	1	2	3	4	5	N/A
2. Course content was appropriate to achieving the course objectives.	1	2	3	4	5	N/A
3. Course objectives were clearly written and well-organized.	1	2	3	4	5	N/A
4. Exercises were relevant to my experience and learning level.	1	2	3	4	5	N/A
5. It was clear to me what points were most important.	1	2	3	4	5	N/A
6. The majority of the course content was relevant to me.	1	2	3	4	5	N/A
7. What I have learned in this course will contribute to my competence.	1	2	3	4	5	N/A
8. I would encourage my peers to take this course.	1	2	3	4	5	N/A

Overall comments:

Strengths: Please indicate which parts of this course were particularly valuable to you.

_____

_____

Areas for Improvement: Please indicate which parts of this course need to be improved, and add your suggestions for improvement.

_____

_____

February 1995.

Exhibit 7.2: Instructor Evaluation Form

COLGATE-PALMOLIVE GLOBAL EDUCATION AND TRAINING
INSTRUCTOR EVALUATION FORM

Course Title _____

Course Date _____   **Course Location** _____

Read each evaluation statement, and mark the number that best reflects the extent to which you agree or disagree with that statement for each instructor.

	Instructor:					Instructor:				
	Strongly Disagree				Strongly Agree	Strongly Disagree				Strongly Agree
Instructor . . .										
1. . . . was well prepared.	1	2	3	4	5	1	2	3	4	5
2. . . . presented information clearly and in terms I understood.	1	2	3	4	5	1	2	3	4	5
3. . . . was knowledgeable in topic instructed.	1	2	3	4	5	1	2	3	4	5
4. . . . managed well in meeting the course objectives.	1	2	3	4	5	1	2	3	4	5
5. . . . shared relevant experiences and insights.	1	2	3	4	5	1	2	3	4	5
6. . . . was enthusiastic.	1	2	3	4	5	1	2	3	4	5
7. . . . seemed interested in participants' success.	1	2	3	4	5	1	2	3	4	5
8. . . . responded well to questions.	1	2	3	4	5	1	2	3	4	5
9. . . . integrated participants' comments well.	1	2	3	4	5	1	2	3	4	5
10. . . . summarized and reinforced major comments.	1	2	3	4	5	1	2	3	4	5
11. . . . should continue to instruct Colgate-Palmolive courses	1	2	3	4	5	1	2	3	4	5

Comments about the instructors:

_____

_____

_____

_____

February 1995.

Linkage Inc.'s Best Practices in Leadership Development Handbook, edited by David Giber, Louis Carter, and Marshall Goldsmith. Copyright © 2000 by Linkage Press and Jossey-Bass/Pfeiffer, San Francisco, CA.

Exhibit 7.4: Participant Feedback Form

KEY ACCOUNTABILITY: MANAGING THE ACCOUNT AS A
BUSINESS EVALUATION OF BUSINESS EFFECTIVENESS
(PARTICIPANT FEEDBACK)

INSTRUCTIONS: We value your feedback concerning the "Key Accountability: Managing the Account as a Business" course which you attended in 1997. Please help us to evaluate the effectiveness of this training program by completing this survey and returning it to Toni Pennisi, Global Sales Training in New York, PK-16, by May 8, 1998. Fax # (212) 310-3220 ☎ (212) 310-3198.

Name (Optional): _____

Title/Function: _____

Subsidiary: _____

RESPONSIBILITY FOR MANAGING KEY ACCOUNTS

Your answer here will help us to better understand your responses to this survey:

_____ I am a certified instructor for this program.

_____ I have direct responsibility for managing a key account(s)/U.S. Dollar Sales:_____

_____ I am responsible for managing key account managers/U.S. Dollar Sales:_____

_____ I am not directly responsible for managing key accounts. My responsibility is:_____

SECTION I - PROFESSIONAL DEVELOPMENT

Has this program resulted in your further professional development? For example, as a result of participating in the program, do you:

YES   NO

☐   ☐   Take a broader commercial approach to managing the account?

☐   ☐   Think about issues and priorities from the account's perspective?

☐   ☐   Act more like a business manager than a salesperson?

☐   ☐   Take a more thoughtful approach to developing the account?

☐   ☐   Feel more confident?

☐   ☐   Other (please specify) _____

_____

_____

What other professional development activities have you done as a result of this training (such as, visiting other subsidiaries? networking with other CP sales professionals? best practice benchmarking with other companies?)

_____

_____

CP COLGATE-PALMOLIVE

SECTION II- ACHIEVEMENT OF COURSE OBJECTIVES

For the statements below, indicate the degree to which you Strongly Disagree (1), Agree (3), or Strongly Agree (5).

Key Accountability: Managing the Account as a Business helped me to:

	Strongly Disagree		Agree		Strongly Agree	Not Applicable
1. Understand the role of key account managers as business managers of Colgate's most important accounts	1	2	3	4	5	N/A
2. Understand the customer's business from the customer's point of view	1	2	3	4	5	N/A
3. Use a framework for developing account strategies and business plans in accordance with CP brand and corporate objectives	1	2	3	4	5	N/A
4. Increase my knowledge, experience, and confidence in managing my most important accounts	1	2	3	4	5	N/A
5. Build stronger relationships with key accounts	1	2	3	4	5	N/A
6. Achieve improved business results	1	2	3	4	5	N/A

SECTION III - USEFULNESS OF LEARNING

Use the scale below to answer the following questions. Circle only one choice for each question.

Not at All; Never/Rarely 1	To a Small Extent 2	To a Moderate Extent 3	To a Great Extent 4	To a Very Great Extent 5	Not Applicable N/A
1. To what extent did you use the knowledge and/or skills presented in this course prior to attending this course?	1	2	3	4 5	N/A
2. To what extent have you had the opportunity to use the knowledge and/or skills presented in this course?	1	2	3	4 5	N/A
3. To what extent have you actually used the knowledge and/or skills presented in this course, after completing the course?	1	2	3	4 5	N/A
4. To what extent has your confidence in using the knowledge and/or skills increased as a result of this course?	1	2	3	4 5	N/A
5. To what extent did you receive the assistance necessary in preparing for this course?	1	2	3	4 5	N/A
6. To what extent has the content of this course accurately reflected what happens on the job?	1	2	3	4 5	N/A

 **COLGATE-PALMOLIVE**

(continued)

SECTION III - USEFULNESS OF LEARNING (CONTINUED)

Use the scale below to answer the following questions. Circle only one choice for each question.

Not at All; Never/Rarely 1	To a Small Extent 2	To a Moderate Extent 3	To a Great Extent 4	To a Very Great Extent 5	Not Applicable N/A

7. To what extent have you had access to the necessary resources (such as, technology and information) to apply the knowledge and/or skills on your job?   1   2   3   4   5   N/A

8. To what extent have you received help, through coaching and/or feedback, with applying the knowledge and/or skills on the job?   1   2   3   4   5   N/A

SECTION IV - BUSINESS APPLICATION

Please indicate the degree to which you have applied the tools and concepts of the key account manager program in managing your key accounts as a business (1 = have not applied); (5 = have fully applied).

	Have Not Applied		Partially Applied		Fully Applied	Not Applicable
Account Information Checklist How applied?/ Why not applied? (describe)	1	2	3	4	5	N/A
Account Strategy Template How applied?/ Why not applied? (describe)	1	2	3	4	5	N/A
Business and Promotional Planning Process How applied?/ Why not applied? (describe)	1	2	3	4	5	N/A
Promotional Evaluation (pre and post) How applied?/ Why not applied? (describe)	1	2	3	4	5	N/A
Category Management How applied?/ Why not applied? (describe)	1	2	3	4	5	N/A
Supply Chain Management How applied?/ Why not applied? (describe)	1	2	3	4	5	N/A
ECR How applied?/ Why not applied? (describe)	1	2	3	4	5	N/A

COLGATE-PALMOLIVE

SECTION V - BUSINESS RESULTS

As a result of this course:

My performance on the course objectives (Section II) has changed by _____% (please indicate +/−)

My overall job performance has changed by _____% (please indicate +/−)

Overall, what would you say have been the business results of attending this training program? Include any results you think are related to the training, such as, increased understanding of the business, increased use of data, improved profitability, increased sales, improved relationships with key accounts, and so on. If results are measurable, please specify.

_____

_____

_____

SECTION VI - FURTHER SUPPORT AND THE FUTURE

Is there further support from Colgate which would enable you to more fully utilize your learning? (Be specific.)

_____

_____

_____

_____

What areas do you suggest be considered in developing future training for Colgate key account managers?

_____

_____

_____

_____

SECTION VII - ADDITIONAL COMMENTS

_____

_____

_____

_____

_____

_____

Thanks for your candid response to these questions.

CP *COLGATE-PALMOLIVE*

Exhibit 7.5: Sales Director Feedback Form

KEY ACCOUNTABILITY: MANAGING THE ACCOUNT AS A BUSINESS
EVALUATION OF BUSINESS EFFECTIVENESS
(SALES DIRECTOR FEEDBACK)

INSTRUCTIONS: We value your feedback concerning the "Key Accountability: Managing the Account as a Business" course which your key account managers (KAM's) attended in 1997. Please help us to evaluate the effectiveness of this training program by completing this survey and returning it to Toni Pennisi, Global Sales Training in New York, PK-16, by May 8, 1998. Fax # (212) 310-3220, ☎ (212) 310-3198.

Name: _____

Title/Function: _____

Subsidiary: _____

SECTION I - PROFESSIONAL DEVELOPMENT

Overall, have you seen an improvement in how your KAM's approach their business? For example:

YES	NO	
☐	☐	Are KAM's taking a broader commercial approach to managing their accounts as a result of attending the program?
☐	☐	Do they think about issues and priorities from the account's perspective?
☐	☐	Do they act more like business managers than salespeople?
☐	☐	Do they take a more thoughtful approach to developing their accounts?
☐	☐	Do they appear more confident?
☐	☐	Other (please specify)_____

_____

_____

SECTION II- ACHIEVEMENT OF COURSE OBJECTIVES

For the statements below, indicate the degree to which you Strongly Disagree (1), Agree (3), or Strongly Agree (5).

Key Accountability: Managing the Account as a Business helped key account managers to:

	Strongly Disagree		Agree		Strongly Agree	Not Applicable
1. Understand the role of key account managers as business managers of Colgate's most important accounts	1	2	3	4	5	N/A
2. Understand the customer's business from the customer's point of view	1	2	3	4	5	N/A

 **COLGATE-PALMOLIVE**

Linkage Inc.'s Best Practices in Leadership Development Handbook, edited by David Giber, Louis Carter, and Marshall Goldsmith. Copyright © 2000 by Linkage Press and Jossey-Bass/Pfeiffer, San Francisco, CA.

SECTION II- ACHIEVEMENT OF COURSE OBJECTIVES (CONTINUED)

	Strongly Disagree		Agree		Strongly Agree	Not Applicable
3. Use a framework for developing account strategies and business plans in accordance with CP brand and corporate objectives	1	2	3	4	5	N/A
4. Increase their knowledge, experience, and confidence in managing their most important accounts	1	2	3	4	5	N/A
5. Build stronger relationships with key accounts	1	2	3	4	5	N/A
6. Achieve improved business results	1	2	3	4	5	N/A

SECTION III - USEFULNESS OF LEARNING

Use the scale below to answer the following questions. Circle only one choice for each question.

Not at All; Never/Rarely	To a Small Extent	To a Moderate Extent	To a Great Extent	To a Very Great Extent	Not Applicable
1	2	3	4	5	N/A

1. To what extent did participants use the knowledge and/or skills presented in this course prior to attending this course?	1	2	3	4	5	N/A
2. To what extent have participants had the opportunity to use the knowledge and/or skills presented in this course?	1	2	3	4	5	N/A
3. To what extent have participants actually used the knowledge and/or skills presented in this course, after completing the course?	1	2	3	4	5	N/A
4. To what extent has participants' confidence in using the knowledge and/or skills increased as a result of this course?	1	2	3	4	5	N/A
5. To what extent did participants receive the assistance necessary in preparing for this course?	1	2	3	4	5	N/A
6. To what extent has the content of this course accurately reflected what happens on the job?	1	2	3	4	5	N/A
7. To what extent have participants had access to the necessary resources (for example, technology and information) to apply the knowledge and/or skills on the job?	1	2	3	4	5	N/A
8. To what extent have participants received help, through coaching and/or feedback, with applying the knowledge and/or skills on the job?	1	2	3	4	5	N/A

CP **COLGATE-PALMOLIVE**   *(continued)*

SECTION IV - BUSINESS APPLICATION

Please describe the degree to which the tools and concepts of the KAM program have been applied in your subsidiary, by answering the following questions:

1. What have you done to apply and reinforce the knowledge or skills acquired in this program in your subsidiary? (for example, implemented Account Strategy Template; adapted Business Planning process; instituted Category Management project; and so on) Please describe:

_____

_____

_____

_____

2. If you have NOT applied tools and concepts in your subsidiary, why not?

_____

_____

_____

_____

SECTION V - BUSINESS RESULTS

As a result of this course:

Participants' performance on the course objectives (Section II) has changed by _____% (please indicate +/−)

Participants' overall job performance has changed by _____% (please indicate +/−)

Overall, what would you say have been the business results of this training program in your subsidiary? Include any results you think are related to the training, such as increased understanding of the business; increased use of data; improved profitability; increased sales; improved relationships with key accounts, and so on. If results are measurable, please specify.

_____

_____

_____

_____

_____

_____

 **COLGATE-PALMOLIVE**

SECTION VI - FURTHER SUPPORT AND THE FUTURE

Is there further support from Colgate that would enable your KAM's to more fully utilize their learning? (Be specific).

_____

_____

_____

_____

What areas do you suggest be considered in developing future training for Colgate key account managers?

_____

_____

_____

_____

SECTION VII - ADDITIONAL COMMENTS

_____

_____

_____

_____

_____

_____

_____

_____

_____

_____

_____

_____

Thanks for your candid response to these questions.

CP *COLGATE-PALMOLIVE*

Exhibit 7.6: Business and Promotional Planning Process

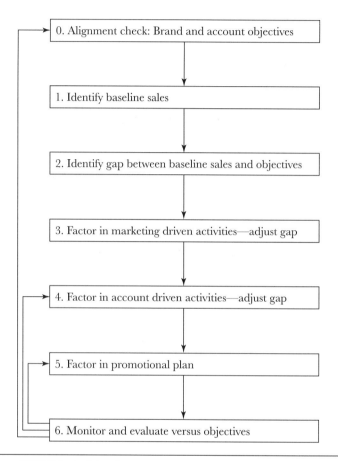

Linkage Inc.'s Best Practices in Leadership Development Handbook, edited by David Giber, Louis Carter, and Marshall Goldsmith. Copyright © 2000 by Linkage Press and Jossey-Bass/Pfeiffer, San Francisco, CA.

Exhibit 7.7: Business and Promotional Planning Template

Customer:													
Products:													
Objectives	**Jan**	**Feb**	**Mar**	**Apr**	**May**	**Jun**	**Jul**	**Aug**	**Sep**	**Oct**	**Nov**	**Dec**	**Total**
Invoiced sales	0	0	0	0	0	0	0	0	0	0	0	0	
GtN	0.0%	0.0%	0.0%	0.0%	0.0%	0.0%	0.0%	0.0%	0.0%	0.0%	0.0%	0.0%	
					Business Plan								
Baseline Sales including seasonality (BLS)	**Jan**	**Feb**	**Mar**	**Apr**	**May**	**Jun**	**Jul**	**Aug**	**Sep**	**Oct**	**Nov**	**Dec**	**Total**
"Net baseline Sales"	0	0	0	0	0	0	0	0	0	0	0	0	0
Marketing Driven	**Jan**	**Feb**	**Mar**	**Apr**	**May**	**Jun**	**Jul**	**Aug**	**Sep**	**Oct**	**Nov**	**Dec**	**Total**
Media effect													0
Consumer Activities effect													
Subtotal Baseline Sales 1 Marketing driven	0	0	0	0	0	0	0	0	0	0	0	0	0
Gap with Objectives	0	0	0	0	0	0	0	0	0	0	0	0	0
Account Driven	**Jan**	**Feb**	**Mar**	**Apr**	**May**	**Jun**	**Jul**	**Aug**	**Sep**	**Oct**	**Nov**	**Dec**	**Total**
Distribution effect													0
Assortment effect													0
Merchandising effect													0
Account Activities effect													
Other effects													

(continued)

Exhibit 7.7: (continued)

	Jan	Feb	Mar	Apr	May	Jun	Jul	Aug	Sep	Oct	Nov	Dec	Total
Subtotal baseline Sales 1 Marketing 1 Account	0	0	0	0	0	0	0	0	0	0	0	0	0
Gap with Objectives	0	0	0	0	0	0	0	0	0	0	0	0	0
Promotional Planning	Jan	Feb	Mar	Apr	May	Jun	Jul	Aug	Sep	Oct	Nov	Dec	Total
Estimated increase over BLS + Mkt + Acc													
Total gross (promotional) sales	0	0	0	0	0	0	0	0	0	0	0	0	0
Consumer related allowances													
Total involved sales	0	0	0	0	0	0	0	0	0	0	0	0	0
Incremental invoiced sales over baseline sales + Mkt + Acc	0	0	0	0	0	0	0	0	0	0	0	0	0
Customer related: Coy B	0.00%	0.00%	0.00%	0.00%	0.00%	0.00%	0.00%	0.00%	0.00%	0.00%	0.00%	0.00%	0
Customer related: Coop													
GtN													
Invoiced sales: gap with objectives	0	0	0	0	0	0	0	0	0	0	0	0	0
GtN: Planned versus Objectives													

(KAM1) © February, 1998 Colgate-Palmolive

Linkage Inc.'s Best Practices in Leadership Development Handbook, edited by David Giber, Louis Carter, and Marshall Goldsmith. Copyright © 2000 by Linkage Press and Jossey-Bass/Pfeiffer, San Francisco, CA.

About the Contributors

Donna McNamara (Donna_McNamara@COLPAL.COM) is director of global education and training for Colgate-Palmolive. In this position she leads the company's initiatives to build the skills and expertise of all Colgate people to compete effectively throughout the world. Prior to joining Colgate, she spent ten years with AT&T, managed an independent consulting practice, and was a college professor. Additionally, she is a past chairperson and Gordon M. Bliss Award recipient of the American Society of Training and Development. For more than twenty years, McNamara has helped organizations accomplish complex change and build their capability through goal alignment, education, performance improvement systems, learning, and organization development. She has written numerous professional articles and regularly presents in her field for national and international audiences. McNamara has a Ph.D. in education and human resources from Peabody College of Vanderbilt University.

Antonia Pennisi (Antonia_Pennisi@COLPAL.COM) is director of global sales training for Colgate-Palmolive. Working with the company's senior sales executives, she is responsible for the creation and implementation of Colgate's sales leadership development strategy in both developed and high growth markets worldwide. Prior to joining Colgate, Pennisi was associate director of management development at the public accounting firm of KPMG Peat Marwick; director of training for Uniforce Temporary Services; and director of program development for the sales training firm of Porter Henry & Company. With Porter Henry she served clients from the consumer products, pharmaceutical, and financial services industries. Pennisi has a master's degree in manpower and urban development from the New School for Social Research.

CHAPTER EIGHT

GUNDERSEN LUTHERAN HOSPITAL

This chapter outlines a self-assessment, personal
change-based program that is designed to develop managers
within this merged healthcare organization.

ABOUT THE CONTRIBUTOR

Introduction

Gundersen Lutheran is a combination of two healthcare organizations that merged in the fall of 1995, Gundersen Clinic, Ltd. and Lutheran Hospital-LaCrosse. The merged organization provides healthcare services to a population of 580,000 in a largely rural "Tri-State Region" comprising nineteen counties in the three adjoining states of Iowa, Minnesota, and Wisconsin.

Gundersen Clinic, Ltd., a not-for-profit corporation, is among the largest multispecialty group practices in the nation. It offers hundreds of medical, surgical, dental, and specialty services and provides care through more than 1,000,000 patient visits a year, an average of 3,300 a day. In addition to the main clinic in LaCrosse, which traces its origins back to 1891, the Gundersen Lutheran system has twenty-six regional community medical clinics and ten regional vision centers in Western Wisconsin, southeastern Minnesota, and Northeastern Iowa, offering patients both primary and tertiary medicine. The system also has sports medicine and mental health centers, home care, specialized housing facilities, and air and ground ambulance services.

Lutheran Hospital-LaCrosse, a 402-bed multispecialty hospital and regional center was established in 1901. More than 15,500 patients are admitted each year, representing more than 77,000 patient days. Over 27,000 patients are treated in the Trauma and Emergency Center each year.

Gundersen Lutheran employs nearly 6,000 employees and is guided by the following mission statement:

> Gundersen Lutheran pursues excellence in the compassionate delivery of comprehensive health services as a leader in patient care, education and research, and is committed to promoting health through community partnerships and learning.

To achieve this mission, employees within the organization embrace and model the values of:

- Excellence in quality and service
- Personalized care

- Integrity
- Respect
- Teamwork
- Communication
- Commitment

In 1997, Gundersen Lutheran was named one of the top 100 healthcare institutions in the United States. William M. Mercer, Inc. and HCIA, Inc., of Baltimore, Maryland, made this recognition public as part of its fifth annual "100 Top Hospitals: Benchmarks for Success" study.

The organization houses a human resource development (HRD) department that provides the majority of organizational nonclinical education and training initiatives. One such initiative is the Leadership Development Program.

Building the Business Case

In May 1990, Lutheran Hospital's administration gave the department of education (now HRD) the charge of developing, designing, and implementing a "comprehensive program by which all managers within the organization would be given the direction and incentive to continually develop their professional expertise." Based on this directive, a proposal was created that focused on the design of an in-house leadership development program that would address the following goals:

- Promoting continuing education as a lifelong objective
- Promoting educated and qualified people who aspire to be managers/ leaders within the organization
- Developing a vehicle by which demonstrated competence on the job can be assessed
- Developing managers into teachers or mentors within their own profession
- Creating a more systematic program for the development of, and reward for, managerial expertise
- Establishing and communicating the expectation of personal growth for staff and managers

Best Practice Study

An intensive study of other "best practice" programs was conducted. The research involved an examination of leadership development models within other United States-based organizations, including the military and the Department of Public Instruction. The investigation yielded extensive leadership development information, especially related to assessment centers. Our benchmark study findings were threefold: (1) some organizations mandated participation in their development programs, (2) others utilized the model as a selection tool, and (3) some based job advancement and pay increases on assessment center performance. These discoveries did not provide the model for learning that matched the previously mentioned goals, so the search continued.

During this research process, the organization was developing a healthcare exchange and growing a relationship with the National Health Service (NHS) in the United Kingdom. In building this association, it was realized that some of the management development schemes utilized within the NHS not only matched the proposed goals, they also utilized assessment (development) centers and offered a parallel industry for comparison and benchmarking.

Based on previous research, and a variety of connections and opportunities within the NHS, a development center model was embraced and the Leadership Development Program became a reality.

Assessment and Development Planning

The structure of the Leadership Development Program (LDP), based on personal and professional development, was in place by August 1991, following the establishment of its competency-based foundation. The program was primarily designed for 250 managers and supervisors within Lutheran Hospital, its affiliate sites, and Gundersen Clinic. Utilizing a survey, the input of all three stakeholder groups was sought in identifying the competencies, or criteria, that were most significant for managerial/leadership excellence within the healthcare system.

The survey included a list of criteria and their definitions drawn from job analysis and performance review processes found within the literature and a variety of organizations in the United States (see Exhibit 8.1). The results were developed and distributed to managers and supervisors on the main campus and throughout the tri-state healthcare system. There was an overwhelming response to the survey and the data was used to develop eleven uniform criteria (including analytical reasoning, adaptability, communication, developing others, integrity, strategic planning, vision, teamwork, self-awareness, interpersonal sensitivity, and decisiveness) for leadership excellence throughout the organization.

Once the criteria were identified, a pilot development center was held and every administrator from throughout the system participated. This provided the opportunity to run a trial of the activities, train internal staff as assessors, and perhaps most important, create the administrative buy-in and support needed to take the program into the future and throughout the organization.

The Leadership Development Program Curriculum

The Leadership Development Program is a two-year, customized learning process (see Exhibit 8.2) that is offered quarterly to twelve individuals; participation is voluntary and application-based. The application process involves self-assessment of performance in the eleven competency areas and requires each candidate to reflect on individual personal/professional strengths and developmental needs. In addition to the self-assessment component, the application process requires the supervisor of each candidate to determine the individual's program readiness in addition to rating the candidate's current performance in the eleven competency areas.

Applications are accepted on an ongoing basis and those on file enter a deliberation process one to two months prior to the beginning of the next LDP. The application materials are reviewed, and selection occurs, utilizing a focused attempt to create the best mix of twelve participants based on gender, professional background, representation of the various constituencies within the healthcare system, and length of employment within the system.

Once selected, the participant begins the two-year Leadership Development Program process which includes a briefing day, a three-day development workshop, a feedback session, a debriefing day, and the formation of a learning team.

Briefing Day. Once accepted into the program, the twelve participants meet for the first time at a Briefing Day. This session, held approximately one month prior to the Development Workshop, allows participants to ask questions about their involvement, meet their colleagues, and prepare for the upcoming development center. In addition to the teambuilding activities that take place, participants undergo psychometric testing in the areas of numerical, verbal, and abstract reasoning (in relation to the analytical reasoning criterion), complete both thinking preference and team role inventories, and fill out materials related to the solicitation of 360-degree feedback from their supervisors, peers, staff members, and customers (see Exhibit 8.3). Before the day concludes, participants receive several homework assignments to be prepared prior to the Development Workshop.

Homework. Each participant is asked to complete an autobiography, a management report, and a healthcare management assessment inventory. Each of these activities contributes to the participant's overall learning experience. Individuals have reported spending between twelve and twenty hours completing these tasks prior to the three-day assessment center.

Development Workshop Activities. At the Development Workshop, individuals participate in a wide range of assessed activities that mirror the challenges of their leadership roles and styles. The activities, all designed around the eleven criteria, include both individual activities such as self-evaluation, written reports, case studies, an in/out basket prioritizing activity, and stand-up presentations; and group exercises such as budget negotiation activities, problem-solving tasks, and a structured interview. Each activity is designed to mirror the challenges that an individual faces on the job. In this simulated environment, participants are given the opportunity to demonstrate their skills, as well as their areas of developmental need.

While participating in the two days of activities, each individual is directly and closely observed by a pool of trained assessors from within the system who record and rate their performance against the eleven criteria. Within the framework of each workshop, the twelve individuals experience a variety of activities where they work in different groups, with predetermined goals and objectives and concrete timelines for accomplishing their tasks. Each participant enters this process and engages in the activities with an ultimate goal in mind: to receive feedback on his or her performance that can be transferred to the workplace. The following example illustrates the experience of an individual who reflects on an assessed budget negotiation activity:

There I was, a new manager within the organization's marketing division who had limited budgetary expertise and a serious lack of peripheral vision, sitting at a table with my peers in the midst of a budget negotiation activity. I had to ask, "What did I get myself into?" As a former intensive care nurse, trained to make rapid-fire decisions with life and death implications, what did I know about budgets or strategic planning?

In this activity, we [the workshop participants] became management employees of a pharmaceutical business and were randomly placed in administrative positions, such as the director of human resources, director of research and development, director of marketing, and so on. Each individual was given a set of financial parameters and departmental needs for the coming year. As director, it was each individual's responsibility to secure as much financial support (or more) for their division within the timeframe of the activity—or so it initially seemed. Through honest and active dialogue, participants eventually began to realize that certain efficiencies could be achieved through collaborative, system-driven, big-picture planning. The team of directors, in order to achieve success, needed to reach this stage of thinking, which ultimately secured each individual's and division's future.

Fortunately, my activity team succeeded in accomplishing this task, as we learned very quickly that individual "greed" or protectionism just wouldn't work. The learning from this activity transferred easily into my work. Coming into the exercise, I knew about systems—bodily systems, however, not organizational systems. I soon realized that in my role, collaboration with multiple customers, who have complex needs and who operate in dynamic systems, is a must in order to achieve success.

My initial experience in this exercise, coupled with my ongoing involvement as a workshop assessor, has stimulated my passion for, and my commitment to, systems thinking. This activity, and the others within the LDP, have provided me, other participants, and the organization with a positive, challenging, learning environment in which to learn the fundamental skills necessary to carry us into the future.

Assessor Discussions. The transfer of learning that takes place between these "staged" activities and the workplace is a critical element of the process. In order to assist in the transference of learning, eight to ten skilled assessors observe participant behavior throughout the two-day development workshop process. More specifically, each participant is observed by two to three of the skilled assessors in every activity. The participant and assessors are rotated so each assessor has the opportunity to observe and rate each participant throughout the two days. This allows for increased objectivity and enriched feedback.

After each activity, the assessors independently review their recorded notes, categorize their observations according to the criteria being examined, assign a number rating, and provide objective commentary to support the rating. Once this process is complete, the assessors meet to discuss and evaluate their findings. The assessment process continues throughout the two days and Day Three is spent compiling information and collecting materials that will support the feedback session.

The assessors provide participants with information that is critical to personal and professional growth. It is important to note that individuals in the role of assessor have all previously participated in the Leadership

Development Program and bring their personal program experiences and learning to the task.

Feedback Sessions. An individual feedback session, based on the observations of all assessors, is scheduled a week to ten days after the completion of the Development Workshop. The feedback comprises a face-to-face meeting and supporting written summaries, including the 360-degree feedback previously solicited in a confidential manner from the participant's immediate supervisor, peers, and staff members. A primary assessor provides the feedback. A primary assessor is the person from the assessor group who was initially and anonymously matched with the participant and who has closely observed and assessed this individual more than other participants at the Development Workshop. It is important to note that the primary assessor has no supervisory or reporting links to the participant. In the best case scenario, the prime assessor has no prior knowledge of the participant that would perhaps bias the observation process.

The information discussed during the feedback session is related to the eleven criteria and illustrates areas of strength and weakness. It is designed to be the foundation for improving performance via the creation of a PDP (Personal/Professional Development Plan).

Debriefing Day. One month after the Development Workshop, following the feedback session, participants reunite to discuss the assessment process, explore the feedback from their prime assessor, form Learning Teams, meet their Learning Team advisor, and receive additional information about PDPs and Learning Contracts. The twelve participants form two diverse "sister" Learning Teams of six, utilizing the results of the thinking preference inventory, the team roles inventory, and facilitated discussion. The participants leave the debriefing day with their first Learning Team meeting scheduled and their first agenda in place.

Learning Team Meetings. Within the Learning Team, participants meet once a month for a half day, with the guidance of a Learning Team advisor (who has previously completed the two-year process) for the purpose of designing a customized approach to individual learning through the development of their PDPs. The PDP aligns with individual learning preferences and working styles, and its focus becomes twofold: enhancing the skill areas identified within the Development Workshop and developing the areas of need that surfaced during the assessment process.

Creating a PDP entails answering five key questions: (1) Where have I been? (2) Where am I now? (3) Where do I want to go? (4) How will I get there? (5) How will I know that I have arrived? The PDP is a strategic plan for the individual learner. It is individual, confidential, and becomes a personal mission statement. The PDP is the entree to the learning process. It contains the conceptual ideas for development and is later translated into a Learning Contract that assists the individual in developing and carrying out learning goals and objectives (see Exhibit 8.4).

The Learning Contract is the individual action plan for the two years of the program. It is designed to incorporate the goals identified within the PDP. By including components such as goals, actions, target dates, and methods of assessment, this document will allow learners to work toward personal learning strategies, while allowing other members of the team to hold them accountable for their learning (see Exhibit 8.5).

The Learning Contract is a contract between the learner and the other members of the Learning Team. It is not confidential. In many instances, it is suggested that the contract be signed off by the individual learner, the Learning Team members, and the team advisor. In this manner, the contract involves the team, provides the structure for enabling the team to stay on task, and creates high levels of accountability for each member of the team to achieve that which they set out to accomplish.

Other functions of the Learning Team include creating a safe environment for each member to grow, providing peer support for PDP design, implementation, and evaluation, providing feedback, monitoring the effort and progress of each member, and serving the organization in the creation of positive networking and unity within the system. To support these functions, each Learning Team has a self-monitored budget that is designated for materials, courses, and experiences that assist team members in accomplishing their learning goals.

The following excerpts from interviews reveal the stories and journeys of three Learning Teams:

Our two years together as a Learning Team had an impact on each of us. Right from the start we were personally committed to the program and were clear as to what we wanted to obtain from the process. If we were to write a book about our experiences, we would write three distinct chapters: *Why we came*; *Why and how we stayed together*; and *The tie that binds*.

Our two years were shaped, to a large extent, by the activities of the organization as it proceeded through the merger. We weren't always clear about what was happening. We had rainy days when we felt we didn't have anyone to lean on. There were resignations and retirements. We developed a unique friendship that guided our learning. We knew we had a safe place where we could learn, risk, and rely on the confidentiality and nonjudgmental support of our peers. The team became a safe haven to work on professional issues, create learning, and inspire a common vision.

We learned a lot during our two years together. We learned that if you don't like something, change it. If you can't change it, change the way you think about it. We now know that our legacy will be determined by those who participated in the program before us, those who participated with us, those who participate after us, and how we work with each one of them.

◆ ◆ ◆

At first we were skeptical. We had no solid clue regarding expectations of us. We convened, somewhat uneasily, to begin our collective journey and individual sojourns. We wondered, "Would it be worth the effort?" and "Were all of the homework assignments an efficient use of our time?" It all seemed rather peculiar at the time. But we went along with it because we had a sense of humorous adventure (and we were getting paid).

What we know now is that it was all worth it and that the process actually does work. The interaction, the feedback, and introspection provided within the framework of the LDP has had a lasting effect on each of us. As one member said, the program, "truly challenged me more than any experience I can recall. Though uncomfortable, the process is necessary and allowed for self-acceptance and growth."

Strict adherence to confidentiality allowed our team to proceed in an atmosphere of openness, congeniality, and trust. We felt free to challenge each other to improve our weaknesses and make optimal use of our strengths. When it came time to write about the impact the program had on individuals, results were remarkably similar. Our team repeatedly cited heightened interdepartmental cooperation and peer support as attributes of the program. Appreciation of the talents, concerns, and the efforts within other departments provides a greater awareness of the "big picture." This overall awareness helps counteract the tendency toward specialization that sharpens expertise but narrows the field of vision.

Each of us took risks when we entered the program. Our organization shared in that risk. It could have been wasting precious time and resources. Now we know that it wasn't.

◆ ◆ ◆

Learning Team Thirteen started out like most all others following the Development Workshop. We began as seven strangers—six team members and a team advisor. No one knew for sure what to expect from the process we were just beginning, we just knew we were excited and looked forward to an adventure, an adventure in learning.

Early team meetings were similar to a couple dating—we took our time and got to know each other. The chemistry within our team was particularly strong and we bonded quickly and intensely. The bonding allowed us to develop a critical ingredient for learning—trust. This element allowed us to move forward efficiently and confidently in developing our PDPs.

At the time that our team was formed, our organization was going through a merger. The team served a role greater than guiding members in the development of PDPs. More critically for us, and the organization, many discussions and debates took place within our team, which led us to a place of greater understanding related to the profound changes that we were all experiencing. Members of the team were from all levels and divisions of the organization, including regional affiliate hospitals, management, and staff. This mix provided us with a microcosm of the organization and the ability to learn more about how we and the organization were responding to the change around us.

We learned from each others' strengths and weaknesses. Based on the comprehensive assessment and feedback that we each experienced, the team was very diverse and very balanced. This balance allowed us to view many different personality traits and learn to deal with, accept, understand, and learn from those who were different than us.

Through the two-year process, we each became better people, better employees, and better managers. For these reasons, we cherish the experience and process of the LDP. We owe it more than can be expressed in words.

Team Education. Learning Teams reunite with their "sister" teams at six, twelve, and eighteen months after the Development Workshop to receive additional information related to leadership development, to provide feedback to program coordinators, and to participate in team-building activities.

In addition to the previously mentioned "reunions," Learning Team members are offered many optional educational courses through the human resource development department that may assist in the achievement of their Learning Contracts.

Recognition Ceremony. At the end of the two-year commitment, the two teams come together to celebrate their learning at a ceremony that recognizes the personal and professional journey of each Learning Team member. Each team discloses their experiences to an audience comprising Gundersen Lutheran administrators, the next group of Leadership Development participants, invited guests, and potential program candidates. The sharing of individual and team journeys takes many forms—whether it be via discussion, slide shows, videos, or a skit—and the message is clear: This program makes a difference. This public evaluation allows the program coordinators and key players within the organization to monitor the return on investment of the program, and it provides an exciting opportunity to recreate buy-in and support from administration, management, and previous program participants.

Program Evaluation and Measurement

The program has been well received and supported in its eight years of operation and to date, twenty-one Development Workshops have taken place, and more than 200 administrators, managers, supervisors, physicians, and employees have participated in the two-year learning experience.

Quantitative and Qualitative Approaches

In evaluating the Leadership Development Program, both quantitative and qualitative methods have been utilized. In 1994, two years after the inception of the program, an external consultant was hired to study the effectiveness of the program from the viewpoint of the participants, the program coordinators, and the organization as a whole. To capture this information, a two-stage process was designed. The first phase utilized a qualitative approach and was based on a number of one-on-one interviews with program participants and coordinators. The second phase was quantitative in nature and was led by a survey that was sent to all previous program participants.

A summary of the study indicated several critical findings: (1) the potential for significant personal/professional development and growth had been achieved; (2) the program was rated by most participants as by far the single most significant development activity of their careers; (3) the major organizational impact of the program is related to the connectivity and networking that is established via participation; (4) the program is in alignment with and promotes the organization's mission and values; (5) and the program has profound and subtle informal effect on the culture of the organization.

Since the time of the commissioned study, internal evaluative measures have continued. While both quantitative and qualitative methods are rigorous and trustworthy, the ongoing evaluation had to provide information and data that was beneficial to the organization in indicating whether or not the program had made, and continued to make, a difference. Prior to selecting an approach, it was critical to gain buy-in and support for the choice from the organization. Input on the study design was sought from administration, corporate research and development, the finance department, and program assessors, advisors, and participants.

Based on the feedback, a qualitative approach became the primary method for studying the program. Although quantitative analysis surfaces at times, a qualitative process takes the lead. Three drives behind using a qualitative versus quantitative approach were (1) there is a preference to allow themes to emerge from the data, (2) it is difficult to quantify "learning," and (3) there is ample qualitative data available and numerous opportunities for data collection built into the structure of the program.

In asking the question, "How have participants incorporated and applied the concepts and ideas from the Leadership Development Program into their personal and professional life?" several measurable components of both ongoing, informal, and formal studies became apparent.

Informal Evaluation

Learning Teams meet at one-, six-, and twelve-month intervals after completing the Development Workshop component of the Leadership Development Program. At each progress check, feedback is solicited through either a survey or interview process. Upon completion of the two-year program, an exit interview and recognition ceremony are held. These opportunities allow for feedback and information gathering throughout each participant's two-year experience. Valuable, rich evidence of learning has surfaced as a result of these interactions:

> At first, the two-year commitment seemed like a lot. Through my experience, I now feel that this program is the best way you can spend your time learning. LDP offers the most bang for the buck related to personal and professional development. I used to rush through each day in an attempt to get things done. I've learned to slow down and enjoy life.
>
> Facility Operations Supervisor

Objective assessment is important to personal growth. Just as important is the support and mentoring that the Learning Team provides. My management capabilities have expanded tremendously and this has allowed me to become more self-confident and able to contribute more to our organization. LDP is invaluable and will change your life.

Director of Radiology

LDP taught me how to set goals for my professional and personal lives and helped me understand how to take the steps necessary to accomplish these goals. I feel that I have improved the skills needed for my position. Also, I have increased my network of colleagues within the healthcare system. LDP is a program which gives each individual the support and tools necessary to become a better leader.

Community Relations Manager

Formal Evaluation

Although informal methods have dominated the evaluation process, some formal approaches have also been implemented. At the time of the merge, the "new" organization was surveyed to determine if the eleven performance criteria were still the critical indicators for success. The survey was distributed to a much broader audience this time, soliciting feedback from not only managers and supervisors throughout the system, but from employees at all levels of the organization. Surprisingly, in light of the merger and the broadened audience, the feedback indicated that the criteria identified in 1991 were still the key factors for leadership success in the future.

In addition, there is currently a plan to design, implement, and evaluate a new performance management system within the organization. This program will be designed around the identified competencies and will involve annual self-assessment, 360-degree feedback, and performance contracting specifically related to each job within the organization. At the same time, the Leadership Development Program will undergo a formal review to ensure alignment with the new performance management model. Each individual within the organization will have a clearly defined job description that highlights the performance expectations and will then be appraised on their strengths and weaknesses as related to the job. Based on the appraisal, they will then be given the opportunity to grow both personally and professionally via participation in the LDP.

On a larger scale, the LDP has had a cultural impact on the integration of the new organization. As the 1994, pre-merger study indicated, interviewees were unanimous that the most significant positive organizational impact of the LDP was the enhancement it gives to the sense of system connectivity. At that time, participants and administrators confirmed the reality of the program's major contribution to breaking down professional, departmental, and facility-based barriers.

As the two organizations merged, the LDP was in its fourth year of operation, and more than twenty-five Learning Teams were active. The Learning Teams provided ample opportunities to develop, sustain, and utilize enduring relationships within the system. Both informal and personal, as well as professional support and advice, was, and still is, actively communicated and nurtured through these networks. The establishment of these wide organizational networks assisted in preparing managers and employees for the many structural, political, human resource, and symbolic changes that occurred at the time of the merger and continue to occur during the transition period.

Best Practice Areas

Throughout the Leadership Development Program, comprehensive assessment has been a major cornerstone of each participant's experience. Each participant is given several pieces of an assessment puzzle that will help in creating a meaningful learning journey. The assessment is multifaceted and comes from a variety of perspectives. It involves self-assessment; input from immediate supervisors, co-workers, colleagues, and employees; psychometric test results; a thinking preference inventory; a team roles survey; a compilation of feedback from nine to twelve assessors that is based on Development Workshop performance; and ongoing assessment and feedback from Learning Team members and advisors.

The Learning Teams offer a nontraditional, customized approach to learning for each participant that encourages personal improvement, skill building, and change. The teams combine diversity of gender, thinking preference, and professional background in creating a rich, self-directed learning environment for each individual. The success of these teams, and the individuals within them, is based on two key elements. The first is the primary focus on the needs of each learner. The second is the fact that the learning content is determined entirely by the learner on the basis of assessment feedback and the individual's personal and professional aims and goals.

The support and mentoring that takes place within these teams contributes to team-building that grows the individual and the organization. The connection that is formed within these teams is, at best, inexplicable.

At a recent Recognition Ceremony, a participant of a 1994 Learning Team shared the following:

> The Learning Team becomes a second family. I feel better when one of my team members walks into the room. Without words, without contact, I just feel more at ease, more comfortable. Together, we learn, we grow, we celebrate our successes and we grieve our heartbreaks. It is an honor and a privilege to be a part of this Learning Team.

Exhibit 8.1: Performance Criteria Survey for Gundersen Lutheran

Below is listed a comprehensive range of performance criteria that have been drawn from job analysis and performance review processes in a variety of large organizations in the United States. Please review the list and definitions, and then prioritize them according to how you feel they best reflect the criteria most significant for managerial and leadership excellence in Gundersen Lutheran.

Please indicate, using the 1–6 scale below, the degree to which each of the criteria below are, in your view, critical for the success of Gundersen Lutheran managers *in general*:

1. This criterion is critical—an essential "must have" for achieving excellence.
2. This criterion is very important.
3. This criterion is important.
4. This criterion is not particularly important.
5. This criterion is of little importance.
6. This criterion is not important at all.

_____ **Adaptability**
Maintains effectiveness in varying work environments where circumstances and priorities are changing

_____ **Ambition**
Is driven to do well, be effective, achieve, succeed, and progress quickly through the organization

_____ **Analytical reasoning**
Analyzes, interprets, and evaluates complex information and arrives at logical deductions and conclusions

Linkage Inc.'s Best Practices in Leadership Development Handbook, edited by David Giber, Louis Carter, and Marshall Goldsmith. Copyright © 2000 by Linkage Press and Jossey-Bass/Pfeiffer, San Francisco, CA.

_____ **Appraisal**

Evaluates subordinates' performance accurately and fairly, and provides effective feedback on a regular basis

_____ **Compliance**

Adheres to policies and/or procedures, or seeks approval from the appropriate authority before making changes

_____ **Decisiveness**

Exhibits a readiness to make decisions, render judgments, take action, or commit oneself

_____ **Delegating**

Appropriately designates responsibility and refers problems or activities to others for effective action

_____ **Developing others**

Develops subordinates' competence by planning effective experiences related to current and future jobs, in the light of individual motivations, interests, and current work situation

_____ **Empathy**

Understands the feelings and attitudes of others and is able to put oneself in others' shoes

_____ **Entrepreneurialism**

Recognizes and takes advantage of new and/or expanded business opportunities

_____ **Fact finding**

Uses investigative skills and research to gather information relevant to organizational issues, trends, and problems

_____ **Flexibility**

Is able to modify approach in order to achieve a goal

_____ **Following through**

Establishes procedures and monitors the progress and results of plans and activities to ensure that goals are achieved

_____ **Independence**
Takes actions in which the dominant influence is personal conviction rather than the influence of others' opinions

_____ **Influencing**
Uses appropriate interpersonal styles, methods of communication, data, and argument to gain agreement or acceptance of an idea, plan, or activity

_____ **Initiative/creativity**
Is proactive, self-starting, seizes opportunities, and originates action to achieve goals

_____ **Innovation**
Is change-oriented and able to generate and/or recognize creative solutions in varying work-related situations

_____ **Integrity**
Maintains and promotes organizational, social, and ethical standards and values in the conduct of internal and external business activities

_____ **Interpersonal sensitivity**
Deals with others in a manner that shows a capacity to understand and respond appropriately to their needs

_____ **Intuition**
Uses hunch, feel, and "sixth sense" to identify issues and possible solutions

_____ **Learning ability**
Assimilates and applies new, job-related information in a timely manner

_____ **Listening**
Draws out opinions and information from others in face-to-face interaction

_____ **Negotiating**
Communicates information and/or arguments effectively, gains support and acceptance of other parties, and compromises when appropriate

_____ **Numerical reasoning**
Analyzes, interprets, and evaluates complex numerical and statistical information and arrives at logical deductions and conclusions

_____ **Oral communication**

Expresses thoughts effectively and convincingly using appropriate verbal and non-verbal behavior to reinforce the content of the message

_____ **Performance orientation**

Is concerned to optimize the effective and efficient management of available resources

_____ **Personal impact**

Creates a positive first impression, commands attention and respect, and is socially confident

_____ **Political and organizational awareness**

Considers probable support or opposition to ideas or action in terms of external, organizational, professional, or sectional interests and constraints

_____ **Prioritizing**

Accurately assesses the relative importance of objectives, activities, and events in relation to organizational goals

_____ **Resilience**

Is able to maintain high performance levels under pressure and/or opposition and is able to maintain composure in the face of disappointments, criticism, and/or rejection

_____ **Risk taking**

Ability to stretch or go beyond personal/professional comfort with confidence in own skills and abilities

_____ **Self-awareness**

Is aware of personal strengths, needs, and limitations and the part they play in the exercise of effective management

_____ **Self-confidence**

Demonstrates a genuine belief in the likelihood of personal success and communicates a positive self-esteem to others

_____ **Sociability**

Is socially outgoing and able to mix easily with others

_____ **Strategic planning**

Sets goals and objectives based on a clear vision of the future and works towards their achievement while ensuring that short-term goals are met

_____ **Teamwork**

Cooperates with others and is able, where appropriate, to complement the roles of others by taking on the role of leader, peer, or subordinate

_____ **Tenacity**

Stays with a position or plan of action until the desired objective is achieved or is no longer reasonably attainable

_____ **Time management**

Is able to plan and organize own use of time, meets deadlines, and doesn't have to rely on the last minute

_____ **Troubleshooting**

Able to gather information and quickly and accurately identify the causes of problems in work-related activities and processes

_____ **Vision**

Is able to view events and possibilities from multiple perspectives, develop future-oriented scenarios, "helicopter" above the current situation, and see the "bigger picture"

_____ **Vitality**

Maintains a high activity level, is enthusiastic, motivated, and energetic

_____ **Written communication**

Expresses thoughts in writing in a grammatically correct, well-organized, and well-structured manner

Exhibit 8.2: Program Map

LEADERSHIP DEVELOPMENT PROGRAM

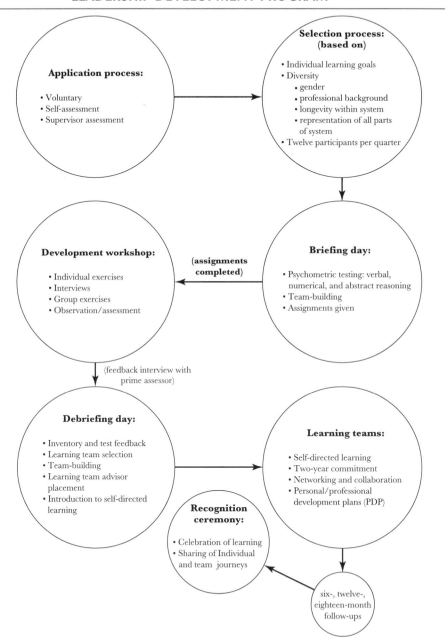

Linkage Inc.'s Best Practices in Leadership Development Handbook, edited by David Giber, Louis Carter, and Marshall Goldsmith. Copyright © 2000 by Linkage Press and Jossey-Bass/Pfeiffer, San Francisco, CA.

Exhibit 8.3: Participant Assessment: Rating Form

LEADERSHIP DEVELOPMENT WORKSHOP

The rating scale is:

1. Very effective in all aspects
2. Effective in all aspects
3. Effective in the majority of aspects, but less than effective in some aspects
4. Effective in some aspects, but less than effective in the majority of aspects
5. Ineffective in all aspects
6. Very ineffective in all aspects

A. Name of the person you are assessing: _____

B. Analytical Reasoning: Analyzes, interprets, and evaluates complex information and arrives at logical deductions and conclusions

__ (1)　　__ (2)　　__ (3)　　__ (4)　　__ (5)　　__ (6)

Comments—Analytical Reasoning: _____

_____

_____

C. Strategic Planning: Plans ahead, sets long-term goals and objectives, and works toward their achievement while ensuring that short-term goals are met

__ (1)　　__ (2)　　__ (3)　　__ (4)　　__ (5)　　__ (6)

Comments—Strategic Planning: _____

_____

_____

D. Vision: Views current events and possibilities from multiple perspectives and develop future-oriented scenarios

__ (1)　　__ (2)　　__ (3)　　__ (4)　　__ (5)　　__ (6)

Linkage Inc.'s Best Practices in Leadership Development Handbook, edited by David Giber, Louis Carter, and Marshall Goldsmith. Copyright © 2000 by Linkage Press and Jossey-Bass/Pfeiffer, San Francisco, CA.

Comments—Vision: _____

_____

_____

E. Teamwork: Acts cooperatively to achieve results in an environment of mutual respect and is able to complement the roles of others in a variety of teamwork settings; appropriately assumes responsibility and/or refers problems or activities to others for effective action

___ (1)   ___ (2)   ___ (3)   ___ (4)   ___ (5)   ___ (6)

Comments—Teamwork: _____

_____

_____

F. Developing Others: Develops and acknowledges colleagues' competence by planning effective experiences related to current and future jobs, in the light of individual motivation, interests, and current work situation

___ (1)   ___ (2)   ___ (3)   ___ (4)   ___ (5)   ___ (6)

Comments—Developing Others: _____

_____

_____

G. Adaptability: Maintains effectiveness in varying work environments where circumstances and priorities are changing; recognizes opportunities, is flexible, innovative, and change-oriented

___ (1)   ___ (2)   ___ (3)   ___ (4)   ___ (5)   ___ (6)

Comments—Adaptability: _____

_____

_____

H. Decisiveness: Is proactive and exhibits a readiness to make informed decisions, render judgments, take purposeful action or commit oneself, and take risks

___ (1)   ___ (2)   ___ (3)   ___ (4)   ___ (5)   ___ (6)

Comments—Decisiveness: _____

_____

_____

I. Self-Awareness: Is aware of personal strengths, needs, and limitations and the part they play in effective leadership

__ (1)   __ (2)   __ (3)   __ (4)   __ (5)   __ (6)

Comments—Self-Awareness: _____

_____

_____

J. Communication: Communicates thoughts effectively both in writing and orally, using appropriate verbal and nonverbal behavior to reinforce the content of this message

__ (1)   __ (2)   __ (3)   __ (4)   __ (5)   __ (6)

Comments—Communication: _____

_____

_____

K. Interpersonal Sensitivity: Relates to colleagues in a considerate manner that shows dignity, respect, and understanding, and responds appropriately to their needs

__ (1)   __ (2)   __ (3)   __ (4)   __ (5)   __ (6)

Comments—Interpersonal Sensitivity: _____

_____

_____

L. Integrity: Maintains and promotes organizational, social, and ethical standards and values in the conduct of internal and external business activities

__ (1)   __ (2)   __ (3)   __ (4)   __ (5)   __ (6)

Comments—Strategic Integrity: _____

_____

_____

Exhibit 8.4: PDP Guidelines

Gundersen Lutheran
Leadership Development Program

- *What do I want to achieve?*
  Specifically, based on your prime assessor feedback of strength and deficit and, most important, your own personal reflections since that time, write down a succinct statement of what you want to accomplish.
- *What are you doing at the present time to get what you want?*
  Scrutinize the behaviors that you are consciously and unconsciously using to achieve your goals. Which ones work, which don't? Make a commitment to stop using non-productive behaviors and focus on those that work.
- *Is your behavior helping?*
  Examine why or why not. What purpose do you have for using that behavior(s)? Is it positive, helpful, and meaningful? If is isn't, are you willing to change your behaviors—how will you do it? Why do you think it isn't working? Focus on you, your actions, and your behaviors.
- *What is your plan to accomplish your goals?*
  Here's where you really need to be action oriented. Your plan needs to focus on "to do's." Include:

Who:	needs to know; are barriers; provides support?
What:	*specifically* do you want to do?
When:	is your timeline?
Why:	do you want to do this?
Where:	will you go?
How much:	will it cost in time, money, resources?
How did you do:	your plan to evaluate and report back?

- *Whose support do you need?*
  Are you willing to ask for support? Are you willing to share with others what you want to accomplish and your plan to do it? Are you willing to ask for their input and ideas?
- *When things fall short are you willing to recycle and start over?*
  How will you do this? Anticipate the roadblocks and create new venues around them to a road that leads toward the successful meeting of your objective.
- *Other ideas?*

Exhibit 8.5: Learning Contract

Learning Objectives	Method of Learning	Evidence of Learning- Outcome	Activities to be Undertaken	Help Needed	Date to be Done

Linkage Inc.'s Best Practices in Leadership Development Handbook, edited by David Giber, Louis Carter, and Marshall Goldsmith. Copyright © 2000 by Linkage Press and Jossey-Bass/Pfeiffer, San Francisco, CA.

About the Contributor

Michelle Fellenz (pfellenz@execp.com) is a human resource development consultant at Gundersen Lutheran in LaCrosse, Wisconsin. Within this position, she works with administrators, physicians, managers, and staff in the areas of leadership development, change management, team-building, and performance management. Fellenz enjoys working with people and organizations in designing, implementing, and evaluating innovative training programs that contribute to organizational growth and development.

Fellenz has a master's degree in industrial/organizational psychology from Mankato State University in Minnesota and she is currently working toward a doctorate in education and leadership from Saint Mary's University in Minnesota.

CHAPTER NINE

IMASCO LIMITED

This chapter outlines an action learning-based program that is
designed to develop the strategic thinking capabilities of
senior and middle management.

Company Description

Imasco Limited is a $10-billion (Canadian dollars) diversified conglomerate focusing on consumer goods and services in North America. They compete in the tobacco, financial services, drugstore, and land development industries. Like most conglomerates, Imasco faces the challenge of leading and allocating resources across a diverse group of companies. This is complicated by a company culture valuing decentralized control.

The Concept of Action Learning

The characteristics of a typical action learning experience include (1) an emphasis on learning by doing, (2) team performances, (3) actual and substantive company issues that put participants into problem-solver roles, and (4) team decisions that are formalized into presentations.[1] This chapter describes the lessons from one such program and its implications for designing action learning experiences with greater impact. In this case, action learning has been carefully tailored to meet very specific organizational needs and objectives.

Building a Business Case for Action Learning at Imasco

As a training tool, one of the most effective contributions that action learning can play is in the area of developing a general manager's *mindset* for mid-level managers. Through a careful selection of projects and experiences, action learning can create for participants a condensed experience of the strategic and organizational leadership issues that the general manager faces. Imasco Limited, in collaboration with the authors, has designed an action learning program that quite successfully instills an understanding of that leadership mindset. Its success is tracked through the promotions of participants into general management positions after the program, the general assessments of their performance once in those positions, and ratios of internal versus external hires for senior positions.

In terms of day-to-day operating issues, the corporate headquarters takes a basic hands-off approach. Instead, they manage longer term through three major planning processes: the financial, strategic, and human resources reviews. On an annual basis, operating companies provide the corporate headquarters with plans in these areas to which they are held accountable. Over the years, there has been a growing recognition that the center could play a significant role in developing the leadership potential of managers across all of the operating companies. For example, certain operating companies are too small to afford extensive training programs or fast-track career opportunities. There is also a desire to deepen the strategic thinking capabilities throughout the middle and senior management ranks in all the businesses.

In addition to leadership development, other issues have shaped the design of the Imasco management program. There was a concern that few managers in the operating companies were aware of the guiding principles and philosophy of Imasco corporate. Rather, operations had been run in such a decentralized manner that many division managers knew little about the corporate headquarters and the overall corporation. Part of this was due to an acquisition strategy that historically had sought profitability and growth in a portfolio of companies over strategic integration of the businesses. Originally starting out as Canada's largest tobacco company, the firm's strategy had been to diversify away from a dependence on tobacco products by acquiring retail businesses and food and beverage manufacturers, then moving into a trust company, a savings and loan, a fast-food chain, a drug store chain, and a land development business. A new corporate CEO, Brian Levitt, was revamping the overall strategy so as to build a more unified strategic synthesis of these varied consumer businesses.

In addition, corporate human resources executives were driving an effort to formalize succession planning and career development for high-potential managers across all the operating companies. It was felt that numerous managers could be groomed for positions demanding their talents in other operating companies. For example, a talented information systems manager might be transferred and promoted to an executive position at another operating company needing his or her business acumen.

Finally, there was a sense at the executive level that successful initiatives undertaken by individual operating groups were not being transferred across the company. Rather, they remained isolated within their operating group. For example, one division had developed superb market segmentation skills, another had developed state-of-the-art inventory control systems. Yet these competencies failed to travel beyond the operating company.

Objectives of the Action Learning Team

In response to these concerns, a management development program was initiated by corporate human resources. Action learning was chosen as the vehicle to accomplish the task. With the issues outlined above, the Imasco Senior Management Development Program, as it would be called, set out as its mission to accomplish three major objectives:

1. To develop the general management and strategic skills of the participants
2. To expose the participants to Imasco Limited's guiding principles and philosophy, as well as each company's key issues, core competencies, challenges, and action plans
3. To identify and accelerate the leadership development of high-potential managers in the Imasco companies

It was also hoped that the program would help to foster relationships and communication links between individuals in the different companies, and that this in turn would lead to cross-fertilization of best practices and heighten organizational learning.

The Action Learning Program

To accomplish these objectives, an annual three-and-a-half-week program was designed around three interlocking components that are specifically structured to meet the program's objectives. The components include (1) on-site operating company visits, (2) a one-week customized management education program, and (3) a work project called "Imasco: The Next Generation." Facilitators (in this case, the authors) play an active role in the learning experience as we will soon explain. Every year, the participants, a select group of twelve to fifteen "fast trackers," all holding responsible middle management positions, are nominated by the senior executives of each operating company. The program has been successfully run for five consecutive years.

The idea behind the three components of the program is that the modules will not only build on what is being learned by participants but do so in a manner that reinforces learning at every step. For example, the operating company visits serve two primary purposes. The first is to provide a general learning experience about the corporate headquarters and the operating companies. Underlying this exposure is the goal of affording participants a "general manager's view" through the perspectives shared by senior executives in presentations and discussion sessions. The second purpose emerges as a learning experience about executive leadership, strategy formulation, and organizational change issues. Each company visited essentially serves as a live case study in which all of these issues can be explored.

The second component of the program—a customized educational program—is designed to integrate learnings from these "live" case studies around the latest knowledge in leadership, strategy formulation, organizational change, and other topics relevant to Imasco company issues. The classroom affords an opportunity to reflect and more thoughtfully critique and comprehend how each operating company is facing its challenges.

The third component—the "Imasco: The Next Generation" project— is the integrative mechanism for participants to assemble not only their overall learnings but to put forth actual recommendations. These recommendations take shape in the form of formal presentations to Imasco senior executives. The experience serves the dual purpose of putting participants in a general manager's mindset and of promoting further exploration of company issues through direct interaction with the senior-most team. In conclusion, each of the three components serves to build on the other and foster more integrated and more profound learning.

We will now explore each component in detail to see how it actually works.

Operating Company Visits

The operating company visits typically last one and a half days per company and are divided between presentations by senior management, question and answer periods, and site visits to production facilities, outlets, or service centers (see Exhibit 9.1). Given the number of operating companies, this stage takes two weeks.

A typical company visit begins with the CEO of the operating company reviewing the major competitive challenges he or she is currently facing and strategic initiatives that the company is undertaking. Then follow presentations by the functional executives. For instance, at one time, Shoppers' Drug Mart—the company's drug store chain—was responding to the arrival of Wal-Mart in Canada. One of the company's primary strategic initiatives was a major overhaul of inventory and distribution systems to ensure that the company's retail outlets would be cost-competitive with Wal-Mart. This company's presentation was built around the initiative itself and how the various functions were involved in the effort.

In addition, each of the operating companies has a distinctive strength or core competence in one or two functional areas. A portion of the presentations are therefore devoted to understanding the operating company's expertise in these areas to facilitate a transfer of knowledge across the corporation. In the case of Imperial Tobacco, its marketing function has a significant amount of time on the agenda. This reflects their outstanding expertise in brand management as they control close to 70 percent of the Canadian market with three major brands. The presentations are followed by onsite visits to an operational location where products are produced or delivered to customers, as well as to competitor outlets.

In the early editions of the program, presentations were by functional area. For example, the chief financial officer would provide an overview of the company's financial picture. The marketing executive would present on the organization's marketing strategy. What we discovered, however, was that these became "silo" presentations. There were few or no interconnections made between functional areas and the overall strategic initiatives of the operating company. As a result, participants failed to gain an integrative or general manager's perspective—a principal aim of the program. In the third year, the presentation formats were redesigned around the themes of a company's one or two major strategic initiatives. Initiatives were chosen that cut across multiple functions and involved both major strategic and organizational changes. This presentation format forced functional executives to present not only their functional role in an overall strategic context but also its cross-functional dimensions. In addition, the operating companies were provided with a generic outline of topics and were asked to cover the following points framed around current strategic initiatives:

- Strategic orientation: vision, values, objectives, and strategies
- Competitive and regulatory environment
- Internal organizational environment (current and future)
- Principal strategic initiatives and organizational changes
- Key resources, distinctive competencies of the organization

The aim has been for the participants to gain an understanding of a strategic initiative along all its possible dimensions:

1. What changes had occurred in the environment, or internally, to initiate the change?
2. How was the decision made?
3. What is the vision of where the company wants to go?
4. What areas of the company have to be brought into alignment for the new strategy to be successful?
5. How is the initiative being implemented?
6. What aspects of the organization's internal architecture have had to be changed?
7. Has there been resistance from any stakeholders?
8. What were typical political problems?
9. How was employee commitment developed to support the new direction?

An essential part of the operating company visits are question and answer periods that follow each presentation in addition to a dinner with the CEO.

Given that the operating companies organize the agenda, these question and answer periods are extremely important. They are an opportunity for the participants to ask candid and probing questions to ensure that a solid understanding of the real issues is developed. Effective questioning is important to get at the more sensitive issues. In the initial two years of the program, presentations were often designed to impress the participants rather than provide realistic descriptions of the obstacles that had to be overcome for their strategies to succeed. By the third year, however, a significant level of trust had developed in the program. At the prompting of facilitators and participant "alumni," the operating company presentations shifted fundamentally to very candid descriptions of operating and competitive challenges. What we learned is that trust is a critical part of any program such as this. It cannot be gained overnight; rather the operating companies needed "proofs" in terms of alumni learnings, respect of confidentiality, and the absence of negative repercussions from the corporate headquarters to develop full trust in the agenda of the program. Only then did presentations shift from highly optimistic to highly realistic overviews.

The quality of facilitation played a crucial role in not only ensuring realistic presentations but also in gaining trust. For example, participants are encouraged by the facilitators to actively look for confirmation of, or divergence from, what they have heard during the presentations. This serves as an opportunity for them to see and understand the issues associated with implementing organizational strategies. For example, if an executive team says they are committed to "customer service," participants are encouraged to look with a critical eye for all signs that affirm or contradict that strategic intent. For instance, if the operating company is a bank, participants would examine and question the level of consumer research, depth of knowledge of customer requirements, customer complaint mechanisms, employee reward systems, ease of doing business, time it takes to be served, customer support systems, and so on. During site visits, employees could even be questioned to determine whether the principles that guide their decisions are based on internal procedures or customer satisfaction.

One of the key characteristics of the Imasco program is the amount of time that participants spend with the executive management teams. In addition to the presentations, participants have the opportunity to meet with senior management at lunch, at the end of the onsite visit, and at dinner. They are encouraged to have open and frank discussions with all members of the senior team. In this way they are exposed to different leadership styles and philosophies across the different companies. This provides a unique opportunity to see how the different leaders approach similar problems. Furthermore, it gives participants an opportunity to question senior executives on multiple occasions as their understanding of company operations deepens. It is interesting to note that participant questioning does indeed become more strategic and persistent as time goes on.

Briefing and debriefing sessions are run by the facilitators, and these precede and follow each operating company visit. The pre-visit briefing is designed to help the participants sort through all of the information on the business they have received beforehand and to focus on the key issues that the industry and company are facing. Therefore, prior to their site visit, the participants have developed some understanding of the following:

- Critical success factors of the industry
- Industry evolution and trends
- Market opportunities and threats
- Company strategy and major operational challenges
- Competitors' strategies
- Specific company strengths and weaknesses

This allows participants to listen to the presentations with a more critical attitude and to ask more strategic questions than if they were hearing about the industry and company for the first time. It also forces them to think in a broader perspective, rather than concentrating on the operational areas of their own functional expertise. During the visit, participants are asked to look for concrete evidence of what they have heard, areas that are not aligned with the corporate strategy, and areas of learning both for and from the operating company. The debrief at the end of the each site visit is designed to consolidate, critique, and analyze what they have seen during the visit. With the "Imasco: The Next Generation" project in mind, they are asked to think about recommendations for the future of each operating company and Imasco Limited. The debrief sessions are also used to apply strategic models that participants were introduced to at the beginning of the program. The models include Boston Consulting Group's Product Portfolio, Michael Porter's Five Forces, Waterman and Peter's 7-S model, and Boynton and Victor's Dynamic Stability Model. Participants are then encouraged to use these models as a framework during the operating company visits and briefing sessions.

Conclusion. The idea behind the operating company visits is to expose participants to actual general managers grappling with both strategic and organizational issues. Through exposure to a range of live case studies, participants develop a significantly enhanced understanding of the general manager's mindset and the skill set they themselves must hone and/or acquire to be effective leaders. In essence, it serves as an opportunity to develop a true multifunctional and strategic mindset. It also heightens opportunities for the transfer of competencies across the operating groups. After implementation of the program, initiatives and expertise began to flow across operating company boundaries. For example, the fast-food company had been reexamining its market segmentation and repositioning its product offerings. One of the participants from the company arranged for a team of marketing specialists from Imperial Tobacco—a company widely recognized as the leader in brand management—to assist in the repositioning. Of particular note is the fact that this exchange can actually occur because the participants have been given enough power and resources within their own organizations to implement ideas or programs.

Customized Management Education Program

The third week of the program is devoted entirely to management education (see Exhibit 9.2 for a typical schedule). The topics and presenters are carefully chosen to reflect the issues that both the operating companies and corporate Imasco are currently dealing with and to expose the participants to leading edge thinkers. For instance, at one point, Imasco was starting to move into international markets such as China, and extensive coursework on globalization has been offered. In the most recent program, a day was devoted to information technology because Imasco is leveraging this tool for competitive advantage.

Subject areas that have been included to date are:

- Globalization
- Consumer demographics
- Organizational change
- Leadership
- Getting value from information technology
- Market segmentation
- Strategic use of financial controls

Separate discussion sessions are held to tie classroom learnings directly to the "real life" situations that the participants have experienced in the operating companies. For example, one operating group altered certain new products in response to information learned through sessions on demographics. A new approach to organizational change was implemented by another unit based on classroom applications. A more formal debriefing takes place at the end of each day to specifically discuss how the theories and models can be applied to each of the operating companies.

Each year, the educational portion is redesigned to reflect new needs within the operating companies. For example, in the first and second program years, the corporate headquarters had instituted a more sophisticated strategic review process. In response, coursework was designed around strategic skill development. In the third year, many of the operating companies were involved in implementing strategic changes and the issue of organizational change became paramount. A heavier emphasis and more sophisticated coursework on organizational change was then added to the curriculum.

Work Project: "Imasco: The Next Generation"

During the management education week, participants are put into multidisciplinary and multi-industry teams of five individuals and are asked to prepare a presentation on what they believe the corporation should look like ten years from now. This project encourages participants to combine both the practical and theoretical learnings, to think in a strategic fashion, and to work closely with their colleagues from other operating companies. In essence, it provides them with a real life case study. This approach is far more rigorous that the normal case study method as the situations are real, current, and the audience has an intimate knowledge of the companies. Recommendations, therefore, have to be realistic and have the potential to be implemented. For instance, the recommendations concerning the drug store operations (Shoppers' Drug Mart) have included investing extensively in information technology to control inventory costs and product availability, centralizing distribution to lower their purchasing and transportation costs, and entering the mail-order business to reach price-sensitive customers. One team also recognized that Shoppers' Drug Mart had very little expertise in distribution—an area of distinctive competence for the fast-food chain. Individuals from the two companies met to transfer and apply the knowledge of the fast-food chain and solved the issue more quickly and effectively.

In general, the presentations are detailed analyses of proposed action plans for Imasco corporate strategy, as well as for each operating company. They may incorporate the full range of internal organizational changes that will be required in each situation to realize the strategic initiatives being proposed. The projects become an exercise in systems thinking for the participants.

On the final day of the program, the teams present their recommendations to the Imasco limited chairman, chief executive officer, and chief financial officer. The seniority and caliber of this panel heightens participants' efforts toward an effective synthesis of learnings to date, and it provides further opportunities to learn from the feedback of senior management. An element of competitiveness among the groups is introduced by having multiple teams present. Each presentation is followed by an open exchange between participants and company executives on the pros and cons of the various recommendations. The program ends with a closing dinner, where the exchange between participants and senior management continues.

The facilitators act as advisors to the teams throughout the week as they are preparing the work project. Through continuous questioning they encourage the teams to see patterns throughout the organization, to think strategically to guide them through the use of the models where applicable, and to get the groups to view their recommendations from a senior management and customer point of view. The goal is to keep the thinking as strategic as possible, while making solid recommendations and understanding issues of implementation. Team members are also encouraged to work on companies other than their own to broaden their perspective.

Lessons Learned

After five years of experimentation and feedback from both participating managers and operating companies, we have concluded that action learning projects such as Imasco's depend on several critical success variables for their effectiveness. Specifically, we discovered that (1) the operating companies must be fully committed to the process in terms of time, resources, and candor; (2) participant team dynamics directly affect the quality of project outcomes; and (3) facilitators play an absolutely essential role—far more than we originally would have imagined.

It took three years to gain the full trust and commitment of the operating companies. This is a remarkable time span given the generally high level of rapport and trust that existed beforehand between the corporate headquarters and the operating groups in advance of the program's initiation. The most likely contributing factor is a historical one—the company's autonomous operating culture. We also learned that operating groups initially preferred the path of "least preparation" in designing their presentations. Essentially, company executives would dust off their most recent internal functional presentation and simply deliver that. The problem was that such presentations were geared toward internal audiences that possessed an already deep understanding of company issues and were interested only in narrow functional perspectives. This did not serve the learning goals of the program, which required presentations geared to audiences with a more limited knowledge of the business and needing a rich and integrated view of both multifunctional and strategic issues. It took three years of participant alumni whose enthusiasm for the program and internal championing for agenda changes led companies to invest the time necessary to innovate.

A second critical lesson we learned was that team dynamics could significantly affect the quality of the "Imasco: The Next Generation" project outcomes. Teams that developed strong norms around candor and diversity of perspectives produced more insightful and more creative project recommendations. Teams where a single individual or perspective dominated tended to be far less innovative and effective in their presentations. In one case, a participant led other participants to believe that he had superior knowledge, and in turn his recommendations constituted the majority of the team's proposals. In the end, his team produced a report that supported essentially the status quo and showed limited insight. Ultimately, it becomes the responsibility of the facilitators to ensure that team norms support openness of ideas and constructive confrontation.

Finally, facilitation turned out to be one of the critical success factors of the program along two dimensions. In the first case, participants found themselves constantly bombarded with information from field visits and had some difficulty in making sense of the complexity. As one participant noted: "Facilitation served to bring order to the chaos we were experiencing from the rapid pace of the operating company visits, and the volume of information." We found that more facilitation was better than less. For that reason, overview briefing sessions are now held at the start of a company visit. A debriefing session is then held at the end of the operating company visit, but *before* the participants have their end-of-day meeting with the executives. This helps them to consolidate the information they have gathered during the day and to crystallize the questions they would like to have answered in the evening session. The evening sessions end with a final, short debriefing session. Debriefing sessions are also held at the end of each management education day. The goal is to spend the time working through how the models and frameworks can be applied to the different operating companies. Facilitators have to play highly objective roles and be willing to lead off in the initial operating company visits with the more challenging questions to executives—role modeling norms of candor and constructive challenging. They essentially act in the same manner when briefing participant groups.

Conclusion

The Imasco program illustrates the application of an action learning format based on internal operating groups as " live case studies" to assist high-potential managers to learn about leadership, strategy, and organizational change. More important, it relies on multiple design mechanisms to heighten opportunities for learning—team-based applications of lessons, careful participant selection, multiple windows for reflection and discussion, extensive facilitation, and project accountability to the company's senior-most executives. These are all crucial to ensure that such programs have impact beyond the experience itself.

Exhibit 9.1: Operating Company Site Visit Schedule of Activities

Day One:

8:00 a.m.–9:00 a.m.	Pre-visit briefing on operating company:

- Critical challenges
- Leadership
- Industry and competition

9:00 a.m.–10:30 a.m.	Opening presentation by operating company CEO with question and answer period—key organization and marketplace challenges
10:30 a.m.–4:00 p.m.	A series of presentations by senior executives on critical challenges facing the operating company
4:00 p.m.–5:30 p.m.	Visit to actual operations
5:30 p.m.–6:30 p.m.	Debrief of day—focus on key learnings
6:30 p.m.–10:00 p.m.	Reception and dinner with executives: —question and answer session with CEO and senior team

Day Two:

8:00 a.m.–10:30 a.m.	Visit to additional company operations or competitor outlets
10:30 a.m.–12:00 a.m.	Functional presentations on company challenges and core competencies
12:00 p.m.–1:30 p.m.	Lunch and closing debrief of visit to operating company

Exhibit 9.2: Management Education Program Schedule

Day One	Day Two	Day Three	Day Four	Day Five
a.m.	**a.m.**	**a.m.**	**a.m.**	**a.m.**
Globalization: Cross-cultural teamwork	Strategic thinking	Organizational change	Market segmentation	Leadership
p.m.	**p.m.**	**p.m.**	**p.m.**	**p.m**
Managing subordinates in a cross-cultural context Application exercises	Applications of strategic thinking to company case studies and site visits	Applications of organizational change tactics and approaches to company case studies and site visits	Demographic trends Application exercises of market seg-mentation and demographics to company case studies and site visits	Leadership 360-degree feedback Self-assessment and application exercises
Evening	**Evening**	**Evening**	**Evening**	**Evening**
"Imasco: The Next Generation" project work group preparation	"Imasco: The Next Generation" project work group preparation	"Imasco: The Next Generation" project work group preparation	"Imasco: The Next Generation" project work group preparation	"Imasco: The Next Generation" project work group preparation

Linkage Inc.'s Best Practices in Leadership Development Handbook, edited by David Giber, Louis Carter, and Marshall Goldsmith. Copyright © 2000 by Linkage Press and Jossey-Bass/Pfeiffer, San Francisco, CA.

Notes

1. Dotlich, D. L., and J. L. Noel. *Action Learning.* San Francisco: Jossey-Bass, 1998.

About the Contributors

Jay A. Conger (jconger@sba.usc.edu), executive director of the Leadership Institute at the University of Southern California, is one of the world's experts on leadership. An outstanding teacher, he has been selected by

BusinessWeek as the best business school professor to teach leadership to executives. Author of more than sixty articles and eight books, he researches leadership, boards of directors, the management of organizational change, and the training and development of leaders and managers. His articles have appeared in the *Harvard Business Review, Organizational Dynamics, Business & Strategy, Leadership Quarterly, Academy of Management Review,* and *Journal of Organizational Behavior.* One of his books, *Learning to Lead* (1992), has been described by *Fortune* magazine as "the source" for understanding leadership training. His newest book entitled *Building Leaders* (Jossey-Bass, 1999) explores how corporations are developing future generations of leadership talent. Some of his other books include *The Leader's Change Handbook* (1998), *Charismatic Leadership in Organizations* (1998), and *Spirit at Work* (1994). In recognition of his work on leadership education, Conger was invited three years ago to join the Harvard Business School to assist in their redesign of the school's organizational behavior course around leadership issues. In addition, he has been actively involved in executive education at INSEAD, a European business school located in France. He received his bachelor's degree from Dartmouth College, his M.B.A. from the University of Virginia, and his D.B.A. from the Harvard Business School. Prior to his academic career, he worked in government and as an international marketing manager for a high technology company.

Bridgit Courey (bcourey@corp-mailbox.com), manager of human resources planning and development at Imasco Limited, leads action-oriented executive development initiatives. During her five-year tenure in this role, emphasis has been on the early identification and cross-functional development of leadership talent throughout the Imasco group of companies. Courey began her career as a chartered accountant and subsequently applied her financial expertise to the executive compensation area. She draws on her own multidisciplinary experience to help shape organizational learning at Imasco.

CHAPTER TEN

THE MATHWORKS

This chapter outlines a "just-in-time" transition to a cross-functional team structure, bolstered by action learning, exposure to senior executives, and team leader rotation, in order to make dramatic improvements in the efficiency of the operations department.

Introduction

The MathWorks is a leading developer and supplier of technical computing software. Founded in 1984 in Natick, Massachusetts, the company has seen exponential growth in the last five years and now employs more than 500 people. A privately held company, The MathWorks has been profitable every year since its inception. Its global customer base includes some of the world's most innovative technology companies, government research labs, financial institutions, and more than 2,000 universities.

Objective

This case study involves the operations department whose forty-person staff reports to two senior managers directed by Elizabeth Haight, vice president of operations. The case study begins in 1994 and details a two-year period of transformative change. The strategic objectives of the change effort were to "dehassle operations" and decrease cycle time. Haight believed the poor business results were symptomatic of an operations culture that accepted poor performance as the norm. From a leadership development perspective, the objective was to create a new culture (a "leaderful" culture) where every individual, at all levels, accepted full responsibility for the success of operations. This chapter outlines how Haight and her senior managers made that happen with the help of Options for Change.

The Presenting Problem

The operations initiative was launched when Jack Little, founder and president of The MathWorks, sent out an informal questionnaire asking all employees to name the company's biggest internal hassle. The operations department won hands down. The department was consistently behind in fulfilling orders and customer complaints had reached all the way to the president's office. Operations staff felt victimized by their customers. Their mantra was, "Poor me, I'm overworked."

Haight and her senior management team assessed the situation. The process was fragmented. Each staff person operated as an isolated unit, responsible only for his or her territory. No one asked for help or felt the need to cooperate. Multiple handoffs resulted in orders taking seven to ten days to turn around. Because the staff couldn't see the whole process or feel a sense of ownership, they didn't consider it a big deal if a folder sat on their desks for two days. With six people in an order fulfillment chain each sitting on a folder for two days, the department was in big trouble. There was constant complaining, blaming, and "scapegoating."

A Radical Structural Change

Haight and her managers agreed that the situation had become urgent and little changes were not working. They wanted to try something radical and were gratified to receive the support of the executive group. The high value placed on innovation and risk taking are clear signs of a primarily random organizational culture (see Figure 10.1). From President Jack Little

FIGURE 10.1.   SYSTEM TYPES.

		Enabled Version	Disabled Version
☆	Random: • Individuality and autonomy • Creative excellence • The individual comes first	• Entrepreneurial • Competitive • Flexible	• Chaotic • Crisis-oriented • Hard to get closure
△	Closed: • Hierarchy • Policies and procedures • The organization comes first	• Clear chain of command • Strong leadership • Quick decisions	• Tyrannical leadership • Disempowerment • Secrecy, fear
⇒	Synchronous: • Alignment • Vision-driven • The values come first	• Strong purpose and vision • Aligned values and beliefs • Harmony	• Cult-like • Inbred • Minimal communication
◯	Open: • Collaboration • Teams and consensus • The process comes first	• Inclusion • Diversity • Empowerment at all levels	• Can't make a decision • Reaches false consensus • All talk, no action

David Kantor, Larry Constantine © 1999 Options for Change

on down, the company took pride in its entrepreneurial spirit, symbolized by its motto, "Change is good."

Typical for a rapidly growing company, The MathWorks had begun to show increasing signs of a hierarchical, functionally-segmented or *closed* culture. In fact, this compartmentalization was exactly the problem in operations. At this stage, it is critical that an organization acquire effective communication and collaboration skills, in order to bridge the gap between the subcultures and avoid resistance.

Fortunately, the innovative and risk-taking values won out. With the support of the executive group, operations management decided to set up a cross-functional team structure, a good example of the open system. In the best entrepreneurial spirit, they said, "Let's try it, learn from our mistakes, and keep refining it." In a matter of weeks the managers privately reengineered the entire department, documenting and analyzing the workflow process, then mapping out and implementing a new structure comprising six cross-functional teams. In a closed system, this strategy would have reduced trust and increased fear and apathy. In the context of operation's random culture, it was just another new idea to try.

Haight called the whole staff together on a Friday afternoon and announced that the new process would be implemented on the following Monday. She explained the new roles and relationships and said that the management team, for the first month, would be a triage unit, available on the floor to clarify, invent, and reinforce the new process. Physically, managers of operations actually left their offices and set up desks in an open common area.

The department had fun with the new random-open system. It was a joy for people to be able to pass their "problems" to the managers. The triage unit worked hard to remove all obstacles and excuses to change, and reinforced the new way of working. Instead of rescuing their staff, the managers encouraged them to be creative, take initiative, and cooperate across traditional boundaries. The results speak for themselves. Within thirty days, operations was shipping in twenty-four hours. The staff enjoyed their newfound success as much as management. The new culture had begun.

Key Features of the Leadership Development Program

The leadership development program at MathWorks contained several key features that are critical to a successful leadership educator program.

Action Learning

The leadership development efforts detailed in this case succeeded in large part due to an action learning approach. The overnight transition to a cross-functional team structure required operations staff to sink or swim. Vice President of Operations Elizabeth Haight, and her managers leveraged the chaos and uncertainty they had created into a kind of survival learning that was quickly internalized. When formal training was called for, the model was always based on participants' real work situations as opposed to generic examples, and it was always delivered on a just-in-time basis.

Exposure to Executives

Buy-in to the new structure and leadership readiness would have been impossible without the support and guidance of senior managers. From the triage mechanism through their ongoing mentoring role, operations managers modeled the leadership qualities and behaviors that the new team leaders needed to adopt. Learning in parallel with team leaders, managers' example proved a powerful motivator throughout the system. In addition, the executive team's initial acceptance of and support for the department's radical course of action was critical. With buy-in at the top secure, operations staff was able to trust in the wisdom of the restructuring and accept their new responsibilities with a feeling of safety.

Cross-functional Rotation

Creating a "leaderful" culture in the department meant fostering a sense of mutual accountability across all departmental functions. This was modeled in the initial restructuring by managers who became familiar with every aspect of operations in addition to their own area of expertise. In the current organizational structure, team leaders are encouraged to rotate to other teams in order to expand their competencies. Managers must now be able to mentor not just those staff members reporting to them, but anyone within the department who seeks their assistance.

The Need for Leadership Development

The new structure would become the catalyst for a new culture. Cross-functional teamwork would force a more mature level of interaction and empowerment. The newly formed culture—now filled with leaders—would be the key to better business results. Each person would see themselves as part of this interconnected business unit, responsible for its success or failure. A strong culture would outlive any one individual.

At the time of the restructuring, the culture was young. Staff were dependent on their managers and asked them constantly what to do or how to solve a problem. At the same time they resented being told and complained to each other. Most of the people in operations were just out of school. There was inexperience characterized by complaining, cliques, and gossip. They bonded around the impossible workload. It was clear that merely changing the structure would not change these collective behaviors and norms. The change leaders needed to provide them with the experience and support to mature.

Using managers as a triage team proved to be an excellent mechanism for providing that support initially and was probably the most important reinforcement of the new way of working. It worked as an instant mirror or feedback function. Managers were able to observe the old patterns as they happened and to redirect the behavior.

At the beginning everybody was euphoric with the new team structure. Managers stayed closely involved with the teams, going to team meetings, and working to make it easy for them to succeed. The sense of euphoria lasted about a year. Then, team members hit an emotional wall—a tide of resistance. Individuals were frustrated by the new organizational structure. In the past there had been a definite line of command, the rules had been clear, people knew how to get ahead. Each person was only accountable for himself or herself. But now the rules had changed. People complained, "I can't get ahead because you changed the rules" or "You changed the structure on me just when I thought I knew where I was going." Again, management did not rescue them, but made them look at their own behavior. The old structure had provided a crutch for dependency. Removing the crutch by changing the structure made some people angry.

The biggest problem was a lack of leadership ability within the teams. It was hard to get people to show their leadership abilities or to develop those abilities to the next level. And with the amount of responsibility management was giving them, if they didn't learn to work together, they would start to feel stressed and weighed down, out of control. They had all the permission in the world, but they didn't see themselves as leaders. Everyone wanted to be a follower or a challenger.

In this new, webbed structure, it was necessary to refine collaborative skills. Breadth of knowledge was emphasized over depth in one particular area. As the staff began to realize that the managers were not going to solve all the problems, they saw the need for teamwork. As the responsibility shifted from managers to team leaders, an urgent need emerged. At that point, team leaders were chosen and change leaders became more focused on training and giving the teams and team leaders the tools they needed to work within the team structure.

The Leadership Development Program

The operations' management team felt they could leverage the chaos they had created to provide new learnings throughout the structure and develop team leadership from the ground up. Their approach contained three critical components.

1. Managers as Models or Coaches
   - Operating in the new paradigm
   - Transitioning from manager to coach

2. Training for Teams
   - Working collaboratively, especially problem solving
   - Working cross-functionally
   - Operating in a flat hierarchy
   - Observing group process to make course corrections, especially conflict resolution
   - Being proactive and self-directed
3. Training for Team Leaders
   - Meeting management
   - Facilitation
   - Influence tactics
   - Decision making
   - Conflict resolution

Managers as Models or Coaches

Framing the transformation as a systemic change for operations (as opposed to a leadership problem) minimized resistance and maximized buy-in from the managers. The importance of management living the new collaborative behaviors themselves cannot be overemphasized. Too many change efforts are torpedoed by management's inability to "walk the talk." The managers needed support from the top that the new rules also applied to them, for example, that they wouldn't be punished for risk-taking and making mistakes, only for not trying. Then and only then could they model the new behaviors for their staff.

Managers launched into honest conversations about their roles in the new cross-functional structure. Up to this point they had all been operating in a fairly traditional leadership hierarchy. Starting with the triage structure, that hierarchy had been inverted. Managers knew they would have to learn and model different behavior, stretching themselves even if they weren't sure what that meant. The managers got support from their vice president to live with the ambiguity. Subsequently, managers began to trust the process of changing their leadership behaviors.

The inverted hierarchy flattened the power structure, making management and staff more like equals. Managers were not just talking about teamwork and collaboration, but they were actually enacting it. They began to communicate and interact in a different way. Staff responded by becoming more proactive, participatory, and "leaderful" themselves. Both managers and staff began to see leadership through new lenses.

Management spent a lot of time coaching and mentoring, teaching people how to manage their emotions, how to get people to support their views on real business issues. They taught them how to have a good argument, how to express a point of view or make a claim and support it. If somebody was flying off the handle and making emotional claims, a managers' job was to bring them back and say, "Let's talk about the reasoning behind that claim."

Managers benefitted from the parallel process of coaching each other, the team leaders, and anyone who came knocking. They read a lot of current management thinking and attended conferences. They were sponges absorbing best practices. They weren't trying to reinvent the wheel, but they did screen all their new ideas for fit to their culture. They learned from daily experiences about the competencies they needed in this new weblike system. They used a competency database to develop a 360-degree review process for themselves. It was an opportunity for feedback and to model the open system. They started to view themselves not as managers, but as change agents, coaches, and internal consultants.

As fairly inexperienced individuals, many team members had not learned to differentiate between their own emotional reactions and projections and other realities. This approach afforded many opportunities to hold up the mirror in real time and teach team members to find better ways to react. Managers reinforced the desired behaviors; they believed they would learn best through teaching.

An early success on the coaching front was an initiative called open-door-Friday. It provided a weekly opportunity for people to contribute new ideas or vent their emotions in a safe, receptive forum. Managers also used it to introduce some basic tools and analytical problem-solving skills to get team members through some difficult roadblocks early in the process. For example, when all the teams were "storming," the ever-popular Tuckman model of group development gave them a reference point to normalize their behavior (see Figure 10.2).

FIGURE 10.2. STAGES OF TEAM DEVELOPMENT.

1. Forming
   - People come in with their own agendas; no common purpose yet
   - No team infrastructure is in place
   - Everyone is feeling each other out
   - Members look to the leader for direction
2. Storming
   - People are jockeying for power and position
   - Differences and conflicts escalate
   - Leadership authority is challenged
   - Original ground rules are tested
3. Norming
   - The group is looking for cohesion and stability
   - Everyone has to follow a more elaborate set of norms
   - Feedback and group accountability begin to occur
   - Efficiency increases with greater alignment
4. Performing
   - People differentiate according to the requirements of the work; everyone pulls their own weight
   - Leadership is shared and rotated; decision making becomes situational
   - Teamwork becomes almost effortless
   - Team output is measured against goals and timelines; accountability occurs

Source: Tuckman, Bruce. "Developmental Sequence in Small Groups," *Journal of Personality and Social Psychology,* vol. 1, no. 6, June 1965. © 1999 Options for Change

Not all managers were happy about the emerging independence of the teams and team leaders or their own shifting roles. The required hands-off management style and just-in-time coaching capability presented new challenges. As the open system culture stabilized, it became clear that some managers were not a good fit. They were eventually counseled to move on, as they continued to be resistant to or incapable of meeting changing expectations. This is always a byproduct of changing cultures and the leadership expectations that emerge. At The MathWorks, most participants embraced the changes enthusiastically.

Support and Training for Managers

As management in the department gave this level of coaching and modeling to their staff, they needed considerable support for themselves. Again, this was done primarily in an action learning mode.

The primary level of support and training was one-on-one coaching of her direct reports by the vice president. When trying to make culture change happen rapidly, there is no substitute for direct hands-on involvement by the senior sponsor, champion, and department head. With both a strategic and tactical vision of the change she was trying to accomplish, she could make instantaneous course corrections with her staff. She was there to continuously reinforce the direction for change, which was to create a "leaderful" and proactive environment. One of her direct reports remarked on a lesson he constantly needed to relearn until it became internalized, "I finally learned that my team's plan B was better than my plan A every time."

All the managers in operations received additional training on change leadership and coaching (see Figure 10.3). They applied the just-in-time approach to themselves. With a baseline of experience under their belts, they were ready to refine their tactics and learn from other change leaders. They learned how to be ever more "planful" about the culture they were trying to create, and how to influence others to participate.

FIGURE 10.3.   TACTICS FOR CHANGE AGENTS WORKSHOP AGENDA.

Day One	Day Two	Day Three
• A systems perspective: — getting buy-in from the top • Planning a strategy that fits: — types of culture — enabled versus disabled — assessing your back-home culture — predicting and avoiding resistance	• Influencing change: —when your 1st, 2nd, and 3rd coaching attempts don't work • Entrenchment: —learning to let go • "Live" case study 1 —resistance and intervention	• Structural mapping: —pinpointing resistance • "Live" case study 2 —resistance and intervention • Boundary profile —expanding the change agent's comfort zone

© 1999 Options for Change

Team Training

As the vice president and her managers looked at team learning models for their new teams, they wanted to be careful not to dictate training from above and undermine the emerging sense of power. They realized that each team would have different needs. In looking to an outside consultant, they were clear about their requirements. They did not want a canned program. They needed nuts and bolts—the tools people needed to deal with the real issues they were facing daily. In keeping with their risk-taking approach, they decided to pilot the alpha version of a four-hour, just-in-time team intervention. It provided the teams and leaders with tools they needed to get the job done while building in the ability to make course corrections over time.

Within the intervention framework, they identified the twelve patterns of behavior that were interfering with optimal team achievement—the "Team Killers" (see below). All the teams shared certain problems, such as the inability to reach closure, overt and covert conflict, uneven participation, and weak leadership.

Team Killers

1. False consensus	7. Lack of mutual accountability
2. Inability to reach closure	8. Unrealistic expectations
3. Rigid hierarchy	9. Forgetting the customer
4. Weak leadership	10. Leaving key stakeholders out
5. Uneven participation	11. Overt conflict
6. Calcified interaction	12. Covert conflict

© 1999 Options for Change

Each team leader was interviewed to get his or her perspective on their team and his or her leadership role. The interview was also meant to reinforce their role as leaders. Each team member then filled out a Process Check on his or her team (see Figure 10.4). The Process Check is a simple instrument for evaluating team process and identifying team killers. This

FIGURE 10.4.   TEAM PROCESS CHECK.

Process Check

Rate your team's effectiveness on each of the twelve items below:
1 = lowest performance, 7 = highest performance

1. False Consensus

1.0	2.0	3.0	4.0	5.0	6.0	7.0

People agree to one thing but
think or do another

Each team member fully
supports team decisions

2. Inability to
   Reach Closure

1.0	2.0	3.0	4.0	5.0	6.0	7.0

Long, circular discussions rarely
conclude decisively

Team makes decisions efficiently
after the right amount of discussion

3. Rigid Hierarchy

1.0	2.0	3.0	4.0	5.0	6.0	7.0

Right or wrong, authority rules

Each member is encouraged
to take appropriate responsibility

4. Weak
   Leadership

1.0	2.0	3.0	4.0	5.0	6.0	7.0

Leaders fail to provide clear
direction and focus

Leaders provide strong vision
and move the work along

5. Uneven
   Participation

1.0	2.0	3.0	4.0	5.0	6.0	7.0

A few key members dominate discussion   Everyone contributes to team decisions

© 1999 Options for Change

assessment pinpointed the specific issues that each team would address during their four-hour session.

A facilitated team meeting was conducted with each team, based on the feedback from the process check. While the content varied from team to team, the agenda for the four-hour session was the same:

1. Teams watched and critiqued two videos showing teams with patterns of interaction that closely resembled their own.
2. They analyzed their own interactions systemically using the Four-Player Roles (see Figure 10.5).
3. Using examples from the participants' manual, they proposed concrete solutions to their teammates for discussion and adoption.

Team participation was voluntary. A few teams and leaders stepped forward immediately—the traditional early adopters. Their enthusiasm sold the others. Within six months, all teams had gone through the four-hour, just-in-time session. The kinds of tools adopted at The MathWorks were very concrete and playful, as might be expected given their random-open

FIGURE 10.5.   FOUR-PLAYER ROLES.

All teams need four roles for successful task completion:

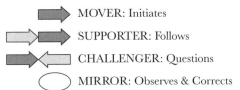

MOVER: Initiates

SUPPORTER: Follows

CHALLENGER: Questions

MIRROR: Observes & Corrects

Effective teams have:	Problems arise when:
Roles that are	Members are
• All present and balanced	• Stuck in predictable roles
• Matched to task at hand	• Unhappy in roles
• Rotated freely among members	• Overusing one role

Source: David Kantor © 1999 Options for Change

culture. For example, a rubber fish became symbolic of covert conflict—the dead fish under the table. Whenever there was an undiscussable issue, someone would fling the dead fish on the table. It would break the ice, bringing a humorous perspective to a tense situation. From there, they could have a genuine dialogue.

For most teams, a single four-hour session was enough to internalize the desired processes and culture change, as they had the takeaway tools and rules to rely on. A small number of teams required a second follow-up session, when new members joined, or to resolve more deep-seated conflict. Part of the initial design, however, was to give additional training to the team leaders.

Issues for Team Leaders

The new team leader's role was difficult and complicated. No longer responsible for just their own area, they bridled at their new responsibilities. "What do you mean, I have responsibility for all this? I just got control over my own area. My area is fine." But that wasn't good enough. Operations management wanted them to "share the pain." Is operations doing well overall? Could one team do something to help out the next?

How was each team adding value to the whole thing? If one failed, all would fail.

The two most difficult areas for team leaders—both within their own teams and across team boundaries—were decision making and influence. Sometimes they would go way over boundaries and make decisions they never believed they would try to make. Other times they became totally paralyzed. Conflict resolution was also challenging. Managers heard comments such as, "This is my peer. How can I tell her what to do? I'm not her manager, but she's making me nuts."

Team leaders were also bumping up against their relationships with managers. This was a rich area for looking at leadership behavior. A dependency mentality persisted in which team leaders wanted to get a manager's solution and/or approval on everything. And yet they avoided direct communication—preferring to ask someone else or skirt the issue. This was a core pattern, very entrenched in the culture.

Training for Team Leaders

Team leaders received an initial two-day training beyond the training they took with their teams. The main goals of the session were to help them clarify their roles, get a base line for what was working and what wasn't working on the team, make the course correction themselves, or know when to ask for outside intervention. The training was intended to develop leadership capabilities and foster independence. Team leaders came away with newfound confidence and tools for their next set of knotholes, whatever those might be. Of course, they continued to receive coaching on a regular basis from senior leaders.

However, one of the lessons learned was that the team leaders can't have too much support or training. This is one of the key factors in teams sustaining permanent culture change. The most important core competencies for team leaders at The MathWorks are:

1. Leading and facilitating change
2. Engaging team members and stakeholders

3. Observing and intervening in group process
4. Developing strong decision-making methods
5. Resolving conflict
6. Keeping the team focused on results without being authoritarian

Consistent with their continuous learning model, The MathWorks is currently designing an advanced course for team leaders based on the experience of the past few years. The course will focus on the above six competencies, and follows a half-day, every two weeks action-learning model that provides the team leaders with some takeaway tools. Each team leader will have the opportunity to work on a problem with their team and report back to their peers. In addition to taking their team leadership abilities to the next level, they will be forming a peer group. This will further reinforce their independence from management. It will also bring new team leaders into the fold.

Additional Supports

Additional supports for the new structure were put in place:

- A resource team was added to serve as a sort of internal temp agency shared by all teams. A team could go to the resource team when they needed extra help, as long as they could justify the need to their team leaders and other teams. The action learning in this structure was resource utilization, interdependency, and building internal capacity.
- A mentoring program was initiated. Each team leader could consult his or her own manager for guidance and leadership. But they could also go to any other manager for mentoring. This again reinforced the cross-functional structure.
- An adoption program was also instituted in which individuals could rotate through other teams to learn new tasks. The individual got training and the department gained flexibility. An exchange occurred so that teams were not caught short-handed and wouldn't come to resent the adopted member.

Review and Assessment

The culture of operations has been totally and permanently transformed. It was neither simple nor easy. But it is complete. Today, the vice president of operations believes that her vision was realized. Within operations, everyone at all levels has grown. They understand that they are responsible for the whole. They are more mature and have become independent problem-solvers. Cross-functional teams are now the norm throughout the company. Each member of operations represents the department on at least one other cross-functional team. When operations staff sit on other cross-functional teams they lead by example or speak up directly when they see disabled team or individual behavior. They are proud of the model and the culture they have created.

The business goals driving the whole transformation have exceeded expectations. Cycle time is still twenty-four hours or better. All the teams keep their own metrics. Everybody is learning about process redesign and how he or she can make a difference. They have gone beyond their initial goals of "Out the door in twenty-four" and "Wow the customer." They have really embraced the idea that everybody is a customer. Now The MathWorks gets mail every day, from people raving about their customer service.

Keys to Success

What made this initiative successful? A summary analysis is shown below. All these components are interconnected and work together.

1. *Start with the presenting problem.* The whole initiative was based on an urgent business need that was causing pain to the entire operations department and the company. Relating the need for change with the pain of each person's day-to-day reality is the first step. The vision of a better future must relate back to and solve the presenting problem.

2. *Create chaos.* Human systems have a lot of inertia and homeostasis. Creating chaos can disturb that inertia quickly. In The MathWorks's case, the decide-and-announce strategy, coupled with the new cross-functional structure, changed the equilibrium literally overnight. This created the push to get things moving.

3. *Engage the system in the possibility of change.* A compelling vision of a better future and a safe learning environment will invite people into the change process. "Out the door in twenty-four" was the motto for the vision, and the managers' modeling the new behavior created a learning environment. Expectations were set, but openness was created to explore what those expectations meant and how they would be met. Fear was never used as a tactic. They did not use 360-degree feedback at the beginning because they felt it was too intimidating.

4. *Provide opportunities for action learning.* Give people an experience that requires new skills and strategies to be successful and people will be self-motivated to learn. The formal training was introduced only after the desire to learn was urgent. The three formal training components, team training, team leader training and change agent training for leaders, were all delivered just in time.

5. *Model desired behavior at the top.* At The MathWorks, senior staff modeled the desired behavior. They related to each other, the team leaders, and the staff in truly honest, open, nonarrogant ways. They became agents of change by modeling a complete range of behaviors that included closed, random, synchronous, and open interactions, to create a flexible and cohesive culture.

6. *Build internal capacity.* While consultants were brought in at strategic times, the company was never overly reliant on outside resources. The development of leaders as change agents and coaches was key to implementing and sustaining the desired culture. Managers wanted the changes in behavior to become entrenched and to succeed into the next generation of management. Certain roles were critical to this end. The leaders' role was to be the mirror, reflecting back in the moment what was working, what was not. The external consultants coached and trained the senior managers, who became the primary change

agents. The team leaders became the first line facilitators and mirrors. They learned to tell when their team was enabled, when it was disabled, and how to fix it. They also identified technical experts who became internal consultants.

7. *Focus on the collective behavior.* The human system or culture with all its reinforcing loops is stronger than any one individual. Rather than trying to change the leadership individual by individual, operations' managers focused on the system. They did that by depersonalizing the expectations, while holding individuals personally accountable. Using the principles of critical mass, they understood that if as few as 20 percent of operations internalized the desired behavior, others would catch it or self-select, with some help, out of the system.

8. *Sacrifice the short term for the long term.* Systemic change outlasts any one individual. Changing the collective behaviors, norms, and values won't provide short-term quick hits; it will produce lasting systemic change.

While The MathWorks story is unique, the principles and lessons learned are generic. Creating a leaderful culture is a conscious choice that requires commitment from the top to "walk the talk." Defining the new collaborative competencies, giving people proper training and support, and holding them jointly and singularly accountable can dramatically improve your business results as it did at The MathWorks.

About the Contributors

Deborah and Alan Slobodnik (change@optionsfc.com) have been married and working together for thirty years. In the process, they "married" state-of-the-art systems thinking from family therapy with contemporary organizational development theory to create a dynamic and practical model for intervening in human systems on the behavioral level. Hundreds of leaders and consultants from around the world have taken their seminars on change, while hundreds of teams from many companies have gone through FASTEAMS®, their four-hour accelerated learning lab for teams.

Their recent association with Jessica Lipnack and Jeff Stamps of NetAge has launched them into building tools for virtual teams. A typical client list includes Analog Devices, Avery Dennison, Canadian Imperial Bank of Commerce, Ford Motor Company, Harvard Pilgrim Health Care, Kennedy School of Government, The New York Times, Inc., Niagara Mohawk Power Corporation, Quantum, and the U.S. Department of Commerce.

Elizabeth Haight (ehaight@mathworks.com) has over twenty years' experience leading and managing operations in the high-tech industry. Haight has held management positions at The MathWorks, Index Technology, and Litton-Datamedix. As vice president of operations at The MathWorks, she is responsible for the Call Center, Logistics, Business Systems, and Facilities.

CHAPTER ELEVEN

THE MITRE CORPORATION

This chapter outlines the Management Development Program
and Leadership Academy that emphasizes action learning teams
as the key to performance enhancement and
cultural change in a technical environment.

Company Background

The MITRE Corporation is a systems engineering, integration, research, development, and information technology company that operates Federally Funded Research and Development Centers (FFRDCs) for the Department of Defense, the Federal Aviation Administration, and the Internal Revenue Service. Independent and not-for-profit, MITRE works in close partnership with its government sponsors to address systems integration and other complex technological challenges facing today's military, intelligence, aviation, and tax administration communities.

The corporation operates in the public interest and is dedicated to providing the resources necessary to make available collaborative solutions to complex issues. MITRE's 4,500 employees are located nationally and internationally with corporate offices in Massachusetts and Virginia.

Overview

The management and leadership programs at the MITRE Corporation include action learning components that are an innovative and effective approach to leveraging training, development, and performance improvement. This method of learning has been successfully used and evaluated with over 800 managers participating in MITRE's corporate-wide Management Development Program (MDP) as well as seventy-five managers and team members participating in a new initiative called Leadership Academy. Each of the programs is unique in its design, objectives, and methodologies—yet they are closely aligned with each other and the desired outcomes. The action learning components of both programs provide the forum for team members to see not only assumptions they make about others and the organization, but also about themselves as individuals. They are able to reframe how they think and work, and they integrate that information into their leadership and team development styles.

This chapter explores how the MITRE Corporation recognized the challenges of technological advancement, cost consciousness, sponsor demands, and environmental changes. MITRE responded by creating management and leadership curricula, focusing on action learning components that asked MITRE's technical and administrative managers to examine their operating style and to demonstrate new ways of working.

Strategic Issues Facing MITRE

The MITRE Corporation, like all organizations, was challenged by unprecedented business, political, and technological change. The complexity of the evolving business has required multiskilled, multidisciplined managers and leaders who can keep pace with change by enhancing competencies that improve performance.

In 1993, the officers recognized the need to develop a cadre of effective managers and leaders to enhance the organization's capabilities to serve its sponsors and to manage projects and people more successfully. MITRE faced a business environment vastly different from that in which the corporation initially achieved its success and reputation for excellence. In order to respond to the challenges and opportunities that were being defined by the new environment, the organization had to reinvent itself for the new circumstances in which it would be operating. It was determined that the quality of MITRE's management and leadership had never been more crucial and that the corporation needed creative management and leadership that would be responsive and visionary, that would communicate with and remain accessible to the clients, and that would share energy and ideas.

In response to this call, the MITRE Institute—the Corporate Education Center—designed and presented a comprehensive leadership curriculum, the Management Development Program. It was created to help the organization accelerate its development as an effective, integrated organization where appropriate knowledge, skills, and styles are learned and implemented.

The Management Development Program

The Management Development Program (MDP) is an experiential learning process that is tailored for and delivered across three management levels: first, middle, and senior. The MDP was designed to harness and shape a leadership cadre that can respond to increasingly changing environments. The program was premised on the conviction that developing the knowledge, skills, and impact of our leaders is crucial to achieving the corporate goals and objectives of the future.

During the pilot, the initial sessions of the MDP were presented to 225 new and experienced first- and middle-level technical and administrative managers. Content included in the modules for all levels was designed to help MITRE managers and leaders acquire and use awareness, information, knowledge, and to explore values and attitudes.

The process of enhancing competencies and changing behaviors was ongoing and continuous and was used for evaluation.

Challenges

To paraphrase an old axiom, "The real job in helping organizations learn is not getting the organization to drink from the fountain of knowledge, but to make the organization thirst for the knowledge in the first place." The staff of the MITRE Institute was aware that MITRE's managers had been promoted because of their technical expertise and competencies; that many managers were in those positions for several years and had been rewarded for their work; and that the majority of managers did not recognize the role of manager or leader as being critical to their success. In addition, the managers already had intense work schedules and did not see the benefit in participating in programs that spanned several months.

Therefore, the challenge was not only to create a management/ leadership program that produced results, but also to include a component that produced a culture change and new ways of thinking and working. What the program needed was a mechanism to provide:

- Opportunity to improve transfer of learning
- Continuity and linkage throughout the MDP
- Structure for networking and peer support
- Process to model effective teams
- Vehicle to encourage change from the bottom up
- Implementation of key action learning concepts

The answer was an action learning process called "Learning Teams."

The Learning Team and Its Purpose

A Learning Team is a small group of MDP managers with complementary skills and experience who become committed to a common purpose, performance goals, and an approach for which they hold themselves mutually accountable. The purpose of Learning Teams is to:

- Enhance learning, personal growth, and professional development
- Serve as a model for effective team development
- Establish cross-organizational networks
- Create the "managers' lounge"
- Decide and collaborate on a project that has personal and organizational value
- Provide mutual support and problem solving

Manager's lounge was an expression that was used to describe the learning team process. The analogy was used that teachers have lounges, doctors have lounges, and other professionals have lounges where informal learning, discussions, and networking take place. The learning team provided a forum for the managers to use each other as sounding boards to seek feedback on resolving problems or making decisions. They also got a perspective of work in other centers, divisions, and departments. In particular, the learning team structure provided an opportunity for the administrative and technical managers to appreciate its work and impact on the organization. Many professional friendships were formed and continue to develop. Collegial interaction and conversation are fundamental aspects of the Learning Teams. As a team works together through active participation, the members develop a mechanism to learn from and with each other through mutual support, advice, and feedback. Team members also develop skills of critical reflection, which allow examination of "taken-for-granted" assumptions that may impede managing in new and more effective ways.

A guidebook, *Learning Team Overview* (see Exhibit 11.1), was created by the MITRE Institute staff to detail the who, what, why, when, and how of a Learning Team. The book was distributed to each MDP participant and included the following:

- Definition, objectives, and purpose of a Learning Team
- Process and the expectations for working in a Learning Team
- Guidelines for selecting a project
- Roles and responsibilities of the program leader and facilitator

Roadmap for Implementation

The roadmap consisted of four primary steps: Selection and Formation of the Learning Teams; Facilitating Learning Team Meetings; Guiding Project Selection; and Adjourning—Final Steps. The activities in each are detailed below.

Selection and Formation of the Learning Teams

The MDP program leaders, who oversee the first-, middle-, and senior-level programs, select teams of six to eight members. Each class, in each level, has four or five teams. Criteria for team selection is based on maximizing diversity of participation through integrating managers from different centers, divisions, departments, technical and administrative functions, and sites.

The development of the Learning Teams is a process and typically spans the four stages of the "Tuckman Model of Group Development": forming, storming, norming, and performing as the members move from *group* behaviors toward *team* behaviors. Throughout these stages, the Learning Teams develop and apply strategies that contribute to individual and team effectiveness. A reference book has been created and is distributed to all team members. The book describes the stages of team development and behavioral characteristics that are exhibited and provides tools to assess team behavior, survey meetings, and check on progress.

Participating at meetings is an essential component of the team's development. Frequency, type, and length of meeting are usually unique to each team. Communication between team members varies and includes a combination of electronic mail, conference calls, video teleconferences, and face-to-face meetings. At the meetings, team members are responsible for the following:

- Identifying group and individual roles
- Selecting a project by consensus
- Agreeing on methods for tracking progress and results
- Enabling members to learn and practice skills for building and maintaining teams
- Providing informal interim reports to the MDP class on their progress
- Strengthening the networking process and techniques
- Supporting each other's individual development plans
- Giving a creative summary at the program's conclusion

Facilitating Learning Team Meetings

A professional facilitator contracted from outside the organization works with each team during four of its scheduled meetings. These are held at the conclusion of the skill development modules. In addition, the teams are expected to meet without the facilitators as often as possible. Frequently teams have members from sites, and they must arrange to meet via video teleconference. Communication is continuous through the use of electronic mail.

As part of the team development process, team members are encouraged to share leadership, take on various roles and responsibilities, and learn from the facilitator. The facilitators serve as coaches and provide structure and tools for team development. They give feedback on the process and often recommend alternative methods and behaviors.

Project Selection

At the beginning of the Learning Team process, members identify a project they can accomplish as a team. When the team selects its project, each member makes a contribution that benefits him or her as well as the overall team effort. As the project evolves, team members are asked to consider how it relates to their managerial and leadership responsibilities, the methodologies that can be used to present it to others, and the potential impact it may have on their departments, divisions, and MITRE.

Projects can be selected from several sources: an idea from team members, former Learning Team projects conducive to ongoing development, or ideas generated from upper management. To begin the process for selecting a project, each team member will talk informally with three individuals (peers, direct reports, or managers) and ask what he or she perceives to be important topics or needs at MITRE. Usually the team project is not sponsored or supported by a particular person in the organization. Guidelines are provided to help the team members focus on both team and task (see Table 11.1).

TABLE 11.1.   GUIDELINES FOR PROJECT SELECTION.

Team Focus	Task Focus
• Focuses on an initiative that each member can contribute to and learn from	• Requires application by Capstone
• Motivates and excites each individual on the team	• Has potential for benefitting the organization and represents a substantial challenge
• Capitalizes on the knowledge and experience of each member	• Has a foreseeable result which will be implemented in the organization
• Provides an opportunity to integrate individual development plans with project work	• Provides a learning lab to share and problem solve while working on the project
• Builds on team members' strengths to share workload	• Is within an area of the team's control and influence

The team facilitators often help the teams decide by taking them through steps in group decision-making process and by systematically helping them scope out the work. Alumni from previous years in the MDP are invited to speak and answer questions about what worked and what did not work for their teams.

Adjourning—The Final Steps

The final module of the MDP is Capstone, which is a day of presentation, reflection, evaluation, and graduation. Each team makes a presentation on the learnings from the perspectives of team development and leadership process, and project learnings and results. The audience comprises the class and MITRE Institute staff. The presentations are traditionally very creative and significant in content. Often the teams have created surveys, researched their work, conducted interviews, and identified stakeholders; all of this material is highlighted and described. Each team completes a summary form (see Exhibit 11.2), which is included in a compilation that is printed and shared among all participants in the MDP that current year.

Following Capstone, the compilations of Learning Team summaries (see Exhibit 11.3) are sent to MITRE's CEO and president and all vice presidents. They are asked to review the work and request team presentations that meet their needs and interest. Several teams are asked each year to make the presentations. Another significant part of Capstone is the graduation luncheon. The learning team members "graduate" each other and use the time to give personal and positive feedback.

Evaluation Process and Impact

The evaluation process of the Learning Teams is based on changes in knowledge, values, and skills. As part of their presentations, the teams report collectively at Capstone what they learned and how they are planning to use the knowledge and skills. In addition, each team member is asked to participate in Level 1 evaluation by ranking the following:

- To what extent their experience provided for a better understanding of the process
- To what extent knowledge, skills, and techniques developed
- To what extent they contributed to making the learning team process as useful as possible

Each MDP manager is asked to comment on the team facilitators' contributions (see Exhibit 11.4). The MDP managers are also asked to detail "impact stories" of how they applied learnings back to their teams and jobs and to give examples of the impact of the actions on themselves, others, and the organization. As a follow-up, the story collection process is done three months after the completion of the program.

Lessons Learned

The following "lessons learned" have been identified by continuous evaluation of the process and the impact on the job:

- Facilitation is critical from the beginning of the team formation
- Projects should be relevant to each member for sustained team momentum
- Projects overshadow other Learning Team objectives; team development and leadership need continuous emphasis
- Group dynamics drive success
- Emphasis on process and self-direction is difficult in a hierarchical and task-focused organization

Outcomes

The ratio of team and task benefits were analyzed and integrated into the project (see Table 11.2).

Working in Learning Teams has evolved from a component of the MDP that was clearly not considered a high priority to a critical part of

TABLE 11.2. BENEFITS OF THE MDP.

Benefits to the Organization	Benefits to the Team Members
• Introduced "manager's lounge" concept and culture change	• Practiced leadership skills using team members as sounding-board advisors
• Emphasized continuous learning	• Experienced working collaboratively
• Provided cross-organizational knowledge	• Established personal and professional networks throughout the organization
• Changed from individual directive to collaborative behaviors	• Formed work teams outside of "own" area of expertise
• Encouraged innovative solutions to organizational challenges	• Acquired a common vocabulary among team members and others on the job

the learning and team development process. Working on the projects creates an arena for team members to capitalize on their strengths and competencies and to share this knowledge and expertise. For instance, the technical managers gained a clearer perspective of how and why the administrative centers are structured and how they work and vice versa.

The learnings from the projects have been significant from both the individual and corporate perspectives. Examples of learning team outcomes that have been implemented in the organization are:

- Creation and implementation of a corporate-wide electronic assignment bulletin board used for posting and responding to temporary assignments
- Workshop design and presentation on factors affecting morale and identifying methodologies to improve it
- Collaborative effort with the corporate officers to determine MITRE staff's perceptions of the corporate mission and vision by using the team's survey and interview data to understand how well the information is disseminated
- Development of a managers' resource home page (MENTOR) on MITRE information systems, infrastructure, and services

Throughout the process, the team members identify their stakeholders and are encouraged to present their findings and recommendations to them at the conclusion of the MDP programs. In so doing, the stakeholders often use the survey and interview data compiled by the teams to influence decisions and contribute to creating new systems.

In addition to learning from the project work, the managers learn from each other; they learn from reflecting on how they are addressing problems; they learn to question their assumptions on which their actions were based; and they learn to give and receive feedback from their team members. Over the years, several of the managers continue to network and sustain the collegiality and peer respect that has developed.

Leadership Academy

Leadership Academy is a MITRE Institute program designed specifically for intact work teams. The purpose of this program is to improve total organizational performance by enhancing the leadership role teams play, team effectiveness, and individual leadership capabilities. The academy provides an environment for an experiential learning process that incorporates theory and applies this theory to just-in-time training. The program meets for five days over a six-month period and is offered in four parts (see Figure 11.1). A few of the features that make the program different from the MDP Learning Teams are that the participants are self-selected; there is at least one member who is a graduate of the MDP; and each intact team works on its existing project.

FIGURE 11.1.   THE LEADERSHIP ACADEMY STRUCTURE.

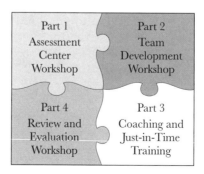

Objectives of Leadership Academy

There are many objectives and anticipated outcomes, which include:

- Solving and managing business problems
- Strengthening collaborative relationships
- Increasing customer focus and responsiveness
- Aligning individual and team performance and output to meet and exceed strategic goals
- Developing a sense of leadership as a team and the individual roles to sustain that over time

Leadership Academy Implementation

One of the unique features of Leadership Academy is that the Assessment Center is presented first. The Assessment Center is a method, not a place. It is a way to see and evaluate people's effectiveness by observing them in action. In the center, the teams work through simulations—realistic, job-related tasks. Specially trained assessors, who are contracted to work with institute staff, observe the people at work, meet in consensus sessions to evaluate their effectiveness, and give detailed feedback to the participants on a one-to-one basis. In addition to the feedback that each individual receives from his or her assessor, the team gives peer feedback to each other. All of the feedback is for the participants' use only. It is not shared with others at the center, nor is any record of the feedback kept at MITRE.

The strength of the Assessment Center lies in the disciplined structure that promotes objectivity, validity, and reliability. As is required by the International Congress on the Assessment Center Method, the center:

- Is competency-based
- Is behavior-oriented
- Uses trained assessors
- Uses a consensus evaluation process

Leadership Academy is presented in four parts, which are outlined in Table 11.3. The focus of Part 1 is on the "individual" as he or she participates in

TABLE 11.3　LEADERSHIP ACADEMY COMPONENTS.

Part 1: Assessment Center Workshop (2 days)	Simulated team exercises Team dynamics and communication Giving and receiving feedback Individual assessor feedback Self-insight instrument: Individual
Part 2: Team Development Workshop (2 days)	Team dynamics Effective team leadership Conflict resolution Self-insight instrument: Team roles and responsibilities Measures of effectiveness
Part 3: Coaching and Just-in-Time Training (4 months)	Coaching Action learning Just-in-time training Application of skills and behaviors • For improved effectiveness • Work on task/project
Part 4: Review and Evaluation Workshop (1 day)	All teams reconvene Work teams share lessons learned Post-assessment feedback Evaluation and feedback of the program Graduation

the program, while Parts 2, 3, and 4 are devoted to team development and team coaching. Each part is bridged to various components.

Roles of Team Members and Facilitators

The role of the trained assessors and coaches changes in each phase of the program. They work as trainers, as coaches, and as assessors as outlined in Table 11.4.

Part 2 of the program is the skill development module, which is designed and presented by four of the facilitators/coaches. The areas that are stressed are consensus reaching, conflict management, problem solving, and innovating. It is during this module that the teams start integrating the skill building into the project work.

Part 3 of the program is the unique "just-in-time" coaching and training. Each team's assessor/coach works with them on the job up to four

TABLE 11.4 PARTICIPANT AND CONSULTANT ROLES.

Part 1: Assessment Center	Part 2: Skill Development Workshop	Part 3: Four Months of Coaching and Training	Part 4: One-Day Review Workshop
Participant Roles	Participant Roles	Participant Roles	Participant Roles
Feedback on individual strengths and areas for development from peers and assessors	Feedback on team effectiveness from peers and coaches	Work as a team on job-related tasks	Review
Self-insight through videotape review and classroom discussions	Team self-insight through team survey	Coaching by phone, e-mail, and in person according to the needs of each team	Reflection through self-insight instrument
Skills training	Skills training	Training as requested	Recommend
Individual development planning	Back on the job development and work planning	Four days of assistance allocated	
Role of one consultant: trainers Role of other consultants: assessors (one for every two participants in the Assessment Center)	Role of consultants: coaches and trainers (one for every participating team)	Role of consultants: coaches and trainers (one for every participating team)	Role of consultants: coaches and trainers (one for every participating team)

days and helps to increase the team's ability to produce work more effectively.

Part 4 of Leadership Academy concludes the program. The teams make a presentation of their project work. Graduation takes place at the last session, and the team participants, directors, and vice presidents are invited to a celebration reception.

As part of the evaluation strategy of Leadership Academy, the participants are asked to fill out a form at the completion of each module. They give feedback on the completion and relevance of the objectives as well as the course purpose, activities, facilitators, material, relevance to their jobs, and overall rating. At the last module, the participants fill out an overall evaluation form of the program; are asked to detail how they intend to use the learnings; to anticipate the impact this program will have on their teams; and to reflect on their top three "take-aways." Application and impact interviews take place six months after the completion of the pilot program. Participants and their managers are interviewed to measure the effectiveness and return of investment.

Learn, Reflect, Do!

Learn, reflect, do is what action learning is about at MITRE. This philosophy is integrated into the design of the MITRE Corporation's Management Development Program and Leadership Academy curriculum. There can be no change without actions in which the participants gather knowledge, reflect on its application in real-life situations, and do something with it. Personal and team development is equally as important as working on a project. Learning takes place because the team members facilitate it.

The challenges identified in 1993, which required multiskilled, multidisciplined managers and leaders who could keep pace with change, still exist. The strategic issues facing the corporation are perhaps even more complex, and change will continue at an unprecedented pace. By "teaming up," new ways of thinking and working have evolved successfully.

Exhibit 11.1: Learning Team Reference Guide Overview

MANAGEMENT DEVELOPMENT PROGRAM

Definition and Objectives of a Learning Team

Definition. A Learning Team is a small group of MDP managers with complementary skills and experience who become committed to a common purpose, performance goals, and an approach for which they hold themselves mutually accountable.

Objectives

- Establish cross-organizational networks to encourage information sharing and learning
- Provide mutual support and joint problem solving for all aspects of managing and leading at MITRE
- Discuss the MDP course content and ways to apply learning back on the job
- Encourage, support, and contribute to individual members' development plans
- Learn about team development to enhance managers' ability to work effectively in teams at MITRE
- Decide and collaborate on a project that has personal and organizational value

Purpose of a Learning Team

Learning Teams are an important component in the MDP learning experience. The overall purpose of Learning Teams is to enhance member learning and professional and personal development. Specifically, Learning Teams serve as a model for building effective teams from which process

Linkage Inc.'s Best Practices in Leadership Development Handbook, edited by David Giber, Louis Carter, and Marshall Goldsmith. Copyright © 2000 by Linkage Press and Jossey-Bass/Pfeiffer, San Francisco, CA.

and task skills may be acquired, practiced, and applied in other team settings back on the job. For example, Learning Teams provide an opportunity for giving and receiving feedback, sharing responsibilities, resolving conflicts, working across boundaries, and alternating leadership roles.

Collegial interaction and conversation are fundamental aspects of Learning Teams. As a team works together through active participation, team members develop a mechanism to learn from and with each other through mutual support, advice, and feedback. Team members also develop skills of critical reflection, which allow examination of "taken-for-granted" assumptions that may impede managing in new and more effective ways.

Benefits from the Learning Team process include:

- Developing managerial and leadership skills through a process of reflecting on experiences and actions taken when solving on-the-job problems with peers
- Enhancing innovative ways of thinking about and working within the organization by addressing unfamiliar situations
- Identifying ways to analyze problems and change from new perspectives
- Learning to build and examine "theories in use" through mutual collaboration with peers of different backgrounds, facilitators, and other resource people

Learning Team Process

A Learning Team consists of six to eight managers who strive to develop themselves into an effective team. Criteria for team selection is based on maximizing diversity of participation through integrating managers from different centers and divisions, departments, technical and administrative functions, and sites. A professional facilitator works with the team during four of its scheduled meetings.

At the beginning of the Learning Team process, members identify a project they can accomplish as a group. When a team selects their project, each member makes a contribution that benefits him or her, as well as the overall team effort. As the project evolves, team members are asked to consider how it relates to their managerial responsibilities, the methodologies that can be used to present it to others, and the potential impact it may have on their groups, departments, divisions, and the organization. Project status and team process lessons are presented throughout the program. Project results are presented at the final MDP component, Capstone.

The development of a Learning Team is a process and typically spans across the four stages of the Tuckman model, which is described below (forming, storming, norming, and performing) as the members move from *group* behaviors toward *team* behaviors. Throughout these stages, the Learning Team will develop and apply strategies that contribute to individual and team effectiveness.

Forming. During formation, teams will spend time on activities that build understanding and support in the group. Relationship issues emerge early in the team's formation as concerns about moving from individual status to member status evolve. Team members will need to understand how they fit into the team, and questions about roles and responsibilities that emerge will need to be addressed.

Storming. A normal and necessary process that teams go through is storming. The team facilitator is available to help the Learning Team understand the natural tension they may experience and move through in this stage. Guidebooks and relevant references will also be useful as resources to provide tools for this stage.

Norming. One norm that develops in successful Learning Teams is commitment to the team. Members will need to balance team membership with their individual responsibilities and organizational commitments. The team will need to clarify how loyalties will conflict or mesh and how the team effort will support and be supported by the work unit to which they belong.

Performing. In the later stages of team development, members of Learning Teams will experience a process of growth and maturing that can be observed, understood, and felt by the team. It is during this performing stage that teams achieve maximum rapport and effectiveness when working together.

Expectations for Working in a Learning Team

Participation at meetings is an essential component of the team's development. Frequency, type, and length of meetings are unique to each team. Communication between team members varies and includes a combination of electronic mail, conference calls, video teleconference, and face-to-face meetings. During initial meetings, the Learning Team will decide on the frequency and type of meetings they will hold. This decision will be revisited periodically throughout the duration of the Learning Team.

Learning Teams will use guidebooks and resource materials to introduce process techniques. By the program's conclusion, techniques and suggestions outlined in these resources and introduced by the facilitator will have been explored and practiced at appropriate times in the Learning Team.

Learning Team members are responsible for the following:

- Establishing norms and guidelines
- Selecting a team name
- Identifying group and individual roles
- Defining a project by consensus
- Agreeing on methods for tracking progress and results
- Enabling members to learn and practice skills for building and maintaining effective teams
- Providing informal interim reports to the whole MDP class on the Learning Team process and project progress
- Strengthening networking processes and techniques
- Supporting each other's individual development plans and other managerial needs
- Giving a creative summary of the completed project and Learning Team lessons at the conclusion of the MDP

Process and Guidelines for Selecting a Learning Team Project

Projects can be selected from several sources: an idea generated from team members, former Learning Team projects conducive to ongoing development, or ideas generated from upper management. To begin the process for selecting a project, each Learning Team member will talk informally with three individuals (peers, subordinates, direct reports, or boss) and ask what he or she perceives to be important topics or needs at MITRE. The purpose of this first step is to gather data from those around you.

The second step is to meet again as a Learning Team and share data, process it for themes and patterns, and discuss its meaning. This will result in integrating and analyzing findings and generalizing meanings. Also considered will be former Learning Team projects conducive for continued work and topics provided from upper management.

At this point, each member should ask himself or herself what is important from the information generated and share this with the group. Using this information from the process described above, the Learning Team will select a project. To help guide its decision, the group should identify criteria for the project.

The following are guidelines for identifying a team project and its focus:

- Requires application by Capstone session
- Is within each individual's area of control and influence
- Has real value to each member, the individual's work unit, and MITRE
- Represents a substantial challenge and has potential for benefitting the organization
- Motivates and excites each individual
- Challenges each team member to be accountable for progress
- Has a foreseeable end result

Roles and Responsibilities of the Program Leader and Facilitators

Below are ways the MDP *Program Leaders* will help support the Learning Team efforts.

- Form Learning Teams
- Identify facilitator for each Learning Team
- Introduce and explain the Learning Team concept and process
- Describe expectations for a Learning Team

- Explain project selection process
- Review roles and responsibilities
- Provide resources relevant to building teams
- Coordinate report-outs at focus sessions and/or in other components
- Receive periodic communication from Learning Teams
- Serve as a conduit between Learning Teams and other relevant people, activities, and resources at MITRE
- Publicize Learning Team successes

Below are ways the *Facilitators* will help support Learning Team efforts.

- Serve as a coach to the Learning Team, focused on the process of team development
- Provide structure and tools for team development
- Facilitate early meetings to model the process and role
- Provide feedback on Learning Team process
- Recommend alternative methods and behaviors
- Help Learning Team to critically review its own processes and assumptions
- Ensure *A Guide to Effective Teams* and *Learning Team Resource Materials* are used

Exhibit 11.2: Instructions for Completing the Learning Team Project Form

The attached form (see Exhibit 11.3 on pages 322–323) is a means of gathering information about all projects in the Management Development Program (MDP). The form provides a brief, consistent way to think about learning team projects and provides a mechanism for gathering and eventually distributing information about these important projects.

We will assemble notebooks with all summaries from the first, middle, and senior levels of the MDP in Washington and Bedford. These notebooks will be circulated to all current MDP participants and corporate officers. In addition to this form, each team should prepare a complete set of handouts and other back-up materials that are used at the Capstone presentation and provide them to your program leader. These handouts, as well as those from all Learning Teams, will be kept in a central location for access.

Who Completes the Form

Each learning team should complete one form and return it to your program leader. You may use the attached form or access a softcopy.

When Should Forms Be Completed

Each learning team should complete the form and return it to your program leader prior to your Capstone module.

What Do the Categories on the Form Mean

Table 11.5 offers a brief description of the categories on the form.

TABLE 11.5.   CATEGORY DESCRIPTIONS.

Category	Description
Title	The title or name of your project
Purpose	What you hoped to accomplish by doing this project
Methodology	How did you do the project? What methods did you use?
Outcomes	What was the outcome of your project? Did you accomplish what you set out to do?
Lessons Learned	What lessons did you learn about the topic of your *project?* What lessons did you learn about working in *teams?*
Comments and Observations	What would you like to tell others about your experiences working on this project and in this team? Any comments, observations, learnings, criticisms, and so on, are valid.
Team Members	Please include names and departments.
For More Information	If you would like to designate a specific individual on the Learning Team who will be responsible for providing additional information to those who are interested, list that person's name and a way to contact that person (phone, mail stop).

Exhibit 11.3: Learning Team Project Summary Form

Title: _____

Purpose: _____

Methodology: _____

Outcomes: _____

Lessons learned: In the table below, describe the lessons you learned about your project and the lessons learned about working in the learning team.

Lessons about the Topic	Lessons about Learning Team

Comments and observations: _____

_____

_____

_____

_____

_____

_____

_____

_____

_____

_____

_____

Team members: _____

_____

_____

_____

_____

_____

For more information about this project, contact: _____

_____

_____

_____

_____

_____

Exhibit 11.4: MDP Learning Team Evaluation

MANAGEMENT DEVELOPMENT PROGRAM

Please consider your experience on your MDP Learning Team and answer the questions below:

1. To what extent did your Learning Team experience provide a better understanding of the team development process?

   1_____ **2**_____ **3**_____**4**_____**5**
   Not all all   **Somewhat**   **To a great extent**

2. To what extent are the knowledge, skills, and techniques you developed through the Learning Team experience applicable to your job at MITRE?

   1_____ **2**_____ **3**_____**4**_____**5**
   Not all all   **Somewhat**   **To a great extent**

3. What aspect(s) of the Learning Team experience were most useful? Least useful? Please specify and explain why.

4. What did you contribute to make the Learning Team process as useful as possible?

5. In what ways did your facilitator contribute to the process?

Please make any additional comments about the Learning Team experience on the back of this sheet.

About the Contributor

Patricia A. Hurton (hurtonp@mitre.org) is a senior staff development specialist at the MITRE Corporation. She has been with the MITRE Institute for over ten years and was one of the original designers and presenters of the Management Development Program. Prior to joining the MITRE Corporation, Hurton was president of Patricia A. Hurton & Associates, Inc., and worked as a consultant and trainer with leading corporations in banking, insurance, high technology, education, and healthcare industries nationally and internationally. She was the recipient of the American Society for Training and Development (ASTD) Technical and Skills Consultant of the Year Award. She has had numerous articles published and has presented at several international conferences.

CHAPTER TWELVE

MOTOROLA

This chapter outlines a Global Organization Leadership
Development Process (GOLD) for high-potential leaders that
combines training, action learning, and a global online tracking
system to create results-oriented, global, entrepreneurial leaders.

Introduction

Every major corporation wants to develop innovative and visionary leaders. Companies that lack a cadre of globally focused leaders who can interpret the vision and strategy of the organization to drive the business forward lose ground to competitors. Those that successfully develop their leaders share a common characteristic. Their training and HR functions see themselves as partners with the business rather than as adjunct service groups. This is not how training and HR have viewed themselves in the past. In articulating this paradigm shift, training and HR must move beyond being event based, and become true partners in the organization's strategic and operational framework. Staff must understand the business of the business, and their role in making the business successful. Second, training and HR must view the operating managers across the organization as customers and establish strong partnerships with them. Third, they must evaluate the impact of interventions and programs. Training and HR groups that fail to track the impact of their programs run the risk of losing a valuable customer, their own organization, that needs evidence of improved leadership performance.[1]

This chapter outlines Motorola's experience with the establishment of such a partnership in order to accelerate the leadership development of high performing managers. This initiative is known as the Global Organization Leadership Development Process, or GOLD™ (see Exhibit 12.1).

The Business Issues

The impetus behind the GOLD process was not a sense that Motorola's existing leadership programs needed updating. Rather, GOLD was a specially designed response to a business need confronting the Messaging Systems Products Group (MSPG) in Motorola in 1994.

The Messaging Systems Products Group manufactures pagers. During the period 1990–1994, MSPG experienced rapid growth fueled by the globalization of markets and retail distribution to consumers. This led to a dramatic shift in the size and geographic distribution of MSPG's business and began to place unique demands on the organization. Among other things, almost 70 percent of its business was predicted to come from Asia and elsewhere outside the United States within a short period. In Asia, the paging business was expected to more than double by the end of the decade. Globally, paging was expected to be a $10 billion business within six years. In 1994, Motorola HR estimated an additional 200 senior-level global business leaders would be required by the year 2000 if MSPG was to retain market share and keep abreast of this rate of growth. HR did not believe the current approach to leadership development would ensure this cadre of leaders, and they asked the Learning and Development Organization to propose an alternative intervention. Strong steps were needed.

Global Needs Assessment

The Learning and Development Organization in MSPG is committed to carrying out a thorough needs assessment before the design and development of any training.[2] Given the serious nature of the problem facing MSPG, an indepth global training needs assessment (TNA) was performed to ensure any leadership intervention would produce the desired results. Many practitioners lack management support for TNA and are expected to develop a leadership training program based on a set of agreed-on competencies rather than from a model of leadership driven by business needs and validated by thorough needs assessment. In the case of GOLD, critical business issues and the anticipated leadership shortfall drove the design from the outset. The TNA was market driven, focusing on the collection of data around the business need, rather than seeking to validate a set of leadership competencies.

Two people undertook the TNA in two phases over a period of sixteen weeks. In the first phase, data were gathered from GMs and senior managers in the United States. Forty-two individual senior staff members in the United States and eleven global focus groups for 106 individuals were interviewed, seeking input about leadership needs in terms of the strategic direction of MSPG and their vision for the future. The second phase replicated this approach in Asia, with seventy-three senior managers attending focus groups or being interviewed individually. European input was also obtained (see Exhibits 12.2 and 12.3). The TNA sought answers to four questions:

1. Given where MSPG is headed in the future, how aligned are its current management practices to its future business needs?
2. What are the critical leadership competencies MSPG leaders need in order to take the business into the anticipated future?
3. In what ways are current processes for identifying, selecting, and developing leaders ineffective to meet the leadership needs of its growing business?
4. What are the major change issues MSPG needs to take into account going forward?

The TNA data revealed a disturbing picture. Without an innovative approach to leadership development, MSPG would not have leadership with the required competencies, mindset, and expertise by the end of the decade. Key findings from this global business-focused TNA follow:

- Emerging leaders were not being prepared for future business challenges.
- Despite some minor incremental changes, leadership and management skills were not improving.
- In many parts of the business there was no sense of urgency around changing the leadership culture.
- The major change issues suggested by many interviewees revealed a short-range focus.

A total paradigm shift was needed. If the business were to grow and retain market share, MSPG needed managers who would think in terms of leading, not managing, assume a global focus, not a regional one, adopt a customer focus rather than a functional one, and cultivate an entrepreneurial mentality in place of a big business perspective. Leadership development that reinforced the prevailing leadership style would not serve the organization as it prepared for the future.

In the assessment report it was pointed out that if MSPG continued to rely on its traditional training approaches Learning and Development would be unable to develop leaders with the necessary skills within the time frame. MSPG needed an accelerated leadership development process capable of producing next generation leaders to take the business into the twenty-first century. These leaders would transform the business by establishing Motorola's FLEX paging technology as the worldwide standard (see Motorola's Web site at www.mot.com for more details), manage the business both as a global enterprise and autonomous decentralized organizations, and move from a technology-driven to a market-driven mindset. They would have to anticipate change in order to remain the market leader in one of the most dynamic marketplaces in the world. These new leaders would be constantly challenged to be creative, innovative, and decisive. Above all, they would need a total commitment to the MSPG vision. Without the right leadership cadre MSPG was in danger of failing to take advantage of the markets with the resultant loss of business impetus. It was this growth dynamic and projected leadership shortfall, coupled with the realization that current approaches would not suffice, that led Motorola to build the Global Organization Leadership Development (GOLD™) process. The design and development phase, from the presentation of the TNA report to the GMs and their agreement to funding to the pilot of GOLD, was extremely short—a mere eight months!

Involving the senior decision makers in the TNA and design was crucial. On the one hand, they provided the insights and strategic thinking about leadership and the business that the company needed to build on, and on the other hand, they acted as champions and sponsors. Without senior management's buy-in, a radically new approach to leadership development would not get off the ground. Listening to the GMs and managers as the primary clients and involving them in the development of the new leadership initiative was a sure way of gaining their support.

Target Population

Who did GOLD target? Firstly, those nominated for GOLD had to be on the list of recognized high potentials (Hi-Pos). They were the company's brightest and best middle managers. Age-wise, they were early thirties and older, and there were approximately twice as many men as women (the result of choosing Hi-Po managers). Second, they came from all regions of the business (Asia, North America, Latin America, and Europe). Hi-Pos came from all functions—not only engineering but finance, HR, sales, marketing, new product development, and so on.

In many companies Hi-Po lists are a closely guarded secret. The prevailing view is that if the names on the list are known, it is a demotivating factor for those who find themselves omitted. However, a program designed to rapidly advance high-potential middle managers must, out of necessity, disclose the selection of Hi-Pos by senior management. MSPG division General Managers (GMs) were responsible for choosing participants to attend GOLD. Nominees had to be on the Hi-Po listing and be approved by all GMs to ensure no one was being "slipped in" who was not considered outstanding by other GMs.

Design and Structure of GOLD

In the early stages of the design of GOLD, the nature of the end product was unclear. The TNA highlighted the need for the leadership development process to be very focused on the demands facing the business and on the leadership qualities needed to drive the business forward on a global scale so that Motorola could identify and exploit new markets, businesses, and technology faster than ever before. MSPG had to develop leaders with different skills and mindsets from many of their role models. As Jim Wright, vice president and director of strategic marketing for MSPG, observed at the time, "It's clear that the old rules of developing the leaders needed for the future will not be sufficient in the years ahead. We must develop the leadership that will enable MSPG to achieve the challenges ahead of us by means of intensive, interactive, experiential sessions focused on our specific business needs."

Structurally, the design team's objective was to provide a unique learning environment for a carefully chosen group of future leaders. This objective necessitated the design of more than a training program. Training sessions alone would not develop true leaders. What evolved through the eight-month design phase was a leadership development process that went beyond traditional competency-based leadership training. The design team laid aside preconceived notions about what leaders should do and think, and let the relevant competencies emerge as they reflected on the TNA data and the business issues these leaders would have to confront and resolve. The competencies underlying GOLD did not resemble typical leadership competency listings. Rather they were derived from and driven by the strategic business imperatives facing Motorola Paging in the mid-1990s.

The design team functioned as a virtual team because no one lived in the same city, and for a time we were not even in the same country. The primary design team comprised Tom Land, an organizational development specialist, and Marguerite Foxon, a performance improvement specialist. Jim Wright, representing the Paging Executive Council (PEC), the top management group in MSPG, was also part of the design team. His support and involvement, despite a demanding schedule, was key to getting GOLD to the pilot stage. As with all new approaches, a senior person must promote the cause if the company is to obtain funding and attendees for the first session. To design and launch a leadership development initiative as radical as GOLD, a supportive senior management champion whose advocacy is respected and honored is essential.

The goal of GOLD is to produce results-oriented, global, entrepreneurial leaders working together for the success of the paging business as a whole, and capable of creating the future of MSPG. The intended outcomes are a net increase of 200+ MSPG leaders by the year 2000, dramatic business results through the application of leadership practices to significant business issues, the creation of a distinctive MSPG model of global leadership, the promotion of networking among the leaders across organizational boundaries, and the involvement of the GMs in the inspiration, support, and monitoring of the leaders going through the GOLD process.

GOLD is not a program. It is an accelerated leadership development *process* with three distinct elements. The most visible is the training piece. The other two are the Business Challenges (action learning) and GOLD Miner, a database and tracking process. These three components are discussed next.

The GOLD Process

A GOLD session covers a three-month period, resulting in four GOLDs per year (one per quarter). At the completion of the pilot with twenty managers, approximately thirty to thirty-five participants signed up for each quarter, netting upwards of 110 GOLD alumni per year. Although at one point forty attendees were accepted, thirty-five was the optimum number. This allows participants to network with managers from several different functions and regions and to be exposed to a variety of viewpoints during discussions without sacrificing their chance to raise issues in class or get "face time" with the faculty.

Each quarter followed the same pattern. In the first month participants met in Asia for seven days. In the second month they met in the United States for eight days, and finally in Europe in the third month for six days. In all three cases optional cultural orientation days were offered for those who could come early. In total this amounted to twenty-one training days with three optional culture days spread over three months. GOLD required a high level of commitment from the participants, their supervisors, and the GMs because of the time key people were away from the business.

Hotel bookings and logistics were outsourced to a specialist consulting group with prior experience with MSPG. One full-time internal administrator handled all GOLD administration such as nominations, printing of files, shipping of prework, faculty contracts, and general troubleshooting. The value of appointing a full-time administrator was learned early on. Apart from anything else, it freed the design team to concentrate on design and development and ensured that logistics were executed flawlessly.

Training

The emphasis is on global and transnational strategic thinking and action, vision and strategy alignment, customer focus, transcultural leadership, and leading and managing change (including an internal culture change that provides an ongoing developmental milieu for future leaders).

Phase One: Ice Breakers. In the first phase of the training, activities break down barriers between participants as they form relationships. From the outset, emphasis is placed on the need to move out of silos and work in teams that cross natural boundaries of function, gender, region, and culture. This begins with three hours of icebreaking activities that require cross-regional teams to work together under time pressure to resolve difficult tasks. In one activity, each eight-person team has a bucket of water with eight ropes attached. Using only the ropes the team must manipulate the bucket and empty the water into a small container without spilling a drop. Teams are given five minutes to plan. Teams win when they collaborate and realize that not all eight participants need be involved to most effectively complete the task. Skilled facilitators debrief participants and draw out the implications for leadership, collaboration, and "out of the box" thinking. Meal times provided a measure of the extent to which the "silo" mentality was breaking down. As the cross-regional activities took effect, table groups became culturally diverse and participants began to socialize with other nationalities in the evenings. This shift was very noticeable after the activities were introduced into the training in 1996. In the earlier sessions there was little impromptu cross-cultural socialization.

On the first day participants also spend several hours with Jim Wright, vice president and director of strategic planning, on the MSPG vision and strategic thrusts. Time is spent discussing the shift in focus that MSPG has been undergoing, from being product-driven to architectural-driven. External faculty in this first phase present sessions on the alignment of vision and strategy and on transcultural competency. Both topic areas are considered fundamental to the development of MSPG leaders. In particular, transcultural competency is vital for MSPG to become truly global in mindset and organization.

Phase Two: Strategic Planning. In the second phase, GOLD participants meet in the United States in a city where Motorola does *not* have an office, in order to minimize interruptions. This phase emphasizes strategic planning, particularly at the transnational level, and developing customer-focused strategies. Participants work on issues around forming and implementing global and divisional strategies, develop tools for the effective use of resources and knowledge in the FLEX architecture development and marketing programs, and address critical leadership issues (for example, how to optimize customer responsiveness, spread innovation, and increase efficiency within the company's global organization). During the final five days of this phase, participants spend much of their time in cross-regional and cross-functional teams working on a customer-focused marketing simulation. The debrief includes discussion of team functioning and team leadership as well as the business issues raised by the simulation.

Phase Three: Leading Organizational Transformation. The third phase, Leading Organizational Transformation, focuses on personal and strategic organizational leadership as well as changing the culture of the organization (which became a subobjective of GOLD). In this segment, participants receive 360-degree feedback from their peers, managers, and teams so they gain a better understanding of their behaviors and actions as perceived by others. They complete a personal inventory and a work group culture analysis. Both dovetail with the 360-degree survey, providing a comprehensive analysis of strengths and weaknesses in terms of the current work group culture and desired work group culture. These analyses serve as the basis for the week-long training and each participant receives private consultation with the facilitators as well as time in triads and work teams to study the implications and applications of the data. The week culminates in an individual action planning exercise that incorporates the full twenty-one days of training. This exercise takes several hours, and builds on issues raised in the personal consultation as well as through the 360-degree feedback, discussions, and activities. Participants then form triads to discuss and refine their action plans and to seek support in implementing their plan back in the workplace. In the evaluation undertaken some months later, it was found that almost every participant had endeavored to implement the items on their action plan, often with quite dramatic results. One participant reported "My personal profile and the 360-degree feedback I received helped me to close the communication gaps with all of my subordinates. The result—an 80 percent improvement on the [upward] appraisals from my team." Another commented, "Based on my action items, I have made a conscious effort to force myself to look into projects and design trends two to five years down the road as opposed to the next twelve months."

Throughout the three GOLD training sessions over the three-month period, participants are addressed by GMs who have demonstrated a high level of commitment to GOLD. For example, Jim Wright arranged his schedule to fly to Asia for the opening of all GOLD presentations (four per year). Approximately twelve GMs, including the CEO of MSPG, flew to wherever GOLD was located to give a ninty-minute presentation on how their business group is supporting and driving forward the MSPG vision. Participants learn about business groups they may know little of, are provided with confidential financial and product development information, and are exposed to strategies and new thinking from the highest levels. There is no other forum within MSPG outside of the Paging Executive Council (PEC) that this comprehensive overview can be gained. As one participant noted: "The discussions we had with the GMs relating to our strategy and future directions from the viewpoint of their numerous functions and regions have broadened my approach to strategy. I gained great benefit from hearing the views of these senior managers and listening to them articulate our vision."

Sourcing and Managing Faculty

The faculty is critical to the success of GOLD, both internal faculty (the GMs) and world-class external faculty. Considerable effort went into finding leading academic and industry thinkers. Faculty were sought who could connect their expertise and experience to the MSPG vision and strategies, and deliver the material in a powerful and motivating manner.

It is a time-consuming and expensive exercise to source, preview, educate, and manage a group of world-class faculty. Each one met with numerous MSPG managers as well as the PEC. Faculty members were briefed on why GOLD was being developed, given access to considerable internal confidential information, and assisted with the development of case material. All faculty members held a discussion for several hours in the early design phase. Three faculty members whose content had a natural connection met with the design team to ensure a seamless flow between modules. By being familiar with each other's cases and examples, they prepared for or built on the material of the others during their GOLD sessions. It takes effort on the part of the design team to achieve this flow. It also requires a willingness by external faculty, who are recognized experts and outstanding presenters in their own right, to work within designers' requirements.

The pay-off is worth the effort. Even at the pilot participants are presented with a seamless stream of content rather than a series of instructors presenting separate modules. In addition, faculty members speak knowledgeably and with insight about the organization, its strengths and weaknesses, the relationship of their content to the vision and business challenges, and the strategic issues facing MSPG. On many occasions, faculty members have been invited by GOLD alumni to join various business groups in a consulting capacity, which only enhances their understanding of MSPG for the next GOLD session.

The success of GOLD is due to more than the selection of relevant content and world-class faculty. GOLD is aligned with the MSPG vision and linked to key business drivers. The CEO's and GMs' involvement provides a level of commitment rarely seen in Motorola training programs. When the MSPG CEO travels to Istanbul or Prague to spend a few hours with thirty-five high potentials to explain his vision for the future and the quality of leadership he is looking for from GOLD alumni, he conveys a strong message about the importance of this initiative.

Action Learning

The second element of GOLD is the application. The design team was convinced that no matter how mind stretching and job-relevant the content might be, training alone could not accelerate the development of a cadre of new leaders. There had to be a mechanism for participants to put the new learning into action. They could not wait until the end of the three months of training. That was too late. Application had to begin when participants arrived at GOLD. If possible, application issues should be raised at the time of their nomination. The company adapted the traditional action learning model as the vehicle for application.

Action learning is a means of placing training into context and enhancing transfer of skills and knowledge.[3] In most programs that incorporate action learning, participants bring either an individual or team project they are working on to use as a means to transfer the newly learned skills and knowledge. Participants are better able to transfer training into their work environment because of the program's continuous cycle of reflection and application of new learning.

The design team's model of action learning differed from the traditional approach in three significant ways. First, no participant worked on an individual project in GOLD. All projects, known as "Business Challenges," were team-based. Team size varied depending on the project. For example, on one Challenge team, there were only two managers. On two other Business Challenges, there were teams of eleven. On average, teams had five to eight members.

The second difference is the team composition. Rarely have team members been from the same office. Most teams have members from two or more countries, and from three or more functions. A typical Business Challenge team might have a marketing manager from Texas, a business development manager from Singapore, an engineer from Singapore, an HR manager from Florida, and a quality director from Beijing. This eclectic mix reflects the nature of global work teams today. Leaders no longer have the luxury of working with a team located in the same building or even the same country in many cases. Global leadership teams solve global problems, and Motorola's leadership development process acknowledged this and built it into the training design.

Third, participants did not nominate the project for their Business Challenge. The GMs made this decision. GMs were advised to select strategic business issues that "kept them awake at night." In the first year of GOLD, many of the Business Challenge teams were charged with developing strategies to get the FLEX protocol accepted in various countries. Each GM nominating high-potential staff for GOLD identified a significant strategic stretch assignment as the Business Challenge and nominated the optimal mix of Hi-Pos as the Business Challenge Team attending GOLD. In many cases GMs incorporated someone from another GM's group to enhance the team membership and give more opportunity for cross-fertilization of ideas.

Prior to attending GOLD, the GM briefed each Business Challenge team. Because the action learning continues after the formal training, team members' supervisors were included in this briefing whenever possible. This ensured buy-in to the process and minimized conflict around priorities after GOLD.

Action learning, in the form of the Business Challenge, was integrated into the training sessions and continued after the GOLD training was completed. Faculty assigned application exercises to Business Challenge teams, and participants were encouraged to use the new tools and skills learned at GOLD to achieve their Business Challenge goals. Teams had to find time to make progress on Business Challenges between the three one-week training sessions during the quarter they were at GOLD. No work time was allocated for the Challenges, and team members found time over and above normal working hours to meet. This was consistent with the belief that outstanding leaders must find ways to achieve outcomes, despite time and resource constraints. Once their three months of GOLD training was completed, teams continued meeting and working on their Business Challenge for as long as necessary. In some cases, the deliverables were required within a specified period of months after the completion of the GOLD training; in others, they were open-ended. At least one team continued to meet and work on its Challenge for two years. The leader of a successful Latin American team commented, "When I look back at the strategies our Business Challenge team recommended to management, I see they are acting in all areas—functional areas and teams are implementing these strategies."

Business Challenge Examples

Examples of Business Challenges are:

- Develop an effective strategy for the paging business to succeed in Latin American markets where digital cellular is being positioned as a substitute for paging
- Identify, analyze, and evaluate the factors contributing to higher manufacturing costs in this region, and develop strategies and action plans that will lead to significant and timely reductions

- Create and establish a pervasive brand identity and dominant market presence in China

These were indeed "stretch assignments" for teams that often lacked specific expertise in the topic area, were located in different cities and even different regions, and that were required to tackle the Challenge while continuing with their normal workload. Successful teams identified internal and external resources to help them, sought out mentors and sponsors to work with them, and applied the tools and insights from the GOLD training in tackling the Challenge.

GOLD Miner

The third element of the GOLD process is GOLD Miner (see Exhibit 12.4). This is both a database of GOLD alumni and a leadership development tracking system. GMs and senior managers can access GOLD Miner from around the world to identify leaders for new projects or business opportunities. It was designed to track GOLD alumni in terms of job rotation, expatriate assignments, cross-functional experience, and promotions.

The database was a valuable tool. For example, a senior manager wished to establish a new group to pursue an innovative use of Motorola paging technology. She required key leaders in each region worldwide. She mined the GOLD database to identify high-performing managers already experienced in resolving strategic business issues via their Business Challenge to lead the project in each region. Every manager appointed to this project was a GOLD alumnus.

Multilevel Evaluation

A multilevel evaluation strategy was implemented throughout the GOLD process. Continuous and real-time evaluation of all aspects of the GOLD process enabled the design team to make real-time program changes, assess the workplace impact of GOLD, and monitor the leadership development of alumni. The evaluation strategy had three foci—during and post-training evaluation, transfer evaluation, and impact evaluation.

During and Post-Training Evaluation

This level of evaluation was far more extensive than the typical reaction assessment or "happy sheet" employed by most companies. During the first two presentations by each instructor, participants provided daily feedback on "strengths of the session" and "what needs changing." This enabled real-time adjustments during the GOLD session. If evaluation is undertaken at the end of the module, changes cannot be implemented until the next quarter. At the close of each module the design team evaluator debriefed the group as a whole. It was found that after their first two presentations, instructors' sessions were no longer in need of adjustment and this evaluation could be discontinued.

Participants completed a survey to identify the most meaningful learning, what they planned to take back and apply in the workplace, and the impact of the module on their leadership behaviors. Instructors were asked to self-evaluate their presentation according to several criteria such as how well their material related to participants' work roles, the effectiveness of learning activities, the value of pre-reading, and whether learning objectives were met. Data were analyzed and a report provided within forty-eight hours to instructors, the design team, the CEO, general managers, and others as appropriate. The design team followed up on an individual basis with participants who had raised specific concerns.

Two months after completion of the third and final training session (that is, five months after commencing and two months after completing the three months of GOLD training), an overall assessment survey was distributed. The response rate for this survey ranged from 56 percent to 100 percent, with an average of 80 percent. This evaluation assessed each module in relation to the other modules as well as to the overall goal of GOLD. It focused on post-training networking between participants, the level of support from GMs and immediate supervisors, application to the Business Challenges (action learning) of the tools and skills learned in training, and an assessment of GOLD as a valuable investment for MSPG (see Exhibit 12.5).

This instrument's value was immediately apparent. From early evaluations it was learned that many of the immediate supervisors (for example, senior managers) did not support GOLD participants taking time to work on Business Challenges. As a consequence, the effectiveness of the action learning piece, the primary opportunity to practice and develop the leadership skills, was being undermined. The design team had predicted this opposition, but the Paging Executive Council (PEC) was not convinced and declined to fund an intervention designed to gain senior manager commitment for GOLD. When this evaluation finding was presented to the PEC they requested a mandatory Executive GOLD program for supervisors of GOLD participants. The design team was given three months to develop a one-week program for the global senior management population. Executive GOLD was delivered to all senior managers over an eight-week period. Within a few months after the problem surfaced, lack of support ceased to be an issue. Without the evaluation data and feedback to the PEC, it would have been difficult to address the inadequacy of supervisor support.

Transfer Evaluation

Transfer evaluation assessed the degree to which skills and knowledge learned in the training, as well as through the Business Challenges have transferred to the work environment. In other words, were participants taking the lessons learned from the classroom as well as the action learning and applying these to their leadership roles on the job? Unless they were, MSPG would fail to achieve its goal of 200+ leaders by 2000. Because GOLD is a process intervention rather than a training intervention, formal leadership development continues after the three months of training. Not only does the Business Challenge continue as a developmental activity, but the selection of alumni for job rotation, expatriate assignments, or special projects is part of the development process and an opportunity to apply the knowledge and skills gained throughout GOLD. Transfer was assessed by focusing on Business Challenges and application of the training to the workplace. Refer to Exhibits 12.6 and 12.7 for an example of a transfer evaluation survey and cover letter.

At the close of the final GOLD training session, Business Challenge teams prepared an action plan for the coming three-month period. This plan itemized the aspects of the Challenge they would work on, who would take what responsibility, as well as when, where, and how the team would meet. Teams with members located in various parts of the world gave careful consideration to meeting management. They did not leave GOLD assuming that meetings would somehow occur.

Three months after GOLD, the evaluator contacted each team and discussed team progress, application of the training to the Business Challenge, team dynamics, and any problems. The design team is now able to predict how a Business Challenge team will perform over the long term based on the degree of transfer of learning within the first three months. Teams committed to the action plan and applying the concepts and tools from GOLD are most likely to surmount the difficulties of working on the Challenge over and above their everyday tasks. Teams with vague action plans or unable to meet more than once or twice in the first three months are unlikely to complete the Challenge.

Action learning was evaluated on a global scale by reviewing all teams annually. A design team member met with each Business Challenge team wherever they were located to review progress. Participants discussed application of the GOLD training, problems encountered, how the Challenge had helped with the development of leadership, and the team's progress in resolving the Challenge. Team members unable to attend the review were interviewed by conference call. From these annual reviews, members gathered rich data on action learning, issues facing multilocated teams, and the dynamics of high-performing teams.

During the second annual review of teams a continuum of implementation stages against which teams can be rated was identified. The stages are (1) the Challenge has been abandoned and the team disbanded; (2) the team has stalled; (3) the team is moving forward with the Challenge; (4) the Challenge has been completed and the team disbanded; (5) the Challenge has been completed and the team is initiating new strategy implementation.

At the most recent review, teams were located on the continuum as follows: (1) Abandoned: one team; (2) Stalled: six teams; (3) Progressing: eight teams; (4) Challenge completed and team disbanded: four teams; (5) Initiating new strategy implementation: five teams. In other words, just under 30 percent (seven teams) were in difficulty or had failed, but nearly 40 percent (nine teams) had successfully completed the Challenges. As an example of "success," one team had been the major force in a win for Motorola worth more than $110 million. This review provided a measure of the level of transfer of GOLD learnings to strategic business issues (that is, the Business Challenges).

Every six months, the evaluator undertook a major transfer study of GOLD participants who had attended GOLD training sessions over the previous eight to twelve months. In the most recent study, the survey response rate was 91 percent ($n = 100$). Data, especially from open-ended questions, provided evidence of GOLD's value as a leadership development intervention. Participants implemented personal action plans, and upwards of 75 percent reported achieving action plan goals. Respondents gave examples of conscious integration of skills and knowledge gained through GOLD. For example, one participant commented, "I learned a lot about cultural sensitivity. Since GOLD I've had business dealings in Japan, Hong Kong, and China. I'm much more sensitive to other cultures and in all cases didn't try to go in and get business done and get out like a typical American." A transfer evaluation report was prepared and circulated to the PEC and senior management.

Surprisingly, participants perceived the Business Challenge as less helpful than the new knowledge and skills (for example, training) in developing leadership skills. Only one-third of respondents identified the Challenge as being as valuable as the training input in developing leadership skills. This suggests some Challenges are a more effective means of leadership development than others are. Team composition was another factor contributing to a successful outcome. Teams composed of intact work groups or with at least one member whose fulltime job is aligned with the Business Challenge valued the Challenge more highly. Team members whose daily jobs did not fit well with the Challenge tended to not receive the same degree of support, resources, or consequences as a manager whose job was aligned with the Challenge. These findings were used to encourage GMs to plan the composition of the teams even more thoughtfully.

The transfer evaluation also assessed the value of sending participants to three different parts of the world and bringing participants together from around the globe. It would have been less costly to stage regional GOLDs. Because effective leaders use their networks to advantage, the design team decided global networking should play a central role in GOLD. The benefit of structuring GOLD around global networking is demonstrated in a European manager's comment, "I source products from our factories on behalf of Europe. I have used my GOLD contacts in Singapore, India, Florida, and China to get things going." There were several instances of business successes and cost savings directly attributable to GOLD networking.

The demographic data indicated that GOLD managers were selected for rotational and expatriate assignments, and were more rapidly promoted than Hi-Pos prior to GOLD. On average, 70 percent of GOLD alumni experienced a change in one or more aspect of their job within one year of GOLD. As previously mentioned, GOLD alumni have been chosen to head up new projects *because* they have been through GOLD and are perceived as having superior leadership skills.

Impact Evaluation

The following impact evaluation e-mail is sent out to measure the outcomes of Business Challenge teams.

Sample Impact Evaluation. "I am contacting spring and summer Business Challenge teams who may have completed their Challenge, in an attempt to gather some general data regarding return on investment and impact on the organization. We know some of the Challenges have resulted in measurable cost savings, increased productivity, and so on. In other cases, the measurements may be inferred, but less easily measured.

"If your team has completed its Challenge and believe the Challenge has led to a return on investment or has impacted the organization substantively, please reply to this e-mail. I do not want to send out a survey, but would prefer to e-mail or phone those of you who believe such a benefit has occurred."

The organizational impact of a leadership development process such as GOLD does not occur until well after it is put in place. The design team waited two and a half years from the commencement of GOLD before investigating its long-term impact on MSPG. The team felt that it would take that long for significant changes to emerge. There was considerable evidence that GOLD alumni had transferred the skills and knowledge to the workplace. They now sought evidence that this accelerated leadership development process was promoting the growth of the business.

The preceding sample evaluation e-mail was sent to leaders of Business Challenge teams seeking information on the impact of the execution of their Challenge. Responses provided encouraging data. Reference has been made to the multimillion dollar contribution of one Business Challenge team. Several teams have been instrumental in contributing to major strategic thrusts, opening new markets, or initiating changes that will result in cost savings and increased productivity in the future. In one country, the Business Challenge team's research and proposals resulted in successful new marketing strategies.

Lessons Learned

GOLD is a successful leadership development process. During the years of their involvement with GOLD, the design team has reflected on reasons for this success. Other organizations wishing to replicate this model can build on their experience with similar results. They have learned several lessons about executing a leadership development initiative:

1. *Commit to the continuous involvement of management.* Senior management support is crucial to the success of major change interventions.[4] The most-senior management levels were asked to take an active role in the development of the GOLD process from the beginning. The design team used every opportunity to enlist their support. They worked hard to keep senior management informed and obtain their input. They encouraged them to be presenters. Ultimately they were successful in getting senior managers to take ownership of GOLD. The design team educated the GMs and managers to think in terms of a leadership development process closely linked to business issues and MSPG goals, rather than in terms of a training program. They kept GOLD highly visible by providing evaluation feedback to managers of attendees, GMs, and the sector CEO. Marketing the evaluation

findings and recommendations within MSPG was a major factor in gaining total acceptance of GOLD, even from the skeptics.

2. *Undertake a thorough needs assessment.* If a global intervention is required, undertake a global assessment. There is no excuse for educated guess-work or a "quick and dirty" needs assessment.[5] Use the assessment phase to get buy-in as well as valuable input from the primary stake-holders. Managers who will not support a thorough assessment are un-likely to fully commit to the leadership development intervention. In this case study, needs assessment were used to clarify the business issues, focus on relevant performance issues, and understand senior manage-ment's vision for the future. These global data provided the foundation for the proposed global intervention.

3. *Link leadership development to critical business issues.* This linkage was the sell-ing point. It provided the direction and focus for the design of GOLD. GOLD does not develop leaders in a vacuum unrelated to the business. The leadership development process accelerates the development of leaders while simultaneously driving the business forward toward strate-gic goals. Every aspect of the GOLD process is aligned with the vision and strategic goals of MSPG.

4. *Look beyond the established approaches.* Let the business issues confronting your organization creatively drive the development of the leadership development process. The typical competency-based approach to lead-ership development did not suit the needs of the design team because they chose to build the design around the critical business issues. Sim-ilarly they considered how to adapt the traditional approach to action learning to more powerfully align it with the pressing business chal-lenges facing GMs. The resulting model allowed GOLD participants to begin shaping the future of their organization as they worked on the Business Challenges.

5. *Allow the intervention to develop incrementally.* GOLD costs $3 million per year. An initial request for this level of funding would have been de-nied. The design team eventually received funding for every element of the design because they demonstrated the business rationale under-pinning GOLD and continuously involved the GMs in the GOLD process. Initially, for example, the team did not have funding for the op-

tional cultural days. At the pilot it was clear they could enhance the transcultural communication module with the inclusion of cultural days in each region. These experiences orient participants and build cultural awareness before an overseas assignment. Rather than seek full funding at the outset it is wiser to request additional funding once the intervention is in place and demonstrates value.

6. *Use best-in-class faculty.* A best-in-class intervention requires best-in-class faculty. Experts are usually expensive, but with careful searching you can locate as yet undiscovered academics and practitioners who charge reasonable fees. Committing to regular presentations over a period of years gives them exposure to a major corporation and valuable consulting work. The design team worked hard at building close friendships with the GOLD faculty. Managing the faculty is as important as good sourcing. The more opportunity faculty have to visit your organization and understand its corporate culture, strategies, vision, successes, and failures, the more powerful and relevant their presentation will be. GOLD instructors appeared to know as much about MSPG as most participants. This level of knowledge did not just happen but was the result of systematic briefings and exposure to MSPG.

7 *Evaluate continuously.* The design team knew it would be difficult to sustain funding past the first year unless we could show GOLD was changing leadership attitudes and behaviors. For this reason GOLD had a highly visible evaluation component. This provided valuable information for sponsors and champions, and it enabled the design team to rapidly implement improvements to the GOLD process. A leadership development intervention requires its own evaluation strategy designed to provide a complete picture of the process and its impact on the organization. Produce informative but easily read reports and circulate them for maximum effect.

Summary

GOLD commenced in the fourth quarter of 1995. Eleven GOLDs were held for approximately 350 managers in an effort to accelerate the development of 200+ leaders needed by the end of the decade. In mid-1998, GOLD II commenced, the second phase of the process, based on a similar three-phase global training model but with a different action learning component. GOLD II participants are alumni who attended GOLD at least one year earlier. Currently the GOLD process is "on hold." Motorola has been negatively impacted by the economic problems in Asia and elsewhere during the past twelve months, and sector-specific leadership initiatives have been suspended.

Within MSPG, GOLD is considered an unqualified success. It is not a "program" that managers attend, but a process that has become an integral part of the organization. GOLD has had a greater impact on MSPG than anyone predicted. For example, managers attending Executive GOLD in early 1997 raised concerns that led to a reorganization of strategic alignment issues at the most senior level of MSPG. In the revised strategic plan, GOLD was listed as a key initiative enabling the organization to achieve its mission and business goals. When asked to rate the value of GOLD as an investment for MSPG, the senior managers attending Executive GOLD gave it 4.9 on a five-point scale.

Throughout Motorola worldwide there has been a great deal of interest in the GOLD process. The semi-conductor sector instituted a GOLD process in 1998, and in Asia a regional cross-sector adaptation of GOLD commenced in 1997. A GOLD participant from the MSPG Learning and Development group designed and instituted a supervisor development program based on the GOLD model in 1998.

GOLD has also attracted attention outside Motorola. Several companies have benchmarked the GOLD process. In 1998, three major business schools in the United States, the United Kingdom, and France collaborated to develop an executive development program for Fortune 100 companies based on the GOLD model. The University of Michigan Best Practices study (1997) rated GOLD as a Best Practice in Leadership Development, and Bowling Green State University identified GOLD as a Best Practice in Leading Change in 1998.

Organizations desiring to be successful in a global and technologically driven world must be able to rapidly develop leaders, but this developmental task is becoming more difficult. Exposing managers to academic and industry consultants for a week will not accelerate leadership development. Effective programs must be linked to business issues, aligned with the vision and strategic goals of the organization, and based on a process model of leadership development. The design team believes other organizations can adopt the GOLD model and replicate their experience. The success factors underpinning GOLD are not complex. The most difficult thing is to obtain senior management buy-in, but this is easier when interventions are linked to the business needs and drivers of the organization. In truth, there can be no other justification for instituting a leadership development process.

Exhibit 12.1: The GOLD Process Map

GOLD™ PROCESS

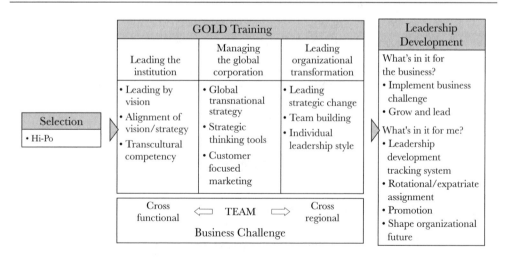

Exhibit 12.2: Senior Management Interview Questions

Business/Challenges

1. In your region, what is Motorola Paging's vision for the future? What must that vision accomplish? How will we know if we are successful in accomplishing it?
2. What critical issues must be addressed in this vision?
3. What are the challenges facing us in your region?
4. How prepared are you and your managers to meet these critical challenges?
5. How do you view the relationship between management and employee now? In the future, given our business challenges?

People Reporting to You

1. Which skills are becoming more important in light of the challenges you identified above for your region?
2. Which skills are becoming less important?
3. How do you perceive the role of the middle managers that report to you?
4. What do managers who are highly effective in your organization do differently? What makes them successful?
5. How do you determine the strengths and liabilities of your managers? What do you measure? Do you use any assessment tools?
6. How do your highly effective managers acquire this skill set?

Talk about You, Your Peers, Your Job

1. How did you get the job you are now in? What path did you take? What training and experience was most helpful to you?

2. How do you perceive your role as a senior manager and leader?

3. What do you see as your immediate and long-term developmental needs?

4. Looking at your peers, what do you see as their immediate and long-term developmental needs?

Management and Training or Development System Issues

1. Looking at the training and development system currently in place, can this system effectively develop your direct reports to staff your job in the near future?

2. If we were building an ideal training and development system for future leaders, how would it operate?

Leadership Training

1. What are the most important benefits you expect from leadership training?

2. Do you currently use training to develop your managers? Is it mostly internal, external, or both? How aware are you of the training available internally?

3. What types of leadership training would you like to see our organization provide?

4. If you had to score how well our training department is meeting your leadership training needs, on a scale of one to ten where would we fall?

Exhibit 12.3: Leadership Development Focus Group Questions

1. Thinking about your region, what business are we in? Where is it going?
2. If there is one thing we need to watch out for in MSPG that could jeopardize our success, it is. . . .
3. Will we be organized differently in the future? If so, how will we be structured?
4. What is the primary difference between the role of senior managers versus mid-level managers versus first-level supervisors in your organization? What should their roles be? What role do you play in the organization?
5. When you think of MSPG's leadership and management style, what do you think of?
6. Thinking about the challenges MSPG faces in the next five years, what do first line supervisors, mid-level, and senior managers do well? What skills, behaviors, and attitudes need to change or improve?
7. What was the most effective training and/or experience you have had that helped you become a leader? Why was it effective?
8. What is the best way for leaders to acquire the necessary skills and attitudes to be successful in our business in the future?
9. If you could change one thing in the way we select, train, and develop our leaders, what would it be?
10. If you could change MSPG leadership or management, what would you change?
11. What is the one leadership or management topic you would like to see offered?

Exhibit 12.4: GOLD Miner Database Form

MOTOROLA PAGING PRODUCTS GROUP

INTERNAL RESUME—MOTOROLA CONFIDENTIAL PROPRIETARY—when completed

PERSONAL DATA

Name (First, Last) _____   SSN _____

Race _____ (1=White, 2=Black, 3=Asian, 4=American Indian, 5=Hispanic)

Sex (M, F) _____   Date of Birth (MM/DD/YY) _____

Citizenship _____   Service Date (MM/DD/YY) _____

Street Address _____

City, State, Zip _____

Home Phone # _____ (Area Code, Number)

Work Phone # _____ (Area Code, Number, Extension)

CAREER OBJECTIVE

_____

_____

MOTOROLA EXPERIENCE

Current Job Title _____   Grade _____

Supervisor _____   Start Date _____

Location _____   Division _____

Functional Expertise (Engineering, Marketing) _____

Technical Expertise (CAD, RF Design, Distribution) _____

If you have management responsibility, indicate the following:

# of Employees _____   Annual Budget ($000'S) _____

Previous Job Title _____   Grade _____

Supervisor _____   Start Date _____

Location _____   Division _____

Functional Expertise (Engineering, Marketing) _____

Technical Expertise (CAD, RF Design, Distribution) _____

If you have management responsibility, indicate the following:

# of Employees _____   Annual Budget ($000'S) _____

Linkage Inc.'s Best Practices in Leadership Development Handbook, edited by David Giber, Louis Carter, and Marshall Goldsmith. Copyright © 2000 by Linkage Press and Jossey-Bass/Pfeiffer, San Francisco, CA.

MOTOROLA EXPERIENCE (con't)

Previous Job Title _____　　Grade _____
Supervisor _____　　Start Date _____
Location _____　　Division _____
Functional Expertise (Engineering, Marketing) _____
Technical Expertise (CAD, RF Design, Distribution) _____
If you have management responsibility, indicate the following:
# of Employees _____　　Annual Budget ($000'S) _____

EXPERIENCE PRIOR TO MOTOROLA

Company Name _____
Job Title _____　　Start Date _____
Functional Expertise (Engineering, Marketing) _____
Technical Expertise (CAD, RF Design, Distribution) _____
If you have management responsibility, indicate the following:
# of Employees _____　　Annual Budget ($000'S) _____

EDUCATION

College _____
Start Date _____　　Graduation Date _____
GPA (Out of 4.0) _____　　Degree (BS, MS, PhD) _____
Area of Concentration _____
College _____
Start Date _____　　Graduation Date _____
GPA (Out of 4.0) _____　　Degree (BS, MS, PhD) _____
Area of Concentration _____

MISCELLANEOUS

International Experience (Country, years) _____
Languages Spoken Fluently _____
Languages Read, Written Fluently _____
Professional Credentials _____

Exhibit 12.5: GOLD Final Assessment

FINAL PARTICIPANT ASSESSMENT OF GOLD

INSTRUCTIONS

Please e-mail back to Marguerite Foxon by [date]

- *Using the scale provided, indicate in each box the degree to which you **agree** with the statement.*
- *All boxes should have a number in them.*
- *Add explanatory comments in the space after each question.*
- *An example has been provided.*
- *There is room at the end of the form for additional comments. The more you wish to write the happier we will be!! Thanks!*

Example

	1		2		3		4		5	

Strongly disagree   *Strongly agree*

	Developing Transcultural Vision	Leading by Visioning	Leading a Transnational Organization	Customer Focused Marketing	Leading and Managing Change
I had sufficient opportunity during the module to practice the key skills.	4	2	3	5	5

Comments:
Seemed too theoretical.
No exercises or applications

	1	2	3	4	5

Strongly disagree   *Strongly agree*

	Developing Transcultural Vision	Leading by Visioning	Leading a Transnational Organization	Customer Focused Marketing	Leading and Managing Change
	Bennett	Davidson	Govindarajan	Carpenter	Petrock Clifford
1. The module met my expectations *Comments:*					
2. There was a balance between theory and application—there was sufficient emphasis on how to apply the concepts. *Comments:*					
3. I gained new insights on the leadership behaviors needed to achieve the MSPG vision. *Comments:*					
4. I had sufficient opportunity during the module to practice the key skills. *Comments:*					
5. My leadership skills will significantly improve if I apply the content of this module. *Comments:*					

	Developing Transcultural Vision	Leading by Visioning	Leading a Transnational Organization	Customer Focused Marketing	Leading and Managing Change
6. The content of this module will help me achieve the goals of the business challenge. *Comments:*					
7. The concepts and tools presented were useful in moving the business challenge forward. *Comments:*					

In the following questions, circle the number that best represents your view. Comments are welcome.

Strongly disagree   1   2   3   4   5   *Strongly agree*

8. GOLD has better enabled me to help create a shared vision of MSPG's future.
Comments:

   1   2   3   4   5

9. I am committed to communicating MSPG's vision to my subordinates and superiors.
Comments:

   1   2   3   4   5

10. I see a leadership role for myself in making the MSPG vision a reality.
Comments:

   1   2   3   4   5

11. Throughout the GOLD process I received inspiration and support from my general manager.
Comments:

   1   2   3   4   5

12. My general manager expressed interest in the progress of the business challenge between GOLD modules and/or following GOLD.
Comments:

   1   2   3   4   5

Strongly disagree   1   2   3   4   5   *Strongly agree*

13. Throughout the GOLD process my supervisor   1   2   3   4   5
    stayed involved and interested, including
    setting high expectations for the
    application of what I was learning.
    Comments:

14. During the coming months I anticipate strong   1   2   3   4   5
    support (including time away from my
    usual work) for the implementation phase of
    the business challenge.
    Comments:

15. The business challenge is an excellent way for me   1   2   3   4   5
    to develop more effective leadership behaviors.
    Comments:

16. I regard GOLD as a cutting-edge process   1   2   3   4   5
    and superior to other leadership programs
    I have attended.
    Comments:

17. GOLD promoted networking across   1   2   3   4   5
    organizational boundaries that will be important
    to future personal and business success.
    Comments:

18. This process is a good investment for MSPG.   1   2   3   4   5
    Comments:

19. The GOLD process is designed to produce results-oriented, global, entrepreneurial leaders who will
    work together for the success of MSPG as a whole and be capable of creating the future of Paging.

    GOLD began the process of achieving   1   2   3   4   5
    this objective.

20. Would you wholeheartedly recommend GOLD to Paging colleagues at a similar point in their careers as yourself?

☐ YES—What is its value-added?   ☐ NO—Why *wouldn't* you recommend
                                               it wholeheartedly?

_____   _____

_____   _____

_____   _____

_____   _____

21. GOLD could be improved by . . . *(consider, for example, topic areas, instructors, materials, program logistics, and so on).*

22. General Comments:

Thank you for your commitment to making GOLD a success!
Please e-mail back to Marguerite Foxon by [date].

Exhibit 12.6: Letter to GOLD Alumni, Distributing the Transfer Evaluation

To: GOLD Alumni

It is approximately one year since you completed GOLD. In line with our commitment to continuous improvement and in order to understand some of the long-term impacts of GOLD on the organization, I would encourage you to complete the brief survey at the end of this e-mail.

The survey is SHORT!! It will take ten minutes or less to fill out. This is the last formal evaluation of GOLD you will be asked to complete. The questions provide an opportunity for you to reflect on your leadership role since GOLD, as well as give us some feedback on the application of GOLD to the workplace. A brief outline of the GOLD curriculum is included to remind you of what was covered.

Please contact me by return e-mail if you require any clarification.

Thanks in advance for your input. Just hit "reply" and type in your responses now!

Marguerite

Exhibit 12.7: GOLD Transfer Evaluation

Curriculum "Memory Jogger"

Developing Transcultural Vision

- Understanding cultural differences, effects on communication
- Communication styles and values
- Stages of ethnocentricism to ethnorelativism

Leading by Visioning

- Role of vision; vision and value creation
- Linking vision to strategy and operations; alignment
- Creating and implementing grounded visions

Leading Transnational Organization

- Strategic intent and strategic renewal
- Core competencies and competency-based growth strategies
- Opportunity management versus performance management
- Implementation challenges

Market-Focused Strategy

- Changes in customers and competitors
- Competitive advantage
- Comprehensive market focused strategies
- Marketing simulation

Leading and Managing Change
- Culture change, motivation, power, resistance to change
- DISC style, 360-degree feedback
- NOW culture and SHOULD culture
- Personal action plans

MSPG Vision
- Director of Strategy
- Sector CEO
- Various GMs

Transfer Evaluation SURVEY

Ten questions—that's all! They won't take you longer than ten minutes.

1. At the close of GOLD you prepared an action plan (based on 360-degree feedback). Have you worked on any of the action items?

   _____ Yes   _____ No

   Have you achieved any of your action plan goals?

   _____ Yes   _____ No

   If yes, give an example _____

   _____

2. Have you consciously used concepts and/or skills learned at GOLD to improve the way you lead and manage?

   _____ Yes   _____ No

   If no, reasons why [check all that apply]

   _____ Concepts and/or skills do not relate to my work situation

   _____ I did not learn anything new

   _____ I have not had an opportunity to use the knowledge or skills

   _____ The pressure of work and/or lack of time made it difficult to apply them

_____ I lack motivation to keep using the skills or knowledge

_____ My immediate supervisor and/or colleagues discouraged me

_____ Other (explain)

3. What was the main thing at GOLD that challenged or expanded your thinking about your leadership role in MSPG? _____

_____

4. Give an example of something you learned at GOLD, that you have integrated into your work practice—what did you learn and how are you using it?

_____

_____

5. GOLD has had an impact on how you lead and manage . . .
   [place **XXX** beside number]

   to some extent   1   2   3   4   5   to a great extent

6. Which has been more helpful in developing your leadership skills:

   _____ The skills and knowledge learned at GOLD

   _____ Being involved with the Business Challenge

   _____ Both equally helpful

   _____ Neither has been particularly helpful

7. Looking back, are there parts of GOLD that seem unrelated to your work environment?

_____

_____

8. Looking forward, what additional skills or knowledge might be helpful to enhance the way you lead or manage?

_____

_____

9. Have you made use of your GOLD global network and contacts with other GOLD alumni who were in your session?

_____ Not at all

_____ A few times

_____ Often

_____ On a regular basis

10. Demographic Data

In which of the following ways has your job changed from the one you had as a GOLD participant? [Check all relevant]

_____ The majority of my direct reports are different

_____ My immediate supervisor is different

_____ I work in a different division

_____ I work in a different function

_____ I work in a different country (how many moves have you made?)

_____ I am at a different grade (promotion)

_____ I have made a lateral change

_____ Nothing about my job has changed

Any general comments?

References

Dixon, N. M. (1998). "Action Learning: More Than Just a Task Force." *Performance Improvement Quarterly,* 11(1).

Duncan, J. B., and E. S. Powers, (1992). "The Politics of Intervening in Organizations." *The Handbook of Human Performance Technology,* eds. H. D. Stolovitch and E. J. Keeps. San Francisco: Jossey-Bass, pp. 77–93.

Phillips, J. J. (1997). *The Handbook of Training Evaluation and Measurement Methods* (3rd ed.). Houston, Tex.: Gulf Publishing Co.

Rossett, A. (1987). *Training Needs Assessment.* Englewood Cliffs, N.J.: Educational Technology Publications.

Rossett, A. (1999). *First Things Fast—A Handbook for Performance Analysis.* San Francisco: Jossey-Bass/Pfeiffer.

Notes

1. Phillips, J. J. (1997). *The Handbook of Training Evaluation and Measurement Methods* (3rd ed.). Houston, Tex.: Gulf Publishing.

2. Rossett, A. (1987). *Training Needs Assessment*. Englewood Cliffs, N.J.: Educational Technology Publications. (1999). *First Things Fast—A Handbook for Performance Analysis*. San Francisco: Jossey-Bass/Pfeiffer.

3. Dixon, N. M. (1998). "Action Training: More Than Just a Task Force." *Performance Improvement Quarterly*, 11(1).

4. Duncan, J. B., and E. S. Powers, (1992). "The Politics of Intervening in Organizations". *The Handbook of Human Performance Technology*, eds. H. D. Stolovitch and E. J. Keeps. San Francisco: Jossey-Bass.

5. Rossett, A. (1999).

About the Contributor

Marguerite Foxon (AMF007@email.mot.com) received her Ph.D. in instructional systems from Florida State University, and has been with Motorola since 1993. Currently, she is a senior performance improvement specialist with Motorola University. Prior to coming to the United States in 1991, she was the national director of education for Coopers & Lybrand in Australia, Indonesia, and New Guinea. Foxon is a director of the International Board of Standards for Training, Performance, and Instruction, has published a number of articles on transfer evaluation and on leadership development in Motorola, and has presented at training and OD conferences in several countries. Honors include twice winning the Outstanding Instructional Designer award from the Australian Institute of Training and Development. In the United States, the Association of Educational Communication and Technology awarded her the Robert de Keiffer International Fellowship for forging professional ties in educational communications and technology between the United States, Australia, and New Zealand. Foxon is listed in the *International Who's Who of Professionals*.

CHAPTER THIRTEEN

PECO ENERGY

This chapter outlines a leadership competency-based process of nomination, individual assessment, development planning, and ongoing coaching support to improve leadership development and bench strength in the increasingly competitive utilities marketplace.

Company Background

PECO Energy Company is a leader in generating and marketing electricity in competitive markets across the United States. Since 1929, the company has provided retail electric and natural gas service to customers in southeastern Pennsylvania, serving more than 1.5 million customers in 1998. With the advent of deregulation, PECO Energy has developed a wide range of competitive businesses that build on its broad asset base, market knowledge, and core capabilities. PECO Energy's generation portfolio of more than 9,000 megawatts is among the most competitive in the United States, and its power marketing division, Power Team, is the leading real-time deliverer of wholesale electricity operating throughout the continental United States. The company also provides a variety of unregulated energy and utility infrastructure services, including competitive wireless and fiber optic-based communications services.

Recent years have brought about unprecedented change in the utility industry, during which PECO Energy steadily evolved from a vertically integrated, fully regulated electric utility to an industry leader in the competitive generation market. During this same period, while going from over 14,000 to under 7,000 employees, PECO Energy has dealt with myriad issues including implementation of two "early-out" programs, unionization attempts throughout the firm, a complete reengineering of the human resource function, changes in its core values and beliefs, and changes in key personnel at the senior management level of the company.

Implementing the Leadership Development Process

Given the rapidly changing nature of the electric industry, PECO Energy's management identified an urgent need to significantly revamp the staffing, selection, and promotion processes. In the fully regulated market, business conditions had been relatively stable and the leadership requirements well-known and predictable. PECO Energy had done a very good job of selecting and promoting talent to operate in this business environment where little change occurred, and the company's bench strength had been more than adequate.

However, with the advent of deregulation came severe ambiguity as to what shape the new competitive electricity market would take, what the rules of competition would be, and in what lines of business PECO Energy would successfully compete. Senior management at PECO Energy, most of whom were career employees, understood that different leadership would be required, but what would leadership look like? How much of that leadership talent was already at PECO Energy? Where were the holes in leadership capability? What would it take to close the gap? Once the talent gap was closed, how would the leadership capability be sustained over time? These questions helped frame the compelling strategic reason to implement the Leadership Development Process—to identify and develop the future leadership team of PECO Energy.

Objectives of the Leadership Development Process

Senior management at PECO Energy established the following objectives for the new leadership initiative:

- Identify the leadership requirements needed to compete in the deregulated market and use them to frame the model of leadership success moving forward.
- Create a structured, disciplined, and rigorous leadership identification and development process to build the leadership bench.
- Inventory the strengths and weaknesses of PECO Energy's current leadership using an objective third-party assessment center. (PECO Energy has partnered with Applied Research Corporation to develop the leadership competency model and assessment center program.)
- Create and implement methods for closing the leadership requirement gaps.

Design of the Leadership Development Process

Prior to implementing the current Leadership Development Process at PECO Energy in 1995, there had been fragmented efforts at succession planning. Some of the business units had worked with key position replacement charts, which served them well in the stable utility market in the late 1980s and early 1990s. Leaders of those business units could gauge bench strength and plot future job assignments for their people with relative certainty. While this worked well for management, some employees felt that there was little objectivity in the process and that favoritism played a big role in career growth.

In 1992, the company attempted to create a centralized, formal Leadership Development Process. This effort was designed to augment the replacement charts with the creation of a pool of high-potential employees whose career growth would be managed through oversight of the senior management team. This process was implemented during a period of tremendous change at PECO Energy, with several other large-scale cultural challenges well in play. Diluted focus and commitment to this process damaged its efficacy and it was subsequently terminated. However, in spite of its failure to take hold, it did provide valuable lessons and ultimately served as the foundation of the current program.

Starting in 1994, PECO Energy's senior management and human resources examined processes for identifying and assessing leadership potential and strongly committed to focusing solely on identifying and developing a company-wide pool of high-potential employees. The company also decided to enlist the assistance of a third-party consulting firm to provide a fresh perspective on the leadership challenge and to lend an objective eye to assessing the leadership bench at PECO Energy. The responsibility for developing bench strength via key replacement chart planning was left to the discretion of division leadership. The formal PECO Energy Leadership Development Process was designed and launched in 1995.

Leadership Competency Model

As part of the leadership development initiative, PECO Energy developed a leadership competency model in 1995. Officers and other key employees were interviewed to identify the current and future leadership requirements for PECO Energy. The information generated during the interviews provides the foundation for the competency model. By defining each competency and illustrating exemplary leadership behavior, the model provides a common understanding of leadership requirements as well as the language to frame discussions of leadership identification and development throughout the company. It is currently being refined for a third time to ensure that it accurately reflects the required leadership competencies appropriate for PECO Energy's rapidly expanding business proposition.

Overview of the Leadership Development Process

The implementation of the Leadership Development Process at PECO Energy in 1995 was the beginning of the evolution of what is now considered a "best practice." Each year since implementation, PECO Energy has improved upon the original concept and design to create a system that responds to the changing business environment.

PECO Energy manages its leadership challenges by dividing the talent pool into three distinct levels: new college recruits, junior to mid-level managers, and upper mid-management. Each level has a separate process for talent identification, leadership assessment, and development planning. All three processes have eligibility criteria that include both internal screening and an external assessment by a third-party consultant.

Summary of Assessment Centers

Following is a brief description of each level within the process.

Level I—Early Insights (College Recruits). Eligibility for participating in the Level I Assessment Center program is limited to those employees who are recruited through the company's university relations program. During the late fall of each year, new college recruits are evaluated in teams of five to seven in a day-long assessment center that examines their performance against a subset of the company's leadership competency model. Participants are provided feedback and development planning consultation, which is used to create plans targeted specifically to their unique needs.

The primary goals of this program are:

1. To provide feedback to the new employee regarding their development needs at this very early stage of their professional life at PECO Energy
2. To provide the employees' management teams with information regarding their development needs so that managers may work with the individuals to accelerate leadership development
3. To provide continuous improvement feedback to the university relations group about the quality of campus recruiting efforts

Level II—Junior and Mid-Level Management. Eligibility for participation in Level II Assessment Center includes serving at least two years at PECO Energy with a consistently high level of performance, which must include a significant and sustainable contribution of a tactical mid-management nature. Participants must also be successfully screened through three very rigorous talent review sessions that start at the business unit and end at the senior management team.

The primary goals of this program are:

1. To provide feedback to the employee regarding their development needs at this stage of their professional life at PECO Energy
2. To provide senior management with an objective, third-party assessment of the employees' leadership potential and development needs
3. To provide senior management and human resources with a detailed aggregate summary of strengths and weaknesses in PECO Energy's emerging leaders

Level III—Upper-Middle Management. Eligibility for participating in Level III Assessment Center includes serving at least one year at PECO Energy, and achieving a high level of performance that must include a significant and sustainable contribution of a strategic senior manager nature. Participants must also be successfully screened through two very rigorous talent review sessions by the management of the business unit and the senior management team. The primary goals of this program are the same as in Level II.

Leadership Development Process—Players and Roles

The Management Development Committee was created to oversee the Leadership Development Process at PECO Energy. It is a corporate governance committee, responsible to the board of directors for leadership continuity, and it includes the entire senior management team. The president, CEO, and chairman of the company chairs the committee, and it meets quarterly to oversee the Leadership Development Process and its results. In addition to topical leadership issues, which are raised and discussed at each meeting, the following schedule reflects the core activity for each quarterly session:

1st Quarter: Agreement on the scope of the Leadership Development Process for the year

2nd Quarter: Final nominations for attending the Level II and III Assessment Centers

3rd Quarter: Review of assessment center results and overall leadership issues identified

4th Quarter: Review and approval of high-potential employee individual development plans

The PECO Development Council is a team of high-potential employees who have been drawn from the Level III high-potential employee pool and play a unique and critical role in the execution of Levels I and II of the Leadership Development Process. The council representatives are assigned a role in one of two sub-teams, either the nomination team or the assessment team. Human resources and the consultants train the teams.

As a member of the nomination team, the council representative is responsible for leading the screening of candidates for participation in the Level II Assessment Center. In this role, they work closely with human resources and the business units' senior management team to ensure fair and rigorous talent review discussions. As a member of the assessment team, the council member serves as one of four assessors in the Level I and II Assessment Centers and is responsible for providing verbal feedback to the candidates.

Line managers are responsible for identifying and nominating the emerging leaders in their units for participation in the assessment centers. Each business unit holds talent review discussions as part of the annual Leadership Development Process cycle.

High-potential employees are those employees who are identified through the process of assessing their potential to move into critical leadership assignments. They are responsible for executing their own development plans with the assistance of the Management Development Committee and Human Resources.

A dedicated human resource professional provides thought leadership and technical expertise for the overall process, creates the agenda for and facilitates the Management Development Committee meetings, and acts as the intermediary of the process through interfacing between the various parties.

The third-party consultant provides advice on leadership issues, designs and implements the leadership assessment centers, and provides focused coaching services. The Leadership Development Process diagram, shown in Figure 13.1, illustrates the selection process for Level II participants.

Screen # 1: Tenure at PECO Energy Company. Participants must have at least two years of service with PECO Energy Company.

Screen # 2: Performance History. Participants must have achieved at least two performance ratings of two or above (on a one to five scale with one being highest).

Screen # 3: Strategic Business Unit or Functional Unit Review. This step marks the beginning of the rise of screened talent throughout the company. A PECO Development Council representative and a local human resource consultant organize and facilitate the talent review discussions in their assigned business or functional units. The Leadership Competency Model is used to guide the discussions of leadership potential. A majority of the people involved in the team discussions must agree that the candidate has demonstrated significant leadership potential for them to move the candidate onto the next screen. At the end of this step, the business

FIGURE 13.1 PECO ENERGY COMPANY'S LEADERSHIP DEVELOPMENT PROCESS—LEVEL II.

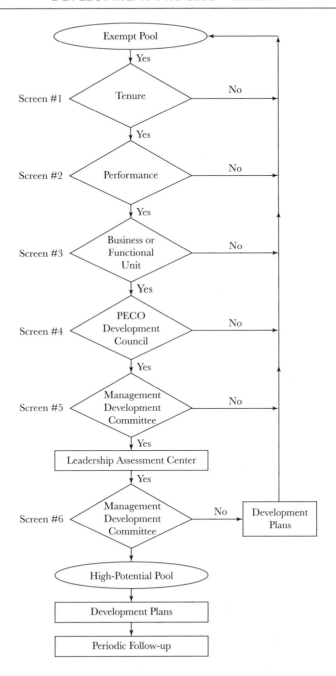

or functional units' shortlists of candidates are passed through to the next screen, the PECO Development Council review.

Screen # 4: PECO Development Council Review. The PECO Development Council reviews the nominations from all of the business or functional units. The council representatives' job is to fairly represent the candidates from his or her assigned business unit. Following rigorous discussion of each individual, the council members vote on whether or not the candidate deserves to move to the next screen.

Screen # 5: Management Development Committee Review. During this step of the process, the PECO Development Council attends the second quarterly Management Development Committee meeting, during which an elected council leader presents the names of individuals who have successfully passed through Screen # 4. The chairman and the committee review the list of names and employee work histories and question the council members, where necessary. Following this discussion, the Management Development Committee takes a final review of the list, discusses any further issues, and votes.

The Leadership Assessment Center. Candidates are sent a congratulatory letter from the head of their business unit, and are invited to attend the leadership assessment center. Although attendance is not mandatory, a nomination to attend the center is recognized as a "feather in the cap." Each leadership assessment center consists of five to seven candidates from mixed business or functional units who participate in the one-and-one-half-day business simulation exercise. The final report summarizing the leadership assessment center findings and recommendations are prepared for the final screen.

Screen # 6: Presentation to the Management Development Committee. The final screen in the Leadership Development Process at PECO Energy includes a presentation to the Management Development Committee of the leadership assessment center results. By this time, committee members have received copies of the assessment reports only for individuals sponsored by their business or functional unit. The entire committee, however, receives a broad overview of the assessment center performances. In addition to the assessment center data, the committee reviews all data accumulated heretofore, such as, performance history and additional information discussed during any of the previous screens. The committee then holds the final discussion during which candidates are voted into the high-potential pool.

Assessment Center Benefits

The use of the leadership assessment center has evolved steadily over the last four years as PECO Energy has learned a great deal about its leadership strength. The first leadership assessment center was piloted in 1995 with candidates from only the top 200 positions. PECO Energy senior management received two significant benefits from the pilot assessment center: They got their first glimpse of how their vice presidents and highest-performing upper mid-managers performed in a competitive business simulation, and, by attending an assessment center data integration session, they saw how the business simulation breathed life into the leadership competency model. The richness of the learning experience was so strong that the decision was made to roll similar programs throughout the professional ranks to inventory the rest of the bench strength and subsequently create the action plans needed to build the leadership for the competitive world.

The leadership assessment center currently being used at PECO Energy features custom-designed behavioral exercises that simulate the future business environment in which PECO Energy's leaders will operate. The center examines an individual's approach, quality of decisions, and actions taken in complex, dynamic organizational settings that mirror PECO Energy's business and leadership challenges. The center also evaluates performance-based leadership actions at individual, peer, and subordinate interaction levels while addressing both strategic and operational needs. The assessment activities include interactive in-baskets that assess strategic and operational problem-solving skills, individual and group problem tasks, individual interviews, and diagnostic instruments. Each particular leadership assessment center level has its own specific business situation that becomes increasingly more intense and strategic in nature at higher levels.

The leadership assessment center provides PECO Energy with an understanding of the depth and breadth of its bench strength. Specifically, the center provides:

1. Confirmation of staffing options for individuals who may be promoted to key leadership positions
2. Verification of the attendees' potential by providing PECO Energy's Management Development Committee with specific, standardized insights concerning participants further potential and development needs
3. An independent assessment of the current overall bench strength of the company
4. Data that reveal the aggregate patterns in strengths and weaknesses that can be incorporated in future leadership development interventions to help close gaps

The leadership assessment center also provides the participant with comprehensive diagnostic information regarding their strengths, development needs, and activities or situations that can provide optimal development opportunities.

Assessment Center Feedback

Feedback from the assessment center includes both verbal and written reports from the consultants to the participants and their senior management sponsors. Two days after they complete their participation in the center, the participant receives indepth individual verbal feedback from one of the center staff, either a consulting psychologist at Level III or a PECO Development Council member at Levels II and I. During this feedback session, privacy and confidentiality are ensured so that the employee can get the most from the meeting by comfortably asking questions about any aspect of the leadership assessment center and its outcomes. This session is a pivotal point in the development of the participant who receives a deluge of information in a candid but friendly environment. The candidate also receives a written report documenting his or her performance, and a copy of this report is sent to his or her senior officer and human resources.

Feedback to the sponsoring senior manager includes a verbal report on performance, a written diagnostic report, and further recommendations for each participant's potential. The Management Development Committee receives a summary of the total leadership assessment center findings, a snapshot of the inventory of talent throughout the corporation, and recommendations for addressing broad leadership issues identified in the assessment centers.

Leadership Development Planning. The leadership assessment center feedback is likely to be the most candid and robust developmental feedback that a participant has ever received. The report is very direct about participants' strengths and weaknesses and provides most of the grist for development planning. It is one of the few optimal moments for learning in their professional life because of the "wake-up call" nature of the feedback. Most employees and their managers have a limited perspective on development planning. The assessment report enables them to focus on areas needing development.

PECO Energy uses the "individual development plan" as the primary vehicle for framing leadership assessment center participants' development activities. All employees who participate in the leadership assessment center, regardless of whether they go into the high-potential pool, create an individual development plan with assistance from human resources and their management. The plan that is ultimately created is very critical to the development of each participant as it sets the stage for many initiatives:

- The employee's road map for successfully developing the leadership attributes PECO Energy seeks
- The contract for development between the employee and senior management
- The aggregate record of development resource needs for the coming year
- The baseline for discussion in the annual review of the high-potential pool

PECO Energy uses a simple format for creating the individual development plan. The employees use both past performance and the results of the assessment center to identify and prioritize their primary leadership development challenges. Challenges fit into one of three categories: (1) an experience need that could be addressed through a particular job assignment, (2) a style issue that may be resolved through coaching activity, or (3) a knowledge deficiency that could be addressed through taking a course or seminar. The plan includes a firm timeline for developmental activities as well as an acknowledgment of support from the sponsoring senior officer.

Articulating one's development challenge can be a difficult exercise. PECO Energy has found that articulating the answers to two questions has helped employees to clarify their developmental goal or challenge.

1. If you were to meet with a coworker two years from now, how would he or she know that you have developed your area of weakness?
2. How would your development in this area support and/or promote PECO Energy's strategy?

The individual development plan of each high-potential employee is reviewed and approved by the Management Development Committee at the fourth-quarter meeting. The committee ensures that the plans are on target and that the development objectives are rigorous. In essence, the committee actually manages the development of the high-potential employees through its actions during this meeting as it solidifies the contractual nature of the plan and clarifies the expectations of both parties. The employees commit to specific development targets; senior managers commit to supporting their employees' growth. The committee may also review the progress of past leadership assessment center participants who have worked at least two years on their development. Any such employee who has made significant progress may be voted into the high-potential pool. Conversely, any current high-potential employee who has not fulfilled development expectations may be withdrawn from the pool.

Throughout the development process, the human resource staff must provide the dispassionate, objective perspective, always seeking to improve the bench strength of the company by leveraging all the information accumulated through the talent reviews, assessment activity, development planning meetings, and ongoing employee job performance. This activity includes coaching and pushing employees for more specific, meaningful, and rigorous development plans as well as challenging the senior management team to fulfill their commitment to developing future leaders.

The resources used to support the employees' development depend on the particular development challenge. To use a new job assignment to satisfy a leadership experience need, for example, employees may be moved to a pre-identified "key developmental position," some other job, or a part-time assignment such as a task force initiative. A key developmental position is a specific job within PECO Energy that is ripe with leadership development opportunities. The positions are identified in what is becoming an annual exercise of uncovering the best development positions within PECO Energy. A team including human resources and line management identifies the few vital positions that can provide accelerated development. Once the list is gathered, it is presented to the Management Development Committee for their approval.

Not every job move for a high-potential employee is to another key developmental job. Assignments are based on a combination of business need, employee development need, and job assignment availability. An employee could also develop leadership skills by becoming involved in civic activities, such as serving on the board of a nonprofit organization.

Employees with leadership style issues are provided the opportunity to work with a personal coach. External consultants or other employees within PECO Energy, such as an officer or other senior managers, may provide the coaching. The coaching assignments are made with consultation among the employee, human resources, and the employee's sponsoring officer. Another method for addressing style issues is to send employees to an external short-term experiential learning course where they have the opportunity to explore their leadership style and impact in more depth.

As for challenges regarding specific knowledge needs, it is common to send employees to internal courses offered at PECO Energy, seminars offered by consulting firms, for example, and universities which offer in-residence, short-term business courses.

Finally, most employees are asked to consider using a diary for recording the daily, weekly, and monthly learning activities. This has been particularly helpful to some employees who have been working on style issues.

Keeping track of the opportunities for improving one's leadership style in the moment can provide acceleration in learning for some people and further motivate them even more to continue to grow.

Evaluation

Four short years after implementing its leadership development process, PECO Energy achieved its goals of:

- Understanding the leadership model necessary for success in the competitive market
- Creating and implementing a rigorous leadership identification and development process
- Gathering a detailed inventory of its aggregate leadership competency
- Improving the leadership bench through targeted development activities as well as adding key external hires to particular positions

In evaluating the impact of the leadership development process and, in particular, the leadership assessment center, PECO Energy has found that:

- The data from the process is both useful and well-utilized by senior management
- There is an improved understanding of leadership potential and how to identify it
- There has been a shift in the way in which selection decisions are being made
- The assessment center has been widely accepted as a useful management tool

The information gathered from the assessment center process provides the senior management team with useful organizational capability data as they create the business strategy for PECO Energy Company. Known leadership strengths and gaps are being factored into the company's planning activities, and critical leadership assignments are being made with consideration to individual development needs. In fact, the average number of new job assignments for the high-potential employees who were assessed in 1995 is approximately 2.5 career moves per person. Although not all job moves have been successful, these assignments provide management the opportunity to stretch and test the employee's ability to develop the weaknesses identified in the center.

The company's experience with a "competitive" leadership competency model and assessment center has altered the view of leadership. Senior management and assessment center participants now understand the difference between the leadership competencies that were required in the stable regulated market versus those that are needed in today's more ambiguous, rapidly changing competitive arena. Their change in perspective came from the experience of being either an assessment center participant or observer. Prior to this "hands-on" experience with the assessment center, the competency model was just another management model, which senior management acknowledged as being appropriate and necessary for business success, but it had not yet "come to life" for them. The assessment center converts the competency model into action, and then plays it back so that senior management can see how the new definition of leadership "looks and feels." Through this process, they can begin to develop a deeper understanding as the vocabulary of leadership potential and actual behaviors converge throughout the business simulations.

The increased realization of changing leadership needs has also impacted the way in which selection decisions are being made. Prior to the implementation of the leadership development process, most selection decisions were made within the framework of a stable, predictable utility market. Selection decisions were made without much emphasis given to the ability of the individual to adapt to the rapidly changing environment, quickly seize new business opportunities, and work effectively in ambiguous situations. Now, however, staffing decisions are increasingly made with these new leadership requirements firmly in mind.

The leadership assessment center is viewed as the linchpin in the leadership development process at PECO Energy Company. Although the performance feedback from the assessment centers has not always been warmly embraced by some participants and their senior management sponsors, the use of the assessment center as the primary tool for the identification of leadership potential has been widely accepted. The senior management team now has a thorough inventory of PECO Energy's emerging leaders, and a new perspective on what will be required of the leadership team of the future. The assessment center participants have gained insight into their strengths and development needs, and have had the opportunity to work on their developmental challenges through their development planning activity and subsequent job moves. Also, the role of assessor in one of PECO Energy's assessment centers (Leadership Development Process Levels I or II, or the PECO Supervisory Assessment Center) is a coveted developmental experience. Assessor training and experience is now being used to develop critical behavioral identification, employee development, and coaching skills in many management employees at PECO Energy Company as it continues to transform itself into a world-class competitive energy company. With each newly trained assessor, PECO increases its collective capability to improve leadership bench strength throughout the company.

About the Contributor

Patrick J. Sabine (Patrick.j.sabine@usa.dupont.com) is the former director of staffing and development at PECO Energy Company in Philadelphia, Pennsylvania. During his tenure at PECO he was charged with building organizational capability at PECO Energy through the development and implementation of effective selection, performance management, and leadership development processes. While at PECO Energy Company he was asked to present his work in leadership development at various seminars, as well as to senior leadership teams of other organizations. Prior to working at PECO Energy Company, Sabine held various human resource assignments at GTE Corporation, Towers Perrin, and MCI Corporation. He holds a bachelor's degree in economics from SUNY Oswego and a master's degree in industrial and labor relations from Cornell University. Sabine is currently the director of human resources at Dupont Safety Resources Business.

CHAPTER FOURTEEN

SIAC

This chapter outlines a competency-based leadership development system that leverages external coaching, 360-degree feedback, and individual development planning for all managers in the organization within the rapidly changing industry of information technology.

Introduction

As one of the top technology organizations in the financial services world, the Securities Industry Automation Corporation (SIAC) has distinguished itself through its innovative approach to building and developing its own leaders. By designing an integrated approach for its technical professionals—often a difficult audience for leadership development—SIAC has created a successful comprehensive process, as is indicated by the name itself: the Leadership Development System (LDS).

By stretching beyond the classroom into on-the-job development and project team work, linking to such human resource systems as selection, performance management, and succession planning, and carefully evaluating both business and performance impacts, SIAC has built a leadership system that has made a measurable difference. As a key element in changing the organization's conversation about the culture and the values of leadership, the LDS has impelled the organization to recognize that not only having the right technology, but also using the leadership to deploy it, is critical to SIAC's operating excellence.

Who Is SIAC?

Behind the scenes at the world financial markets in New York is SIAC, a twenty-seven-year-old technology organization. SIAC, technological hub of the securities industry, processes the data and writes most of the software applications for the New York and American Stock Exchanges, as well as the National Securities Clearing Corporation and the National Market System. SIAC consists of over 1,400 professionals, divided among computer operations, networks, communications software development, and administration. SIAC plans, develops, implements, and merges a variety of automated information handling and communications systems that support order processing, market data tracking and reporting, and clearance and settlement for a broad range of securities. Its current revenues are over $300 million. With its largest site in Brooklyn, New York, SIAC is a hardworking company that aggressively advances its agenda and growth.

In 1993, a line committee focused on human resources identified the need for greater leadership and a cultural shift at SIAC. In a white paper issued by this HR advisory committee, the SIAC HR department and outside consultants stated:

> As SIAC's clients have gained more familiarity with technology, their expectations for using the results of technological innovation as strategic and competitive tools have also increased.
>
> The securities industry will increasingly depend on information and technology. SIAC will operate within a context of shortened development time frames, increased volume, greater system complexity and speed, more complex buy versus build decisions, accelerating technical volatility, the impact of globalization, and clients who are more and more aggressively involved in the processes that control technology decisions.
>
> To meet future challenges and opportunities, SIAC must become a company that:
>
> - Is a first class systems operator of a complex, highly integrated yet hospitable open systems architecture environment
> - Is its core customers' chief IT strategic business partner
> - Is perceived as a leader in the financial services industry whose managers and lead technologists are knowledgeable about the issues that drive the business
> - Delivers creative solutions to client problems within the stringent confines of complexity and absolute reliability
> - Effectively uses value rather than cost as a competitive advantage
> - Can change to anticipate and meet new market demands
>
> PEOPLE, TECHNOLOGY, and TEAMWORK has been SIAC's theme since 1985. Although each of these components has always contributed to SIAC's success, SIAC's ability to develop and deliver TECHNOLOGY in a highly reliable manner has been perceived as the prime driver of that success. Bolstering SIAC's level of organizational competency in the PEOPLE and TEAMWORK components is now perceived as equally important to positioning SIAC for continued success in the future.

These strategic goals continue to define SIAC's mission today.

Strategic Reasons for This Program

SIAC's leadership development program was designed to meet the needs of its customers through a focused competency model that enhances its leaders' core capabilities: technical integrity, customer partnership, team collaboration, and developing people. (See Exhibit 14.1 on page 403, for an overview of the program.)

The Customer Challenge

The stock markets and brokerage firms cannot afford any systems interruptions. The continuing challenge for SIAC is to meet its goal of 99-percent systems reliability, even as the systems become increasingly open, complex, and integrated. As the needs of the customers continue to rise, SIAC must both increase its technical sophistication and understand where the business is headed in order to build the systems to support it. As stated in the 1994 "Foundation Document":

> The SIAC manager of the future must have good business sense; be technically skilled and literate in new technologies and trends: be able to manage risk, change, and innovation in a volatile open-systems environment; and operate in a business atmosphere in which management decision making and control is increasingly shared among clients and providers.
>
> In a business environment driven by extraordinary levels of complexity, a higher level coordination and cooperation among a wider range of "interested parties" is imperative. This will require mastery of sophisticated group and team dynamics.

The Leadership Development Challenge

SIAC's managers began to consider the next level of leadership that would be needed within the next ten years. They soon recognized some important trends. First, the officers realized that the new distributed technology systems required greater degrees of cooperation and matrix management than in the past, both to successfully create new applications and to solve any problems in operating these complex networks. Second, both HR and the line recognized the increasing difficulty of hiring and retaining top IT professionals. Clearly, SIAC needed to be an employer of choice, offering a positive, high-performance environment that provided the career development and coaching that top IT staff expected from their managers. SIAC's reputation was for technical and operational excellence but not for its investment in developing its managers and leaders. For an organization in which people had advanced largely because they knew the technology so well or because they had built the controls that had maintained SIAC's operational reliability, the focus on developing other forms of leadership was new and challenging.

Building a Business Case

In late 1994, SIAC sponsored focus groups discussing leadership challenges with managers at all levels. At the same time, the senior and executive vice presidents completed a competency card sort. This data was integrated into a widely circulated "Foundation Document" that framed the business case for leadership development. In addition, behavioral interviews were carried out to further validate the focus group findings and create specific behavioral indicators. The resulting data was analyzed by consultants from Linkage, Inc., as well as SIAC's internal Organizational Development and Training Department. The resulting model is shown in Exhibit 14.2 (page 404).

A high-impact leadership program requires a model or framework that captures and clarifies the leadership challenges of the company. Often, such models contain inherent contradictions or balances between competing forces that both the organization and the individuals must strike. In SIAC's case, the model represents the balance between technology and people, between technically elegant solutions and business acumen, and the recognition that leadership requires both.

While the model may appear complex, it does present a clear balance of the critical capabilities that both define the organization and characterize its best leaders. At the center of the model are four core capabilities of the company. The top two core competencies (technical integrity and customer partnership) define who SIAC is as an organization, featuring the hallmarks of technical excellence and integrity as well as the commitment to customer partnership, the tight relationship between SIAC and its partners. The bottom two core competencies (developing people and team collaboration), however, were the areas that SIAC needed to bring into greater balance and improve for the future. Developing people was not a primary focus for SIAC in 1993, and while teamwork was adequate, it was becoming more strained during difficult, more complex projects or problem situations that occurred.

The second ring of the model represents the nine leadership competencies, which drive from the four core capabilities. Each competency is aligned with a core focus for the company. This makes the model memorable and allows each manager to see a clear relationship between the requirements for the business and the necessary skills for leaders. Finally, the third ring of the model represents the seventy-two specific behaviors (eight per competency) that define each factor. These seventy-two behaviors were captured in the 360-degree feedback instrument, which drove the assessment phase of the leadership system.

While the initial focus of SIAC's leadership efforts was on increasing people skills, the model gained credibility when senior management began to refer to the core capabilities and integrate the model into their business conversations. In the Orientation to Management sessions, senior leaders spoke about how the organization should focus on maintaining its technological edge and improving its competitive advantage with customers while improving its teamwork, climate, and employee satisfaction. The model has served as a focal point and symbol for the aspirations of the company and its leaders.

The Audience

The LDS program was initially aimed at the top 200 managers in the company; over the years it has been extended to lower levels. While people were nominated in the sequence to attend, there was no attempt to distinguish high potentials. Although this may have detracted from the "prestige value" of the initiative, a conscious choice was made to give the message that leadership must come from everyone.

A major advance was the early and enthusiastic participation of the CEO and senior leadership. Not only did they act as speakers to the orientation sessions, but all completed the 360-degree assessment process and shared their personal learnings with their teams. It is the designers' belief that leadership development is ultimately personal and that the self-disclosure of senior leaders is a powerful, catalytic event. Five years later, SIAC's CEO continues to speak at every program.

The Assessment Phase

A key decision in the design of any leadership program is the makeup of the assessment phase. At its best, assessment represents an opportunity to capture the attention of senior leaders and involve them personally.

SIAC's LDS designers debated between the merits of off-the-shelf, "normed" instruments versus their own customized model. The decision to use a customized, SIAC-specific model and assessment was driven by the recognition of the organization's need to articulate its own point of view on leadership. The designers wanted to use the modeling and assessment phases to focus and sharpen the discussion of leadership dilemmas. It was felt that this could not be seen as an assessment driven by the ideas of an outside consulting firm but by the critical leadership concerns of SIAC's leaders themselves.

To be powerful, an assessment needs the endorsement and participation of senior leaders. In SIAC's case, the CEO and executive vice presidents all participated in the first wave of assessments and shared their results publicly. This created an instant acceptance of the usefulness of giving and receiving feedback where none had existed before. The designers also made the decision to make assessment "safer" by focusing initially on development, not performance. The assessment gave them a statistically valid view of the gaps in the manager population and helped to target the training offerings. These are shown in the competency matrix in Exhibit 14.3 (page 405).

In a technical organization, the validity of the instrument and the data is always in question. Following the first two waves of SIAC officers who completed the 360-degree assessment, Linkage consultants ran a factor analysis to validate the instrument. Surprisingly for a new instrument, over 90 percent of the scales held up at a reliability coefficient of eighty-five or better. With some revisions the basic integrity of the scales and models was maintained. A reanalysis three years later after over 1,450 people had used the questionnaire revealed that the reliability of the instrument had increased. While the 360-degree assessment was presented on its own, many of SIAC's officers have also completed individual personality assessments and feedback instruments such as the Myers Briggs, or Social Styles Questionnaire. The combination of a customized 360-degree instrument plus the "off-the-shelf" personality assessments has been very powerful and well-received.

Phase One: Orientation

The first phase of LDS was introducing the program to the top 200 managers of the company during the first eighteen months. The designers developed and implemented a two-day orientation to the leadership system, containing the following key elements:

- Active, open participation by some key senior managers, including self-disclosure regarding some of their own leadership challenges and issues.
- Mandatory attendance. While volunteerism is a wonderful thing, using leadership development as a change lever may require mandatory attendance at some stages of the program. The strategic importance of leadership development leads to no apologies for this step, which succeeds in getting everyone on the same page regarding the message and expectations.
- Processing of the 360-degree feedback in a group setting. It was found that contrary to all fears, managers shared their data with many of their colleagues. This became an option and also left people an out by asking them to use coaching triads to share development items without necessarily revealing whether it was a strength they wished to enhance or a clear development gap.

- Review of the SIAC's leadership challenge contained in the "Foundation Document".
- Discussions of such areas as coaching, on-the-job development, and leadership. The designers also included a working exercise on creating development opportunities based on the work of the Center for Creative Leadership. Experience taught the designers that leaders are as interested in derailers as they are in success factors, and want to understand how to compensate for their weaknesses.
- Creation of an individual development plan. SIAC's developmental planning form is shown in Exhibit 14.4. The development of the assessment, development planning work, and orientation process created a new context for these training programs. Managers began to regard them not as "training," but as a sequence of programs needing reinforcement and tied to the way they conduct their business and achieve their goals.

Several features worked particularly well and should be noted here. David Kolb's Learning Styles Inventory (LSI) was used to prompt a discussion on the variety of learning styles and the need to use a range of approaches to ensure retention of learning. Most important, however, was the active presence of senior leaders in these sessions to signal their support to the cynical segments of the organization.

Evaluations of these first sessions revealed that approximately one-third of the managers were enthusiastic about the leadership system, one-third were skeptical and viewed it as "flavor of the month," and the final third were ambivalent. Clearly, more work was needed to ensure the long-term success of the program. It was because of this anticipated skepticism that the positioning of the process as a Leadership System was crucial. It was only through the constant reinforcement of the idea that this was not a short-term program that the company began to gain credibility in the organization.

Phase Two: Consolidating the Gains

The second phase of the Leadership System began to roll out even as new groups continued to go through the core two-day orientation program.

This consolidation phase consisted of the following elements: group profiling and teamwork, external coaching, training programs, and evaluation.

Group Profiling and Teamwork

Aggregate group profiles were created for each SIAC department based on the LDS 360-degree feedback. These competency-based group profiles were used in helping groups look at their shared strengths and development needs as a team. Based on these assessments, some management teams continued working on particular shared development gaps. Several groups opted to share their development plans and open up larger discussions about their effectiveness as a team. While some of these teams chose to participate in LDS umbrella programs such as "Social Styles" and training offered by the Wilson Learning Group, others obtained facilitation help from the external coaches to focus on immediate team issues.

External Coaching

The 360-degree feedback had opened up a reservoir of interest in individual coaching and team building among managers. This coaching focused on leadership and interpersonal effectiveness. Many managers are not comfortable with putting together their own development plans, let alone developing them with their own direct reports. SIAC uses external coaches, who are senior professionals with experience in management, organizational development, and technology. While the expense of such services is an issue that will not be reviewed here, it is important to consider coaching as a powerful intervention in a somewhat conservative company. The use of external coaches allowed officers and directors to move ahead with the feedback and team-building processes at their own pace. It gave them a certain degree of control while allowing for some "remedial" work. One of the most difficult challenges in leadership work with senior managers is the challenge of getting them to work on basic skills when they are concerned about their image. The coaching work received excellent reviews from individuals, and follow-up evaluations revealed that people who received coaching were more likely to complete individual development plans and meet their development objectives.

Training Programs

The LDS included three mandatory training programs:

- Leading in a Technical Environment
- Employee Relations Skills for Managers
- Managing Performance Appraisal

There were also a number of programs focused on customer partnership, teamwork, understanding the securities business, and other areas of core competencies. These programs were designed to provide depth, skill building, and practice. While some officers attended these programs, the largest audience was the director and manager levels.

Evaluation

In May 1997, Linkage completed a formal evaluation of the LDS program through telephone interviews of a random sample of fifty-one participants. The study found the following:

- Two-thirds of the respondents had completed development plans; those who had received coaching were more likely to have completed the plan and met their objectives.
- Many respondents reported that their managers were making an effort to change and could identify specific behaviors that demonstrated that effort.
- Overall, senior management support was viewed as adequate. However, respondents questioned whether upper managers were "walking the talk." This gap between more positive views of one's immediate manager and the mixed reviews of upper management clearly demonstrated the depth of cynicism that existed and the need for greater management support.

The research showed that respondents were looking for greater integration between support for the program and systems in the company for promotion, development, and project assignments, as well as recognition for those who exemplified good leadership role models. The evaluation also revealed employee reports of more positive and consistent leadership behavior, resulting in better listening, improved relationships, and better involvement on project teams.

The company continued the evaluations of both the program components and the program overall. The classroom training programs offered are continually adjusted based on the evaluation results and aggregating the needs shown in the Individual Development Plans.

Reinforcing the System

Senior management provided reinforcement through a financial incentive based on support for the LDS program. The incentive was simple: Officers were judged on how far their direct reports had followed through on the IDPs and on program attendance. In later years, participation in program delivery and support by officers was acknowledged. Although the financial incentive component is no longer used, SIAC is reexploring how to connect incentives to the leadership system.

Phase Three: A Shift in Direction

The last two years represent a marked shift in the direction for leadership development at SIAC. It is clear that LDS has significantly contributed to tangible shifts in the organization, though they cannot be attributed to the development system alone. LDS served as a reference point for development efforts, which might have dissipated if LDS were not there as a consistent reference point for the organization.

The key to the impact of leadership development is the anchor point that a leadership system provides over time. It is probable that a minimum of a two-year period is necessary for this to take place.

It was after the third year that even more convincing data on the LDS came back. In 1998, SIAC administered a comprehensive employee survey that provided comparative results going back before the implementation of LDS. It showed significant change in positive perceptions of managers and the climate as compared to 1995. The survey indicated a positive shift in SIAC in terms of its perceived support for employee development and the relationships between managers and staff.

Leadership Reassessment

In 1998, the designers also began reassessments of leaders who had taken the original 360-degree feedback instrument, three years earlier. Research by Linkage, Inc., CCL, and others has shown that in order to assure a valid reassessment, you must do more than simply readminister the original scale in order to accurately detect positive progress by managers in their scores. Due to the "ceiling effect" and other issues with scales, it is not enough to simply readminister the 360-degree feedback form. As shown below, the solution has been a second scale that measures the degree of perceived change. The two scales used were:

NOW SCALE

1	2	3	4	5	6
Almost never demonstrated	Occasionally demonstrated	Sometimes demonstrated	Often demonstrated	Usually demonstrated	Almost always demonstrated

DEGREE OF CHANGE SCALE

−1	0	1	2	3
Decline	No change	Slight positive change	Definite positive change	Significant positive change
In general, this person's performance at this activity or behavior has slipped in terms of quality and/or performance.	In general, this person is performing this activity or behavior at the same level as before.	On occasion, this person has demonstrated some improvement in performing this activity or behavior.	In general, this person has enriched their frequency and effectiveness in this activity or behavior.	This person has made great strides in terms of their performance of this activity or behavior.

Many of the managers completing the reassessment showed some positive gains in their scores, especially in the competencies of developing people.

External versus Internal Programs

One leadership development consideration for many organizations is whether to drive their programs internally or to send leaders for external education. Linkage's experience in SIAC and elsewhere leads us to recommend both. SIAC began to send selected individuals to the week-long Global Institute for Leadership Development (GILD) in 1997. These people were sent in a team, and an "alumni network" was formed. As the network expanded, it became a powerful influence for leadership work. The exposure to external programs helped enrich ideas for the internal LDS.

In 1997, the organization used the competency model as a component of a consistent approach to reviewing senior management talent. The review form uses a condensed set of the competencies while differentiating among personal attributes that are rated as either (1) a strength, (2) capable, or (3) needs development. This has further reinforced the leadership system and helped senior executives to look at the talent they will need in the future.

As the programs have continued to evolve, it became evident that SIAC needed to more closely tie leadership development to "real" work. To do this, an action learning-based program was chosen from GILD in which teams tackle specific business issues while exploring their leadership and teamwork skills. This represented another watershed for SIAC. First, a team of senior leaders would be asked to spend one week focusing on their individual development as leaders. Second, they would be chartered to solve a critical business problem. This team, called "the Desert Group" because they attended a program held in the California desert, represented some of SIAC's emerging future leaders.

The action learning experience allowed them to look at each other as potential future leaders for the first time, sharing many of their aspirations and visions for SIAC's future. The team completed their project of designing a new approach to one of SIAC's customers. Action learning approaches could have been included much earlier. This might have served to accelerate the change in people's thinking about the ability to apply the learning to real, immediate work. The question is whether this new experience will result in a push for greater integration between strategic and customer issues and the LDS. The training programs that support LDS have also been expanded to focus more on teams at all levels and to be more "experimental."

Learnings

As a result of this program, two key learnings were realized.

Valid Competency Models Can Be Completed in an Accelerated Process

Linkage deliberately chose to shorten the amount of interviewing and data gathering involved in creating the competency model. Instead, the emphasis was put on capturing the core strategic issues through focus groups and interactive sessions. The research validity was gained by revising the model using actual participant data. Though the model had some weaker items and constructs at the beginning, this did not hurt the perceived quality of the feedback process.

The Leadership System Provided an Architecture

The Leadership System provided the structure to help external vendors customize their programs to meet SIAC's needs. It provided a common language and foundation for talking about leadership and its development at SIAC. It also provided the map to connect other HR systems over time to the leadership approach. Faster integration and greater reinforcement of the model in management reviews and performance systems might have helped accelerate our progress. After five years now, the model needs to change to reflect new realities in SIAC for increased innovation, cost effectiveness, and other factors that were not as critical in the past.

Tackling Sensitive Issues

While the original program provided exposure to SIAC's strategy and had modules focused on the financial services industry, the decision was made in the first few years to keep the focus on internal development. It may be argued that the lack of direct involvement and connection to customers and other strategic issues dampened the sense of urgency around change. By building management teams' confidence, the initial years may have allowed more of the customer, cultural change, and team issues to be confronted. Ideally, some might argue that more might have been done to strengthen the connections in the earlier phases. Yet it may be said that management first needs to prove its commitment to employee development as its first step before dealing with customer issues.

Human Resource Systems Provide Critical Reinforcement

SIAC continues its attempts to tie such HR systems as selection, succession and performance reviews, and to a lesser extent, compensation to the LDS model and principles. The maximum impact of the system has been felt by groups that:

- Used the system to draw connections between LDS principles and their own work as a team and as individuals
- Took advantage of short-term training programs to extend their learning and clarify the use of LDS principles
- Formalized and scheduled periodic development planning reviews
- Used team sessions to share success stories and recognize role modeling of the leadership principles

Next Steps

The next opportunity at SIAC is to synthesize the learnings from both the action learning team and the slower but continuing diversification and spread of the original learnings from LDS. The system needs to become even more integrated with the company's drive to maintain a technology leadership position and work with customers. Perhaps this can be helped through using more internal staff as "faculty" as well as greater use of action learning approaches. SIAC is continuing to use its external coaches, but is now emphasizing building internal coaching capability among its mangers. Leaders will also be focusing on using teamwork to address the organization's challenges, raise productivity, and address the leadership values and competencies needed for the new millennium. SIAC's LDS shows an effective way to weave a rich set of educational offerings into an impactful leadership system. The key is continued persistence in driving leadership development as a critical priority and conversation in the business.

Exhibit 14.1: Overview of the Leadership Development System

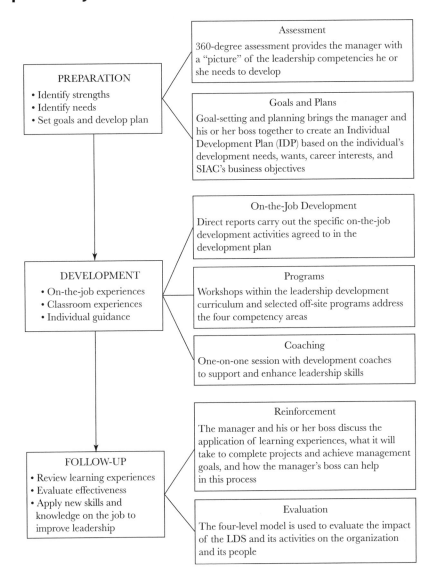

Linkage Inc.'s Best Practices in Leadership Development Handbook, edited by David Giber, Louis Carter, and Marshall Goldsmith. Copyright © 2000 by Linkage Press and Jossey-Bass/Pfeiffer, San Francisco, CA.

Exhibit 14.2: LDS Competencies

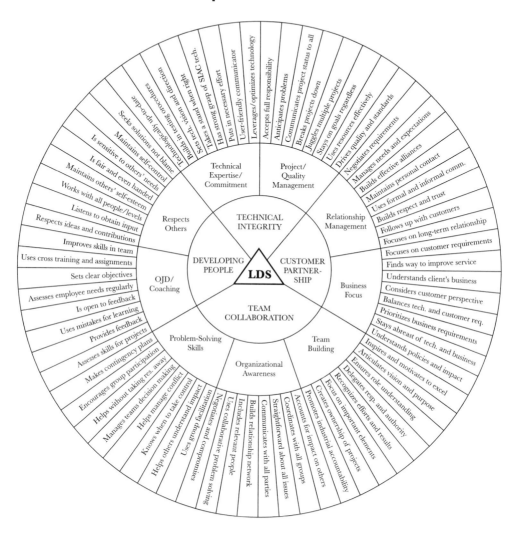

Linkage Inc.'s Best Practices in Leadership Development Handbook, edited by David Giber, Louis Carter, and Marshall Goldsmith. Copyright © 2000 by Linkage Press and Jossey-Bass/Pfeiffer, San Francisco, CA.

Exhibit 14.3: Competency Matrix

Competency Matrix	MANDATORY				RECOMMENDED									MISC.
	Technical Leadership	Employee Relations Skills	Finance and Administration for Managers	Managing Performance Appraisal	Survey of Securities Markets 1 and 2	Overview of Brokerage Operations	Social Styles	OTL Communications	Influence Skills	Team Skills	Earning Customer Partnership	Interviewing Skills	Project Management	Center for Creative Leadership
Customer Partnership														
• Relationship management							△	△	▲	△	▲		△	
• Business focus		△	▲		▲	▲			△		▲		△	
Team Collaboration														
• Team building	▲						△	△	▲	▲			△	△
• Organizational awareness	△	△					△	△	△	▲	△			△
• Problem-solving skills	△						△	▲	▲	▲	△			▲
Technical Integrity														
• Technical expertise/commitment													▲	
• Project/quality management			△				△	△	△	△			▲	
Developing People														
• Coaching/OJD	▲	▲		▲			▲	▲	▲					
• Respects others	▲	▲		▲			▲	▲	▲	△				

▲ Indicates a program's primary focus (60% or more of the program)

△ Indicates a program's secondary focus (30%–40% of the program)

Linkage Inc.'s Best Practices in Leadership Development Handbook, edited by David Giber, Louis Carter, and Marshall Goldsmith. Copyright © 2000 by Linkage Press and Jossey-Bass/Pfeiffer, San Francisco, CA.

Exhibit 14.4: Individual Development Plan

INDIVIDUAL DEVELOPMENT PLAN

IDP Start Date: _____

Name (print): _____   IDP Review Date: _____

Manager: _____   End Date: _____

DEVELOPMENT GOAL

Write your Development Goal using a complete sentence. Do not use bullet points.

_____

_____

_____

List LDS Competencies related to your goal:

_____

_____

_____

_____

Identify business goals and projects related to this competency and your development goals:

_____

_____

_____

_____

DEVELOPMENT STRATEGIES

On-the-job learning assignments and opportunities:	Progress/ review dates:	Formal/structured training, programs, education:	Progress/ review dates:

ANTICIPATED RESULTS AND BENEFITS

What results—with customers, peers, direct reports, and managers—do you expect from learning and applying your new competency?

_____

_____

RESOURCES

List resources (time, people, etc.) that may be needed to help you accomplish your development goal:

_____

_____

_____

Employee's signature:	Date submitted:
Manager's signature:	Date approved:

HR765 10/97

Linkage Inc.'s Best Practices in Leadership Development Handbook, edited by David Giber, Louis Carter, and Marshall Goldsmith. Copyright © 2000 by Linkage Press and Jossey-Bass/Pfeiffer, San Francisco, CA.

About the Contributors

Cheryl Lazzaro (clazzaro@siac.com) is managing director for OD, staffing, and HR integration at SIAC. She is responsible for the development and integration of business-driven HR programs and processes. Previously, she worked for SIAC designing and implementing benefit and executive compensation plans, incentive programs, staffing, planning and recruitment, and mergers.

Jean Patton (Jpatton@siac.com) is a senior consultant in HR for SIAC. In that role, she is the project manager for the Leadership Development System that incorporates a combination of multi-rater assessment, goals-setting for individuals and groups, individual and team coaching, reinforcement, and evaluation. Prior to joining SIAC, Patton was an officer of National Westminster Bank, USA, where she managed a wide range of programs from management development to sales training.

David Giber (Dgiber@linkage-inc.com) is vice president of consulting services at Linkage, Inc., and a co-editor of *Linkage's Best Practices in Leadership Development*. His major focus is on building human resource systems that have measurable performance impact, and he is an expert in developing practical tools for demonstrating the relationship of training and organizational interventions to busines results. For over fifteen years, he has served in director-level positions in training and human resource development, and has consulted with a wide variety of international corporations, universities, and other organizations on such issues as succession planning, leadership development, workforce assessment, competency modeling, and developing performance and compensation systems. Giber is an industrial/organizational psychologist who received his bachelor's degree from Stanford in 1976 and his Ph.D. from Duke University in 1980.

CHAPTER FIFTEEN

SMITHKLINE BEECHAM

This chapter outlines a personal change and assessment-driven
program that is designed for leadership development and
succession planning in a post-merger environment.

Introduction

In 1989, SmithKline Beecham was formed through the merger of SmithKline Beckman Corporation, located in Philadelphia, Pennsylvania, and The Beecham Group in London. Beecham had comparatively few programs in the way of human resources development, while SmithKline Beckman had a process but no consistency in how it was implemented across the corporation. Within a few years, after the company had resolved the most urgent post-merger problems, it had become apparent that SmithKline Beecham needed a consistent, reliable, and standardized leadership planning process. It was believed that such a process would help meld the two companies with their disparate cultures—that it would help change SmithKline Beecham from a multidomestic "we versus them" culture to a global "us." It was also hoped that a company-wide approach would enhance worker loyalty that had been diminished by the merger. Moreover, SmithKline Beecham was experiencing the same pressures felt by the industry worldwide to downsize and reduce its hierarchy, thereby limiting opportunities for advancement.

Creating a Team to Design the Leadership Development Planning Process

In early 1993, the human resources team was asked by senior management to develop three leadership planning initiatives that could be applied company-wide. The initiatives were a succession planning process, an executive development process, and a leadership competency model. Three separate teams were formed to attack these three separate targets. It did not take long, however, to recognize that the targets were all connected. They all led to the single goal of leadership planning. They agreed to work together as one team, with human resources people from all line operations—pharmaceuticals business, over-the-counter products business (Consumer Healthcare), corporate, Europe, and International. There was also an advisory board of line managers.

Data Gathering

The next three months were spent gathering information through interviews with line managers and focus groups. From these, a strong impression was made that people wanted a leadership planning and development process that didn't stop at the top fifty executives but, rather, reached deeper into the ranks of middle management. "Leadership" had never been explicitly defined in the company's initial brief, so the team felt free to broaden the scope. They also reviewed the programs that were already in place, and found there were no fewer than seventeen different executive review and development programs in the merged company. In the area of leadership competencies, on the other hand, the human resources team was working with a blank slate. However, the five core values that SmithKline Beecham had recently defined as part of its merger process helped them arrive at the twenty-one leadership competencies listed in Table 15.1.

TABLE 15.1. THE TWENTY-ONE SMITHKLINE BEECHAM LEADERSHIP COMPETENCIES.

Innovation	Customer	Integrity
• Think strategically	• Improve systems and processes	• Lead courageously
• Innovate	• Commit to quality	• Foster open communication
• Champion change	• Focus on customer needs	• Act with integrity
Performance	**People**	**Personal Effectiveness**
• Establish plans	• Foster enthusiasm and teamwork	• Use sound judgement
• Manage execution	• Reward and celebrate achievement	• Convey information
• Influence others	• Attract and develop talent	• Adapt and develop oneself
• Drive for results	• Build relationships	• Know the organization and the business

Key Learnings of First Round Development Planning

Several key learnings were made during the first round of developing the pilot for the Leadership Planning Process (LPP):

1. Collect data from line managers on the design of the program
2. The process must be "line-owned" and "line-driven"
3. Approach division heads to develop a pilot program. For example, a new division head of the Worldwide Supply Operations (WSO) needed information about the leadership needs and potential of the employees he was managing, and agreed to implement a pilot.
4. Accept successes and failures during your pilot. You can learn as much from your mistakes as you can from your "wins."
5. Link the plan design to the needs and vision of the CEO and senior management team. SmithKline Beecham's LPP was finally approved by the CEO after a great deal of piloting and communication with the CEO.

The Leadership Planning Process (LPP) Design

While a variety of components make up the Leadership Planning Process, the main elements are two subprocesses, the Leadership and Development Review (LADR) and the Group Discussion. A description of each follows.

Leadership and Development Review (LADR)

This is the starting point of the process. It establishes what should be an ongoing dialogue between an employee and his or her supervisor regarding (1) which of the twenty-one competencies are key to the employee's existing position; (2) the gaps between the employee's competency level and those required by the job; (3) the employee's aspirations and what additional competencies will be required to achieve them; and (4) a development plan that will give the employee the experiences that, in turn, will develop those required competencies. (see Exhibits 15.1 on page 432 and 15.2 on page 421).

LADR is not a performance review; nor should it be linked to compensation. While performance reviews focus on past achievements (the "what"), LADR is primarily future driven and focuses on the "how." It requires the employee to articulate his or her aspirations, and the supervisor to determine whether those aspirations are achievable and, if so, what the best steps are to achieving those aspirations. LADR does ask employees to summarize their accomplishments and asks reviewers to comment. But most of this subprocess is devoted to identifying what competencies are required for a particular job, assessing how the incumbent performs against those requirements, and creating a development action plan. The goal is to facilitate a rich and fruitful discussion between reviewee and reviewer, which focuses on the reviewee's continuous improvement and development.

LADR is designed to be processed electronically from start to finish. Information from each individual's LADR is then added to a central electronic database that, as the repository of information about competencies within the company, becomes a valuable tool in SmithKline Beecham's internal candidate searches (described later). The data are also used in the Group Discussion.

Group Discussion

This subprocess has been described as the heart of the LPP. It is a facilitated discussion among a "natural team"—a peer group—of supervisors who review the competencies, aspirations, development needs, and development action plans of their direct reports within the context of SmithKline Beecham's needs. There are both line discussions and functional discussions; thus, a single individual can be the focus of more than one group discussion. Discussions begin at the lowest level at which LADRs are completed, and exceptional employees can be "bubbled" or "cascaded" up for discussion at the next level. The process culminates with the group discussion by the chief executive and his team of direct reports. Leadership Watch candidates (known in other companies as "high potentials") are also identified and reviewed during the Group Discussion process.

For the approximately 7,000 SmithKline Beecham employees who undergo the LPP each year, the company holds about 240 group discussions.

This means that, on average, each group discusses thirty-five to forty people, allocating twelve to fifteen minutes per person; the discussions may be compressed into an intense all-day session or continue over two days. At the lower levels, each individual's development plan is reviewed. At the top, there is a closer focus on succession. Not every member of the group will personally know each reviewee, but the documentation will provide enough information for them to make informed judgments. In fact, one of the great benefits of the group discussion is that it alerts managers and executives to a whole range of leadership potential within their teams and outside their immediate areas of responsibility. In the past, these individuals would have remained known only to the managers with whom they came in contact. Consequently, the group discussion serves as an "inventory-taking" of management talent at SmithKline Beecham.

LPP Training Curriculum

As the illustration in Exhibit 15.3 (page 434) indicates, the Leadership Planning Process is an ongoing, integral part of the job for everyone involved throughout the year.

There are several key events on the calendar:

- *Pre-LADR discussion.* In November and December, a pre-LADR discussion is scheduled to prepare for the review process. The reviewee and reviewer together select at least seven of the SmithKline Beecham Leadership Competencies; in addition, in some cases, technical competencies that are specific to the reviewee's function—against which the reviewee should be measured. They also agree on a date to exchange their completed LADR forms, a date to meet and discuss each other's views, and a list of customers for the reviewer to contact for input. A customer is anyone who depends on the quality, cost, and/or schedule of the products or services the reviewee delivers. Typically, each person selects three.

- *Customer input to LADR.* In December and January, the onus is on the reviewer to follow up the actions set in motion a month earlier. The reviewer gathers input from the customers agreed upon at the pre-LADR discussion, asking them to evaluate the individual in terms of competencies, and integrates their input with his or her observations.

- *Exchange of LADR forms.* Between January 15 and March 15, reviewer and reviewee exchange drafts electronically of the forms they have completed and schedule a follow-up discussion. During this period, LADR training is also offered to reviewees who are unfamiliar with the process. (This is in addition to the instruction on LPP that is included in new employees' orientation or induction.)

- *LADR discussion and completion.* In February and March, reviewer and reviewee conduct the LADR discussion, covering all elements of the LADR form. Specific topics to be discussed in this meeting are (1) summary of accomplishments, based on personal observations as well as input from key customers; (2) rating one's own competencies against SmithKline Beecham leadership competencies plus any additional functional and/or technical competencies; (3) reviewee's career interests and aspirations; and (4) the development action plan. Prepared jointly by reviewee and reviewer, the development action plan identifies specific steps employees should take to improve competence where required. The plan also helps clarify the reviewer's expectations of the reviewee for the coming year. Reviewers have access to a Leadership Development Resources Guide, recently introduced by HR, to help them in development planning. The completed LADR form is forwarded to HR.

- *Group Discussion.* Held from April to July, the group discussion is intended to achieve consensus in four key areas: (1) enhancements to the development action plan drafted in the LADR discussion; (2) the issue of whether a development move should occur within the next twelve months, based on personal development and business needs, and what positions the reviewee could potentially fill; (3) positions that individuals could potentially fill within one to three years; and (4) short-term successors for team members participating in the Group Discussion. Within ten days of the Group Discussion, team members must feed back to their direct reports the team's consensus on the reviewee's strengths, development needs, and recommended moves, if any. Development Action Plans are adjusted accordingly.

Succession Planning Process

Succession planning is an integral part of the LPP and particularly of group discussion, as indicated above. Succession planning has been refined using survey data that indicated a greater need to match organizational needs to individual competencies. In addition, SmithKline Beecham's top management expressed the desire to precipitate greater mobility. Succession planning now breaks down into three subprocesses: business assessment, organizational succession planning, and an internal candidate search.

Business Assessment

This action, which occurs prior to group discussion, is intended to determine the critical positions, areas, and functions within each of SmithKline Beecham's businesses, and assess the level of succession planning required. If the requirement is low, it is sufficient to use the individual succession planning process to identify backup candidates. If, on the other hand, the requirement is high, SmithKline Beecham turns to organizational succession planning.

Organizational Succession Planning

This involves multiple steps for identifying the key requirements for the targeted roles. These include (1) the seven top SmithKline Beecham Leadership Competencies and any future Skills, Abilities, and Technologies (SAT); (2) identifying and discussing potential candidates for each position at group discussion, and finalizing a list; (3) determining the timeframe within which the candidate needs to be ready—less than a year, one to three years, or immediately—and identifying the SAT and experience "gaps" they need to fill in that time (emergency backups are also designated during this initiative); and (4) identifying the candidate's development actions and updating his or her LADR. A team member is assigned "ownership" of the development of a specific individual.

After the Group Discussion, a succession plan matrix is produced and updated continually with both organizational changes and changes involving individual candidates. As part of their regular meetings, management teams review succession plans and progress towards individual development.

Internal Candidate Search (ICS)

Supplementing this ongoing succession planning process, SmithKline Beecham has also implemented a subprocess of LPP called Internal Candidate Search (ICS), which is used when a position opens up at the company (see Exhibits 15.4, 15.5, and 15.6 on pages 435–437). While openings had routinely been posted in the past, allowing interested candidates to apply, the ICS proactively seeks matches between openings and employees. The system, which uses a database of LADR and Group Discussion information called Executrac, runs a company-wide computerized search for candidates with the competencies required for a specific job; it also searches for other criteria, such as job level, willingness to make a development move, and willingness to relocate. The ICS process should be used before seeking an external candidate to fill a vacancy. Thanks to the process, SmithKline Beecham saved $1.8 million in 1998 by filling openings internally, versus using executive search agencies or headhunters.

Continuous Improvement of the Leadership Planning Process

It is not only people who undergo development at SmithKline Beecham; processes do, too. Since its inception, the LPP has been continuously improved to meet SmithKline Beecham's organizational needs. Some of the changes have been logistical. For example, the LPP cycle has been modified to match SmithKline Beecham's budgeting cycle so that both culminate in July. This allows SmithKline Beecham to budget for people development. The LPP cycle also accommodates the Management-By-Objective (MBO) and merit review process that SmithKline Beecham conducts for all its management employees. The determination of merit raises and bonuses concludes in the first week of January and draws on some of the same customer input data that are used in LADR.

Another enhancement has been the formal application of the LPP to the job of general manager, a position that is considered the critical stepping stone to the executive suite. To facilitate the flow of talent into leadership positions, SmithKline Beecham decided to define the specific competencies and experiences required for the general manager position. A general manager profile has been formalized and introduced throughout the company, and employees are encouraged to apply regardless of the function they currently perform. Employees can then use LADR and their development action plans to explore ways of acquiring the necessary competencies that will allow them to move into that job.

New products that have been added to the LPP since its implementation include Leadership Exchange and Leadership Advantage.

Leadership Exchange

This program brings a group of fifty managers (identified through the Group Discussion Process as Leadership Watch candidates) together with the CEO, COO, and senior vice president, and the director of human resources for three days of highly interactive discussions. The exchange provides an opportunity for managers to engage in dialogue with the senior leaders about the external environment, strategy, organizational culture, and leadership. It also gives them an opportunity to reflect on their leadership style and the impact that they are having on their teams and the organization.

Leadership Advantage

Leadership Advantage is designed to provide formal leadership training for middle managers, who are nominated for this program by their supervisors because of LADR. Leadership Advantage involves a three-day workshop that addresses, through a series of simulations, such topics as giving and receiving feedback, coaching, and personal resiliency. It targets fourteen of SmithKline Beecham's twenty-one leadership competencies that are deemed most critical to the success of middle managers. Managers also hear from veteran SmithKline Beecham executives.

Key Learnings of LPP after Implementation

In the past five years, the LPP has undergone continual improvement to meet the existing and emerging needs of SmithKline Beecham. Above all, experience has taught the human resource team a number of important lessons about how best to implement a system like the LPP. Key learnings include the following:

- *Line management must be engaged and involved from the outset.* The LPP is not an HR program; it is a SmithKline Beecham program and would have languished without the strong support of the line. If SmithKline Beecham's Worldwide Supply Operations had not agreed to pilot it, LPP would have been stillborn. Instead, a couple of months into the pilot, WSO management was giving HR positive feedback about the LPP. The initiative was led by the line rather than HR pushing an unnecessary program on the line. When HR people are involved, they must be well informed about the business.

- *Enlist many advocates.* Within a period of a few months, the LPP won the support of the heads of WSO, HR, and Consumer Healthcare, producing a groundswell of interest in the process. The LPP team today includes people from all of our businesses and functions, for example, communications, sales and marketing, and HR. Their individual competencies complement each other's while at the same time enriching the overall perspective of the team. Besides their competencies, they are chosen either because of their advocacy or because they are not "pre-sold" on the process. What they do have in common, however, is the respect of their line management, strong influencing skills, strong team skills, and a drive for results. In addition, they continue to rely on a line advisory board whose members provide constant feedback and who have in effect become champions of the process.

- *Train before pilot.* Few managers at SmithKline Beecham are prepared to deploy the LPP without training. To use LADR, managers need to know how to keep communication lines open, to evaluate people for competencies (rather than performance evaluations with which they may be more familiar), to create development plans, and ensure there is follow-through. When SmithKline Beecham first rolled out the process, it initially gave the company's top 400 managers an overview of the LADR process and training in areas ranging from how best to give feedback to ways to link the competency rating to development planning; subsequently all managers and reviewers were trained. In addition, facilitators who assist at the Group Discussions are also trained. Finally, training is provided in three modalities: computer-based, classroom-based, and self-study.

- *Pilot before launch.* The LPP was piloted by Worldwide Supply Operations in 1993 and concurrently by one of the business's HR department. Subsequently the process was implemented in Consumer Healthcare. Then, the Corporate Management Team implemented the process by all sectors in 1994, culminating in a Group Discussion with the top executive tier. The use of pilots created momentum for the LPP because it resulted in a series of line endorsements. It also enabled HR to make changes in the process before it was rolled out company-wide. For example, it was because of our early experiences with the process that we gave competencies a more integral role in LADR. Reviewees assessed themselves against competencies. The executive review was, at first, more focused on what individuals did (in other words, it was a more traditional performance review).

Results

The Leadership Planning Process has become the way that SmithKline Beecham identifies and supports the development of its managerial-level employees. At one time, development planning was inconsistent and succession planning was restricted to a relative handful of executives. The LPP represents a paradigm shift, focusing on the development needs and potential of a much larger population within the context of the organization.

Most of the people development at SmithKline Beecham occurs in an individual's current job. The LPP is not intended to result in significant mobility within SmithKline Beecham and, in fact, current data show that approximately 6 percent of the individuals discussed have been recommended for development moves. That is consistent with general industry trends of downsizing, which sometimes reduce the opportunity for promotion. By exposing hidden talent, the LPP facilitates the exploitation of transferable skills, enabling more employees to make cross-functional or cross-sector moves.

Exhibit 15.1: LADR/LPP Review Form

WELCOME TO THE 1999 LEADERSHIP PLANNING PROCESS

Last year more than 8,500 employees participated in the LADR process and over 230 Group Discussions were held during the spring and summer.

Based on your feedback through the 1998 LADR/LPP survey, members of the LPP team have decided not to make any changes to the LADR form this year. However, based on the pending European Data Protection Law, it is very important that all employees read the following statement.

> *European Data Law*—As part of the LADR process, the information contained on this form documents strengths, developmental needs, and actions that are used to highlight internal talent and find possible job opportunities within SmithKline Beecham. This data will be stored electronically within the SB computing environment and used by authorised data users to support Group Discussions and the Internal Candidate Search Process. I authorise SB to use the data supplied on my LADR for those purposes.

As a quality control check please ensure that you type your name and position at the foot of each page as shown.

Good luck and don't hesitate to contact your HR manager if you need assistance with any part of the Leadership Planning Process.

(continued)

Exhibit 15.1 (continued)

Leadership and Development Review

SmithKline Beecham

Date _____ (day/month/year)

Reviewee Name _____ Position _____ SS/NI/OTHER _____

(last, first, middle initial)

Sector/Bus. Unit/Country _____ Function _____

Reviewer Name _____ Position _____

(last, first, middle initial)

SUMMARIZE RESULTS ACHIEVED IN PRINCIPAL DUTIES AND LIST OTHER SIGNIFICANT ACCOMPLISHMENTS

(Consider key elements of job responsibilities, special projects, and annual objectives.)

REVIEW SUMMARY OF ACCOMPLISHMENTS

REVIEWER COMMENTS ON REVIEWEE'S SUMMARY OF ACCOMPLISHMENTS

NB. European Data Law—Please ensure you read the cover page.

Refer to the last three pages of this form for instructions and competency descriptions.

The LADR Word document is available in both A4 and *Letter* page sizes.

CURRENT JOB RATING

1. Select the **7 most critical** competencies for your current position by placing an X next to the competency. **You need not rate the remaining competencies.**

PERSON RATING—PLEASE RATE ALL COMPETENCIES

1. **Outstanding Competency.** Numerous examples easily identified.
2. **Competency** clearly demonstrated. A solid, **personal strength.** Further challenge in this area can be attempted.
3. **Competency** evident to some degree, but not a predominant strength.
4. **Competency** not yet evident or underdeveloped.

Using the rating scale, assess your competence against the SB Leadership Competencies

REVIEWEE	REVIEWER	SB LEADERSHIP COMPETENCIES	REVIEWEE	REVIEWER
		INNOVATION		
		Think strategically		
		Innovate		
		Champion change		
		PERFORMANCE		
		Establish plans		
		Manage execution		
		Influence others		
		Drive for results		
		CUSTOMER		
		Improve systems and processes		
		Commit to quality		
		Focus on customer needs		
		PEOPLE		
		Foster enthusiasm and teamwork		
		Reward and celebrate achievement		
		Attract and develop talent		
		Build relationships		
		INTEGRITY		
		Lead courageously		
		Foster open communication		
		Act with integrity		
		PERSONAL EFFECTIVENESS		
		Use sound judgment		
		Convey information		
		Adapt and develop oneself		
		Know the organization and the business		

Reviewee Name: _____   Position: _____

(continued)

Exhibit 15.1 (continued)

using the 4-point rating scale, list any functional or technical competencies important in your current job and rate your competence.

Functional and/or Technical Competencies	REVIEWEE	REVIEWER

Reviewee Name: _____ Position _____

CAREER INTERESTS AND ASPIRATIONS
Identify potential career directions and indicate timeframe.

REVIEWER'S COMMENTS
Comment on reviewee's aspirations in terms of potential fulfillment and timeframe.

Mobility (Y/N) within Next 12 Months: Domestic _____   International _____

REVIEWEE/REVIEWER SUMMARY
Summarize demonstrated strengths and development needs.

STRENGTHS:
1.
2.
3.
4.
5.

DEVELOPMENT NEEDS:
1.
2.
3.
4.
5.

DEVELOPMENT PLAN FOR CONTINUOUS IMPROVEMENT AND LEARNING
Summarize and review results of previous development plan.

Reviewee Name: _____ Position: _____

(continued)

Exhibit 15.1 (continued)

Identify current development needs and develop action plans.

Development Need	Development Action Plan	Person(s) Responsible	Target Date
1.			
2.			
3.			
4.			
5.			

Reviewee has discussed with Reviewer   Yes _____   Date: _____

Reviewee Name: _____   Position: _____

Exhibit 15.1 (*continued*)

LEADERSHIP AND DEVELOPMENT REVIEW (LADR) FORM

The LADR Process: The following is a brief overview of the LADR component of the Leadership Planning Process.

For a detailed process description, please refer to the LPP Learning System, which is available in book format and as a Computer-Based Training application.

See the last two pages of this form for a description of the 21 SB Leadership Competencies.

Step 1 The Reviewee initiates discussion with Reviewer to agree on the:
- functional/technical competencies to include in LADR
- customers to provide feedback
- date of the LADR discussion

Step 2 The Reviewee completes his/her draft LADR form.

IMPORTANT NOTE

In order to keep the Leadership Planning Process as simple as possible, it has been decided to use the existing database until some new technology has been thoroughly tested. As a result, the contents of your LADR will have to be manually entered into the current database. While you will have the opportunity to type an unlimited amount of text on the form, it will be truncated for presentation at Group Discussion. Therefore, please be concise and organize your free text using bullet points and be aware of the following space restrictions:

Career Aspirations	5 lines (72 characters (including spaces))
Reviewer's Comments	5 lines (72 characters (including spaces))
Strengths	5 lines (72 characters (including spaces))
Development Needs	5 lines (72 characters (including spaces))
Development Action Plan	5 × 3 lines (45 characters (including spaces))

Step 3 The Reviewer completes his/her draft of the LADR form considering customer input.

Step 4   Reviewee and Reviewer exchange forms.

Step 5   The Reviewee and the Reviewer meet one-on-one to discuss each others' views/assessments.

Step 6   The Reviewee completes the final LADR form that summarizes the consensus/agreements and forwards it to the Reviewer for approval.

Step 7   The Reviewee sends the approved LADR form to his/her Human Resource Manager.

Step 8   The Human Resource Manager reviews the LADR form data for completeness and reasonableness.

Step 9   The Human Resource Manager forwards the LADR form to his/her Database Champion.

SB Leadership Model Competency Descriptions

INNOVATION

Think Strategically: Considers a broad range of internal and external factors when solving problems and making decisions; identifies critical, high payoff strategies and prioritizes team efforts accordingly; uses information about the market and competitors in making decisions; recognizes strategic opportunities for success; adjusts actions and decisions for focus on critical strategic issues (for example, customers, quality, competition, and so on).

Innovate: Generates new ideas; goes beyond the status quo; recognizes the need for new or modified approaches; brings perspectives and approaches together, combining them in creative ways.

Champion Change: Challenges the status quo and champions new initiatives; acts as a catalyst of change and stimulates others to change; paves the way for needed changes; manages implementation effectively.

PERFORMANCE

Establish Plans: Fosters the development of a common vision; develops short- and long-range plans that are appropriately comprehensive, realistic, and effective in meeting goals; integrates planning efforts across work units.

Manage Execution: Delegates to and empowers others; provides needed assistance; coordinates work efforts when necessary; monitors progress.

Influence Others: Asserts own ideas and persuades others; gains support and commitment from others; mobilizes people to take action; achieves effective compromise.

Drive for Results: Drives for results and success; conveys a sense of urgency and drives issues to closure; persists despite obstacles and opposition.

CUSTOMER

Improve Systems and Processes: Identifies, implements, and continuously improves processes and procedures for accomplishing work.

Commit to Quality: Emphasizes the need to deliver quality products and/or services; defines standards for quality and evaluates products, processes, and/or services against those standards; manages quality.

Focus on Customer Needs: Anticipates customer needs; takes action to meet customer needs; continually searches for ways to increase customer satisfaction.

PEOPLE

Foster Enthusiasm and Teamwork: Builds effective teams committed to organizational goals; encourages and empowers people to achieve;

establishes challenging performance standards; creates enthusiasm, a feeling of investment, and a desire to excel; fosters collaboration among team members and among teams.

Reward and Celebrate Achievement: Acknowledges and celebrates team accomplishments; rewards people for good performance; inspires people to excel; lets people know when they are performing well; recognizes the contributions of people from diverse backgrounds.

Attract and Develop Talent: Attracts high caliber people; develops team and talent with diverse capabilities; accurately assesses strengths and development needs of employees; gives timely, specific feedback, and helpful coaching; provides challenging assignments and opportunities for development.

Build Relationships: Relates to people in an open, friendly, accepting manner; shows sincere interest in others and their concerns; initiates and develops relationships with others as a key priority; creates an open and accepting environment.

INTEGRITY

Lead Courageously: Steps forward to address difficult issues; puts self on the line to deal with important problems; stands firm when necessary.

Foster Open Communication: Creates an atmosphere in which timely and high quality information flows smoothly between self and others; encourages the open expression of ideas and opinions; demonstrates attention to and conveys understanding of the comments and questions of others; listens well in a group.

Act with Integrity: Demonstrates principled leadership and sound business ethics; shows consistency among principles, values, and behavior; builds trust with others through own authenticity and follow-through on commitments.

PERSONAL EFFECTIVENESS

Use Sound Judgment: Makes timely and sound decisions; makes decisions under conditions of uncertainty.

Convey Information: Clearly conveys information orally and in writing; gets point across effectively.

Adapt and Develop Oneself: Handles day-to-day work challenges confidently; is willing and able to adjust to multiple and changing work demands; learns from experience; actively pursues learning and self-development; seeks feedback and welcomes unsolicited feedback; demonstrates flexibility.

Know the Organization and the Business: Understands the organization's mission and strategy; knows how the business is run; stays aware of industry and global developments that affect the business.

Exhibit 15.2: Sample Letter to Customer for Customer Review

TO: Customer   cc:

FROM: Reviewer

SUBJECT: Reviewee's LADR

As part of the LADR process, I am collecting input about _____'s performance. Since you are one of his/her key customers, team members or matrix managers, both of us believe that your input is essential. Could you please provide me with specific information in regards to the following:

- Describe a significant work effort this employee has performed in support of your organization or project team.
- What value was added to your organization's or project team's performance as a result of this employee's effort?
- What observations did you make concerning this employee's actions as reflections of our SB Values?
- Can you suggest any opportunities for improved or enhanced performance which would help the individual in continuing his/her development?

Your time in providing this information is greatly appreciated, and I hope to use it to help this individual be even more effective in supporting you in the future. Your views will be considered with others and will be shared as a composite view. You may either send me this information confidentially in writing or call me at _____ and we can discuss it.

Thank you for your assistance.

Regards,

Customer Input To The Leadership and Development Review

Date _____
(day/month/year)

Customer Name _____   Position _____
(last, first, middle initial)

Based on your experiences with this employee and your expectations of the position, would you rate what you think are the seven most critical competencies for the Reviewee's current position and rate their personal performance against those competencies based on the 4-point rating scale.

PERFORMANCE RATING—PLEASE RATE ONLY THE 7 MOST CRITICAL COMPETENCIES FOR THE REVIEWEE'S CURRENT POSITION

1. **Outstanding Competency.** Numerous noteworthy examples easily identified.

2. **Competency** clearly demonstrated. A solid, **personal strength.** Further challenge in this area can be attempted.

3. **Competency evident to some degree,** but not a predominant strength.

4. **Competency** not yet evident or **underdeveloped.**

PERFORMANCE REVIEWER	SB LEADERSHIP COMPETENCIES	PERFORMANCE REVIEWER	SB LEADERSHIP COMPETENCIES
	INNOVATION		**PEOPLE**
	Think Strategically		Foster Enthusiasm and Teamwork
	Innovate		Reward and Celebrate Achievement
	Champion Change		Attract and Develop Talent
			Build Relationships
	PERFORMANCE		**INTEGRITY**
	Establish Plans		Lead Courageously
	Manage Execution		Foster Open Communication
	Influence Others		Act with Integrity
	Drive for Results		
	CUSTOMER		**PERSONAL EFFECTIVENESS**
	Improve Systems and Processes		Use Sound Judgment
	Commit to Quality		Convey Information
	Focus on Customer Needs		Adapt and Develop Oneself
			Know the Organization and the Business

STRENGTHS

DEVELOPMENT NEEDS

ADDITIONAL COMMENTS (e.g., Project Work)

Exhibit 15.3: Leadership Planning Process Map

LEADERSHIP PLANNING PROCESS MAP

Inputs
As a customer-driven process, development plans require input from customers.

Database
Managing 7,000 records requires the use of technology—that is, a database.

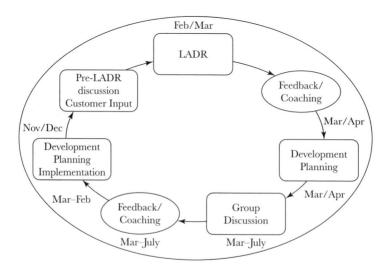

Measures
The success of any process is premised on obtaining one's objectives. At SB, measurement is valued.

Exhibit 15.4: ICS Selection Process Map

ICS SELECTION PROCESS MAP

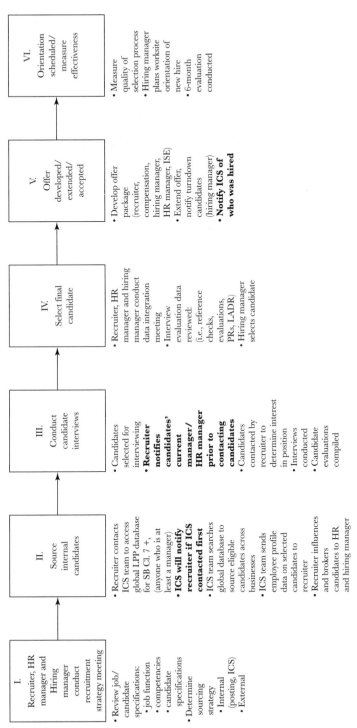

I.
Recruiter, HR manager and Hiring manager conduct recruitment strategy meeting

- Review job/ candidate specifications:
  - job function
  - competencies
  - candidate specifications
- Determine sourcing strategy
  - Internal (posting, ICS)
  - External

II.
Source internal candidates

- Recruiter contacts ICS team to access global LPP database for SB Cl. 7 +, (anyone who is at least a manager)
- **ICS will notify recruiter if ICS contacted first**
- ICS team searches global database to source eligible candidates across businesses
- ICS team sends employee profile data on selected candidates to recruiter
- Recruiter influences and brokers candidates to HR and hiring manager

III.
Conduct candidate interviews

- Candidates selected for interviewing
- **Recruiter notifies candidates' current manager/ HR manager prior to contacting candidates**
- Candidates contacted by recruiter to determine interest in position
- Interviews conducted
- Candidate evaluations compiled

IV.
Select final candidate

- Recruiter, HR manager and hiring manager conduct data integration meeting
- Interview evaluation data reviewed: (i.e., reference checks, evaluations, PRs, LADR)
- Hiring manager selects candidate

V.
Offer developed/ extended/ accepted

- Develop offer package (recruiter, compensation, hiring manager, HR manager, ISE)
- Extend offer, notify turndown candidates (hiring manager)
- **Notify ICS of who was hired**

VI.
Orientation scheduled/ measure effectiveness

- Measure quality of selection process
- Hiring manager plans worksite orientation of new hire
- 6-month evaluation conducted

Linkage Inc.'s Best Practices in Leadership Development Handbook, edited by David Giber, Louis Carter, and Marshall Goldsmith. Copyright © 2000 by Linkage Press and Jossey-Bass/Pfeiffer, San Francisco, CA.

Exhibit 15.5: ICS Request—Job Specification Form

SmithKline Beecham
INTERNAL CANDIDATE SEARCH REQUEST
JOB SPECIFICATION

JOB TITLE	SB GRADE
REPORTS TO (name):	(title):
SB SECTOR	GEOGRAPHIC REGION
SITE LOCATION	
HR MANAGER	EMPLOYMENT MANAGER
CONTACT	CONTACT

KEY RESPONSIBILITIES OF POSITION   (Please attach a job description if you have one)

KEY RESULTS EXPECTED OVER NEXT 12 MONTHS

SUPERVISES: none

BUDGET RESPONSIBILITY	% TRAVEL LIKELY DESTINATIONS 0

Exhibit 15.6: ICS Request—Candidate Specification Form

INTERNAL CANDIDATE SEARCH REQUEST
CANDIDATE SPECIFICATION

EXPERIENCE REQUIRED ESSENTIAL   PREFERABLE
EDUCATION REQUIRED ESSENTIAL   PREFERABLE
LIST BELOW THE 6 MOST IMPORTANT SB LEADERSHIP COMPETENCIES FOR THE JOB ☐ ☐ ☐ ☐ ☐ ☐
LANGUAGES ESSENTIAL   PREFERABLE
RELOCATION Are you willing to relocate a successful candidate for this   YES ☐   NO ☐ position?
OTHER REQUIREMENTS (indicate whether essential or preferable)

Linkage Inc.'s Best Practices in Leadership Development Handbook, edited by David Giber, Louis Carter, and Marshall Goldsmith. Copyright © 2000 by Linkage Press and Jossey-Bass/Pfeiffer, San Francisco, CA.

About the Contributors

Lou Manzi (louis.manzi@sb.com) is the vice president and director of worldwide recruitment and leadership planning. He joined SmithKline Beecham Consumer Products as Manager, Government and Public Affairs, in 1985. He is currently with SmithKline Beecham Corporate Staffs and is responsible for leadership and succession planning and United States/United Kingdom recruitment. In addition, he has responsibility for coordinating all U.S. Human Resources Shared Services initiatives.

Manzi received his bachelor's degree from St. Mary's Seminary College and is currently enrolled in the Executive Master's Program of the University of Pennsylvania. He serves on the Development Committee of the Arthritis Foundation and is a trustee of the Wilkes University Board of Trustees.

June Abramson (June_A_Abramson@SBPHRD.COM) is the Smith-Kline Beecham human resource director of development. She obtained her bachelor's degree in psychology from LaSalle University. She joined SmithKline Beecham Corporation in November 1973 and has held various positions throughout her career in human resources, most recently as human resources director, development, pharmaceuticals research and development.

Abramson's twenty-plus years of experience include design and development of global processes, training and development, and consultation with line management on organization design and implementation. She is the co-architect of the Leadership Planning Process and was responsible for leading a cross-sector team whose charter was to examine and develop internal best practice for Leadership and Development Review. The result was a global assessment process for leaders within SB.

CHAPTER SIXTEEN

LEADERSHIP DEVELOPMENT TRENDS AND FINDINGS

To provide additional context for the case studies presented in this book, we asked our contributors to reflect on seven critical areas of their leadership development systems. These areas include (1) Competitive and Strategic Business Challenges, (2) Leadership Competencies, (3) Most Impactful Key Features of Leadership Training, (4) Critical Success Factors, and (5) Evaluation Methods.

1. Competitive and Strategic Business Challenges

> Q: Please indicate which *two* of the following competitive and strategic business challenges *most* impacted the focus of your leadership development initiative.

No organization, even the most established and successful, can afford to rest on its laurels amid economic revolution, exacting customers, and increasing corporate anxiety over global competition and mounting revenue goals. It is hardly surprising, then, that globalization, improving productivity, competitive pressures, and maintaining a focus on customers were the top factors that helped contributors design and build a business case for their leadership development programs (see Table 16.1). Retention and hiring, on the other hand, may cause sleepless nights for senior executives and OD leaders, but they have had little direct impact on the focus of these leadership development initiatives. Keeping and developing leaders is perceived as the initiatives' direct result, not their strategic rationale.

2. Leadership Competencies

> Q: Please indicate the *top four* Leadership Competencies that *most* impacted the design of your leadership development training program.

Definition of Competencies

- *Builds Teamwork:* Builds effective teams committed to organizational goals and results

TABLE 16.1. TOP TWELVE LEADERSHIP DEVELOPMENT INITIATIVE CHALLENGES.

Challenge	Frequency
Globalization	40%
Improving productivity	33%
Competitive pressures	33%
Customer focus	27%
Rapid growth	20%
Focus on corporate vision	20%
Entrance into new markets	7%
Post-merger integration	7%
Strategic partnerships	7%
Other	7%
Technology	0%
Retention and hiring	0%

- *Understands the Business:* Knows the organization and stays abreast of business and competitive trends
- *Conceptual Thinking:* Conceives and selects innovative strategies and ideas for the organization; balancing innovation with big-picture thinking
- *Customer Driven:* Strives to create value for the customer resulting in mutual long-term success
- *Focused Drive:* Focuses on a goal and prioritizes—and harnesses—energy to meet that goal; balances focus and drive
- *Drives Profitability:* Achieves shareholder and/or stakeholder benefit by securing cost-effective and efficient operations
- *Systems Thinking:* Connects processes, events, and structures; balances process orientation with mental discipline
- *Global Perspective:* Addresses cultural and geographic differences in driving corporate strategies for competitive advantage

- *Emotional Intelligence:* Understands and masters one's own emotions (and those of others) in a way that instills confidence; balances perception and emotional maturity

(*Resource:* Linkage's Global Institute Leadership Model)

By a wide margin, the contributors concentrated on strengthening team-building, business understanding, and conceptual thinking among their program participants (see Figure 16.1). Other competencies, such as leading in a changing environment, managing in a technical environment, and fostering innovation, were cited far less frequently. Emotional intelligence too, was rarely featured, despite increasing concern that executives lack the emotional perception and maturity to lead their organizations successfully.

FIGURE 16.1. LEADERSHIP COMPETENCIES THAT MOST IMPACTED THE DESIGN OF THE LEADERSHIP DEVELOPMENT PROGRAM.

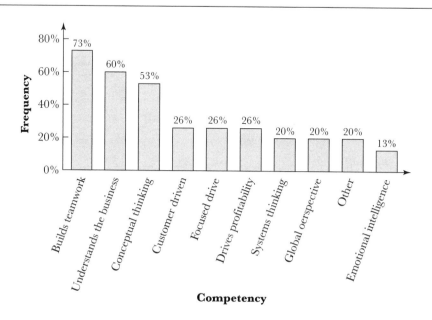

At first glance the responses to Questions 1 and 2 appear contradictory. If globalization, improving productivity, and customer focus were three of the four critical challenges for these initiatives, why do global perspective, drives profitability, and customer driven drop to the bottom tier of key Leadership Competencies? Perhaps this contradiction is because of the contrast between context and solutions. As experts in leadership development, the contributors believe that teamwork and the ability to think both operationally and strategically are the *sine qua non* of high-performing leaders. Once these competencies are established—once the program has laid the groundwork for the leadership *team*—then specific drives and perspectives fall more readily into place.

3. Most Impactful Key Features of Leadership Training

Q: Please indicate the *top four* key features that *most* impacted the success of your leadership development training.

The contributors found that leaders responded primarily to hands-on, practical components (action learning and 360-degree feedback) and to opportunities for exposure to senior executives and the strategic agenda (see Table 16.2). These findings are corroborated both by the Linkage/Warren Bennis study and by a past Linkage research study of leadership development programs within eight pharmaceutical and manufacturing firms (see Foreword). In the eyes of the programs' participants, such targeted, innovative opportunities have far greater impact than traditional methods. Organizations that tread the well-worn path of accelerated promotion, executive MBA programs, and sporadic conferences may find themselves outstripped by competitors who invest in progressive, integrated leadership development systems.

4. Critical Success Factors

Q: Please indicate which *three* of the following competitive and strategic business challenges *most* impacted the focus of your leadership development initiative.

TABLE 16.2.   KEY FEATURES OF THE LEADERSHIP DEVELOPMENT TRAINING.

Feature	Frequency
Action learning	73%
360-degree feedback	67%
Exposure to senior executives	67%
Exposure to strategic agenda	53%
Other	46%
External coaching	26%
Cross-functional rotations	20%
Global rotations	13%
Informal mentoring	7%
Internal case studies	7%
Executive MBA	7%
Formal mentoring	0%
Accelerated promotion	0%
Conferences	0%

Note: Key features identified in the "other" category included individual development plans, leveraging internal faculty, and identification and sharing of best practices and cross-divisional networking.

Just as the contributors recommend featuring 360-degree feedback and exposure to the strategic agenda, so do they point to the critical success factors of continuous evaluation and links to the strategic plan. These factors' importance pales, however, when compared to the emphasis on the role of senior leaders. Based on their experience, the leadership development experts advocate including senior management as champions, faculty, and even codesigners, both to magnify the initiatives' success and to surmount hurdles along the way (see Table 16.3).

TABLE 16.3. CRITICAL SUCCESS FACTORS THAT MOST IMPACTED THE SUCCESS OF THE LEADERSHIP DEVELOPMENT INITIATIVE.

Critical Success Factors	Frequency
Support and involvement of senior management	100%
Continuous evaluation	73%
Linking leadership development with strategic plan	73%
Involving line management in design	20%
Leveraging internal capacity	13%
Thorough needs assessment	12%
"Best-in-class" faculty	6%
Pilot program before launch	6%
Other	0%

5. Evaluation Methods

> Q: Please indicate which of the following evaluation methods
> your organization leveraged to measure the effectiveness
> of your leadership development program.

As Donald Kirkpatrick identified in *Evaluating Training Programs* (Barrett-Koehler Publishers, 1998), the methods of evaluation can be divided into four categories, and include data drawn largely from interviews or questionnaires.

1. *Reaction Evaluations* measure the participant's initial response or feeling from the training.
2. *Learning Evaluations* are administered in the form of tests or questionnaires and measure how well participants have learned facts, ideas, concepts, or theories.
3. *Behavior Evaluations* measure the effect of training on job performance.
4. *Results Evaluations* measure the effect of training on the achievement of organizational goals.

More than half of the leadership development case studies used reaction, behavior, and results evaluations to measure the effectiveness of training, while approximately one-third used learning and alternative methods. Roughly one-tenth of the contributors used other methods of evaluation, including evaluations from third-party sources that measure the effectiveness of individual development plans and of the training program (see Figure 16.2). In these contributors' estimation, the success of a leadership development program should be observed in how participants use their education and respond to it, not merely in how they score on artificial or external tests of knowledge.

FIGURE 16.2. EVALUATION METHOD USAGE.

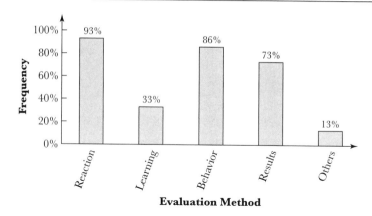

Conclusion

As organizations become more complex and dynamic, so do their leadership development programs. Globalization, productivity declines, competitive pressures, and customer demands are paving the way for more integrated leadership programs and for correspondingly larger development budgets. Nearly half of the organizations included in this book budgeted over $1 million for leadership development in 1999 (see Figure 16.3).

FIGURE 16.3. AMOUNT OF MONEY BUDGETED FOR LEADERSHIP DEVELOPMENT FOR CASE STUDIES IN 1999.

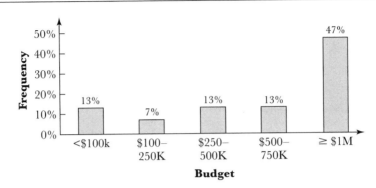

We expect annual budgets for leadership development to increase throughout the next decade. A sizable portion of those funds, particularly for program start-up costs, will be spent on technology. Over 53 percent of organizations cited in this book use their intranet and IT systems for their leadership development programs, particularly in obtaining 360-degree feedback, and over 33 percent use those systems for employee selection. As organizations become more global and electronic communication more ubiquitous, leaders are growing increasingly impatient with papers and forms and increasingly eager to receive feedback and developmental support that is accurate, comprehensive, and immediate.

Over the last two decades, leadership development has grown steadily more sophisticated. Following the lead of such pacesetters as General Electric and Motorola, organizations are committing to education and training that deepen the specific skills, perspective, and competencies they expect of their current and emerging leaders. By combining action learning, 360-degree feedback, and clear links to senior-level strategy and commitment, leadership initiatives are successfully building teams of leaders who see both the forest and the trees, who can understand their customers' demands today and drive strategy and action to anticipate their demands tomorrow. The next two decades promise further innovation, integration, and investment in inhouse leadership education; as leadership at all levels grows more critical, so will the systems for leadership development.

INDEX

ABOUT THE EDITORS

David Giber, Ph.D.
Vice President of Consulting Services, Linkage, Inc.

David Giber (DGiber@linkage-inc.com) is a leading expert in designing and implementing integrated leadership development programs that achieve organizational effectiveness and measurable change. He has served in director-level HR positions for major organizations in various vertical industries for over fifteen years, and has consulted with a wide variety of domestic and global organizations on such issues as succession planning, management development, workforce assessment, competency modeling, and developing performance and compensation systems. He has designed and managed training and development programs worldwide for such firms as SIAC, Digital Equipment Corporation, Keane, Inc., New York Airlines, and Goldman Sachs. He has also developed competency models and competency-based human resource systems for such organizations as the Principal Financial Group, Levi Strauss, LEGO Systems, Harvard Community Health Plan, Unum Insurance, and others. Giber received his bachelor's degree from Stanford in 1976 and his Ph.D. in industrial/organizational psychology from Duke University in 1980.

Louis Carter
Manager of Publications/Consultant, Linkage, Inc.

Lou Carter (LCarter@linkage-inc.com) is a consultant and product development specialist at Linkage, Inc. where he designs and manages "best practice" training and development programs. Prior to joining Linkage, Carter served as vice president in charge of business development and change for an insurance and financial services organization where he designed and delivered several change management interventions. He has also worked as an analyst for two Wall Street investment banking firms, as well as a Cambridge, Massachusetts-based strategic analysis think-tank dedicated to Fortune 500 Internet and online services organizations. He has written articles for *Bankers and Tradesman* as well as for the MIT Society for Organizational Learning Web site. Carter received his bachelor's degree *cum laude* in government and economics from Connecticut College and has studied organizational development and management at Brown University, Harvard University Extension School, and American University/National Training Labs Master's of Science in Organizational Development program.

Marshall Goldsmith, Ph.D.
Keilty, Goldsmith & Company

Marshall Goldsmith (marshall@kgcnet.com) is one of the world's foremost authorities in helping leaders achieve positive, measurable change in behavior: for themselves, their people, and their teams. Goldsmith has been ranked in the *Wall Street Journal* as one of the "Top 10" consultants in the field of executive development. His work has received national recognition from the Institute for Management Studies, the American Management Association, the American Society for Training and Development, and the Human Resource Planning Society. His coaching process has been positively described in both the *New York Times* and the *Financial Times*. He has co-edited (with Frances Hesselbein and Dick Beckhard) the books *The Leader of the Future, The Organization of the Future,* and *The Community of the Future,* which have sold over 400,000 copies in fourteen different languages. Goldsmith has an MBA from Indiana University and a Ph.D. from UCLA. Before forming KGC, he was an associate dean at Loyola Marymount University and a director at the Center for Leadership Studies.

ABOUT LINKAGE, INC.

Linkage, Inc. (http://www.linkageinc.com) is a global leader in creating organizational development, leadership, corporate education programs, research, and resources that achieve measurable business impact. Combining the world's most renowned thought leaders, "best-in-class" educational resources, and a highly experienced team of consultants, Linkage has delivered programs to more than 9,000 individuals, including employees of eighty of the Fortune 100 companies. Clients include Lucent Technologies, Merck, Harvard University, Brigham & Women's Hospital, Skudder Kemper Investments, McDonald's, Toyota, Xerox, and a host of other organizations in the major industries.

Linkage's Suite of Leadership Development Products and Services

Linkage, Inc. prides itself in providing practical, cost-effective, and results-oriented leadership development programs and systems. Linkage provides one-stop-shopping for its clients' leadership development needs.

- Award winning videos, audio tapes, CD-ROMs, conferences, workshops, consulting, on-site training programs, research, and books
- *Leadership Development Consulting and System Development*—Through a multimode systemic model for building a leadership development program, Linkage provides "best-in-class" leadership development consulting. Linkage's Integrated Leadership Development Systems model accelerates and provides ongoing support for leadership development within organizations. Clients include Brown University, Case Corporation, Toyota, American Home Products, Ralston Purina, and ITOCHU International.
- *Global Institute for Leadership Development (GILD)*—Cochaired by Warren Bennis (leadership author and expert) and Phil Harkins (Linkage's president and CEO), GILD provides high-level programs and services targeted at the long-term leadership development of individuals and teams from the world's foremost organizations. One example is GILD's Emerging Leader Program, which is an accelerated leadership development program and process for emerging leaders that combines the best of assessment, training, development, coaching, and benchmarking.
- *The Executive Leadership Development Program*—This program, Linkage's core leadership workshop, is an experiential, interactive session that provides proven models, tools, and processes to help participants become more impactful leaders. The program is designed to provide an intensive three-day session that helps leaders to continuously improve skills, increase knowledge, and develop their leadership competencies.
- *The Leadership Development Conference (LDC)*—Held annually in the United States, Canada, and Europe, LDC brings together human resource executives, corporate leaders, line executives, and practitioners who recognize the bottom-line of developing their organization's existing and future leaders and are aggressively working to build effective leadership development processes. The conference provides attendees with access to proven tools, techniques, and revolutionary approaches to developing leaders and their organization's leadership effectiveness.
- *Leadership Assessment Instrument (LAI)*—Developed by Linkage in partnership with Warren Bennis, the LAI measures the critical capabilities required for high performance leadership across all industries and

functions. The LAI is available as both a self-managed assessment and as a 360-degree assessment.

- *Complete Consultant*—Based on the practical experiences of the authors, observations of other consultants' practice, and research undertaken by Linkage, Inc., the Complete Consultant is an assessment instrument that helps HR and OD professionals clarify their consulting roles and target their development efforts.
- *Action Research*—Linkage's Research Group provides benchmarking and best practice research to help guide decision making on key leadership and organizational development issues, bringing the industry key leaders and best practitioners to work directly with the client.